THE
SPOKEN
SEEN

THE
SPOKEN
SEEN
FILM
& the Romantic
Imagination

FRANK D. McCONNELL

THE JOHNS HOPKINS UNIVERSITY PRESS
Baltimore & London

Chapter four originally appeared, in slightly
different form, as "Film and Writing: The
Political Dimension" in *The Massachusetts
Review*, Autumn 1972; copyright © 1972 by
Frank D. McConnell. The section of chapter five
dealing with *Pickup on South Street* originally
appeared as *"Pickup on South Street* and the
Metamorphosis of the Thriller" in *Film Heritage*,
Spring 1973, and the section dealing with *The
Creature from the Black Lagoon* as "Song
of Innocence: The Creature from the Black
Lagoon" in the *Journal of Popular Film*,
Winter 1973; both are reprinted with
permission.

Manufactured in the United States of America

The Johns Hopkins University Press,
Baltimore, Maryland 21218

The Johns Hopkins University Press Ltd., London

Library of Congress Catalog Card Number 75-11342

ISBN 0-8018-1725-0 (clothbound)
ISBN 0-8018-1726-9 (paperbound)

Library of Congress Cataloging in Publication Data
will be found on the last printed page of this book.

For Carolyn and Christopher,
fellow travelers

The Imagination may be compared to Adam's
dream—he awoke and found it truth.

John Keats

CONTENTS

ILLUSTRATIONS

ACKNOWLEDGMENTS

For whatever is good in this book I owe a large and affectionately recorded debt to a number of friends and colleagues with whom I have had the luck to talk, learn, and sometimes disagree about films, literature, and films-and-literature: Peter Conn, A. Herskovits, Stuart Kaminsky, Bruce Kawin, and S. Schoenbaum. And for the time for thought which made this book a reality I am indebted to the generous assistance of the Northwestern University Office of Research and Sponsored Programs, and to its director, Charles H. Gold. William P. Sisler of The Johns Hopkins University Press has been unfailing in his support and kindness.

A special place on this page, and in this book, is reserved for my friends Alfred Appel, Jr., and Sam Hynes. I have been engaged in a four-year conversation with them on many of the matters discussed here, and I am sure I have learned more from them than I could possibly acknowledge: indeed, it is thanks to Sam Hynes that I was able to teach my first course in film and literature, and it was with Alfred Appel that I taught it.

The two people to whom this book is dedicated, finally, possess my largest gratitude for its appearance. For they not only made its conception possible and its writing easy but made the whole enterprise seem worthwhile.

THE
SPOKEN
SEEN

1

ADAM'S DREAM: THE ROMANTIC PREHISTORY OF AN ART

The art of film has received a number of definitions and is likely to receive a good many more. But one of the most suggestive is that offered by André Bazin, the great French film historian and critic, in his essay "The Myth of Total Cinema." The essay begins as a review of Georges Sadoul's history of the origins of cinema but very rapidly develops into an expostulation of Bazin's own views on the matter:

The way things happened seems to call for a reversal of the historical order of causality, which goes from the economic infrastructure to the ideological superstructure, and for us to consider the basic technical discoveries as fortunate accidents but essentially second in importance to the preconceived ideas of the inventors. The cinema is an idealistic phenomenon. The concept men had of it existed so to speak fully armed in their minds, as if in some platonic heaven, and what strikes us most of all is the obstinate resistance of matter to ideas rather than of any help offered by techniques to the imagination of the researchers.

Film—that is, at least for Bazin— is most correctly regarded as the realization of an aesthetic dream, the incarnation, through inspired technology and visionary science, of an artistic ideal long predating the actual, practical "discovery" of cinema. And, as Bazin develops this argument in his essay, he explicitly allies the art of the film to the specific dream of art as totally representational, totally autonomous counter-reality that we associate primarily with romantic and postromantic nineteenth-century literature.

Such a vision of film, naturally, tends to overidealize the art: as we well know, some of the most important developments in the history of film technology, and even some of the greatest works on the art of the film, have been brought about more by concerns of machinery and economics than by a "myth" of "total cinema." Nevertheless, it seems to me one of the most penetrating attitudes toward film yet articulated. Film means much to us, has indisputably become *the* art of our era, not through a series of accidental developments in public taste, nor yet because of the efficiency and energy with which film has been marketed by the major American and European studios. Rather, film has come to be our art precisely because it continues to raise and explore those problems of reality, perception, meaning, and consciousness which are a vital aspect of our literary inheritance from romanticism. To say that we still live in the romantic era—that our best poets and novelists are direct continuators of the romantic quest—has nearly become a cliché in literary criticism. But the cliché loses its tarnish when we realize that it also makes eloquent sense of the development and aesthetics of the film—and that the aesthetics of film, in turn, can refine and revivify our sense of our literary heritage.

That, at any rate, is the assumption of the "reading" of film which follows. And thus the title of this chapter, "Adam's Dream." The phrase is taken from a letter of John Keats, who perhaps more than any other romantic poet was obsessed and inspired by his own sense of romanticism in the history of thought and of romanticism as a prophecy of the future. On Saturday, 22 November 1817, Keats wrote to his friend Benjamin Bailey: "I am certain of the Heart's affections and the truth of Imagination—What the imagination seizes as Beauty must be truth—whether it existed before or not—for I have the same Idea of all our Passions as of Love they are all in their sublime, creative of essential Beauty. . . . The Imagination may be compared to Adam's dream—he awoke and found it truth."

The reference to "Adam's dream," graceful and lovely as it is, contains a complex bit of literary history. In Book VIII of Milton's *Paradise Lost* Adam relates how, lonely in the paradisal Garden, he had asked God for a companion to share his joys. God then puts

Adam into a deep sleep, during which Adam has a vision of a lovely shape, a creature like himself yet tantalizingly different. It is Eve.

Shee disappear'd, and left me dark, I wak'd
To find her, or for ever to deplore
Her loss, and other pleasures all abjure:
When out of hope, behold her, not far off,
Such as I saw her in my dream, adorn'd
With what all Earth or Heaven could bestow
To make her amiable. . . .

Adam's dream is the vision of Eve, of the human companion who will cause both his fall into history—into our "reality"—and also his eventual recovery from the Fall. And Milton, great preromantic poet that he was, deliberately presents us with the dream-vision, the ideal of Eve, as the cause of her reality, very much as Bazin, great postromantic critic that he was, insists upon the vision of art as the cause of its physical realization.

Keats, in transposing the incident of Adam's dream to the general idea of the Imagination—and, indeed, to the idea of "all our Passions . . . in their sublime"—gives us perhaps the best definition we have of the romantic ideal of literature. For the romantic poet or novelist, as well as for our own most important contemporary poets and novelists, the creation of the literary work involves a complex and potentially dangerous interchange with reality. For the work seeks to become, like Adam's dream, a fantastic, highly structured counter-reality which, through its very power of imagination, makes itself somehow "real," either by restructuring or (more frequently in modern literature) de-structuring our own complacent ideas of what "reality" is like. Ideally, then, as we finish a poem like the "Ode on a Grecian Urn" or Shelley's "Ode to the West Wind" (or a novel like *Ulysses* or Thomas Pynchon's *Gravity's Rainbow*), we should be taken by surprise at the deep resemblance between the visionary world of the work and the quotidian reality out of which we approach the work: we should wake to find it truth, or to find our ordinary world a lie.

But if Keats's metaphor is a brilliant articulation of the ambitions of romantic writing, it is also an uncannily accurate version, it seems to me, of our experience of the art of film. Certainly, no one who has not become impossibly jaded and overintellectualized in his response to film can fail to recognize in the intricacies of Adam's dream a deep similarity to the experience of simply *going* to a movie. We sit in the dark—or we sit waiting impatiently for the Muzak to run out and for the lights to darken—all of us together in the audience and yet each one of us, somehow, alone with the screen, each one of us a romantic Adam about to rediscover for ourselves the world, and we wait for the moment when, in a darkened hall, figures of light will actually begin to move on the screen before us. We may even be lulled into a semihypnotic state by the film we see: surely most film-goers have experienced that curious, nearly frightening moment when, in the middle of a movie, you realize that although you are merely watching a movie, you are powerless to take your eyes from the screen, powerless to stop following the actions being played out before you. And finally, if the film experience has worked, we do wake to find it true: the film ends, the lights come back on, and we file out of the theatre into the world of (usually) dark, mean streets, parked cars, and each other's company—a world which has been there all along, and which the film has helped us rediscover as our world, perhaps simply because it has been so unlike that world.

Filmmakers in general have shown themselves to be, perhaps subliminally, conscious and fond of the power of film to intrude upon and reapportion our ideas of reality. In 1903, Edwin S. Porter made his epochal film *The Great Train Robbery*, the first "Western" movie and perhaps—so runs the argument of some critics—the first truly narrative film. But when it was distributed, *The Great Train Robbery* included a short scene (the advertisements to theaters insisted that it could be shown to advantage either before or after the film itself) in which a fierce-looking Western-style bandit draws a gun and fires it point-blank at the camera—that is, at the audience. People, reportedly, screamed; women fainted, strong men ducked. It is not the only case of an early film audience responding with shock and terror to devices that we now tend to think of as simpleminded and overused. But, in fact, the response of the original audience may well have been the most perceptive. For what is shocking about the bandit firing his gun at you is precisely the fact that *nothing happens;* you duck or scream, but the bullet, even if it were not a blank, can never reach you, never touch you. Nothing, despite the screen's overwhelming illusion of reality, is really there. In the extra scene from *The Great Train Robbery*, in other words, we have an early example of one of film's most potent aesthetic devices: its power to remind us, with a sudden jolt, that we are indulging in a mere illusion, even though this illusion, by its very nature, has a closer connection to *felt* reality than most of our actual experiences. We might remark, by the way, that the *Train Robbery* gambit, old-fashioned as it may seem, apparently has a perennial fascination for filmmakers. In the opening, pretitle sequence of

Magnum Force, the 1973 sequel to *Dirty Harry,* we see a hand (that of hero-detective Harry Calahan) holding a gigantic looking .44 Magnum pistol which gradually swings around to point at the audience and finally is fired.

At a perhaps more complex level, Bernardo Bertolucci's *Last Tango in Paris* moves inexorably and pompously toward the firing of a gun with much the same purpose. A man and a woman, Paul (Marlon Brando) and Jeanne (Maria Schneider) meet and make passionate, often brutal love in a bare apartment in Paris; they pledge at the beginning of their relationship never to reveal to each other their names or their personal histories, in a pathetic attempt to block out the urban world that is depersonalizing them both. And neither of them ever says to the other, "I love you." But at the conclusion of the film, when the girl has decided to break up this bizarre ménage, the man drunkenly pursues her to her own luxurious apartment, proposing marriage and protesting his love. At the last, fatal moment, he asks her name; she replies, "Jeanne," and at the same time takes a pistol out of a drawer and kills him. The point is a significant one for our reading of film, even if rather leaden-footedly made in this specific instance: human communication, the emergence from the dream into society, history, and love, shatters our sense of the film "fantasy" as violently and irrevocably as does a gunshot.

Gunshots, of course, are a relatively crude, if permanently effective, way of making a point about the surprising reality of the film's structured dream. But that image of the bandit from *The Great Train Robbery* helps us see an important relationship between film and the literary imagination of the last two centuries, one which has heretofore generated a good deal of confusion and anger on the part of film theorists. Film, to be sure, is not writing. The difference between the medium of film (photographic replicas of human figures moving on a screen) and the medium of literature (artificial representations of vocal sounds marshalled on a page) is an essential one, and one which we cannot afford to forget for long. But to say that the difference between the two arts is essential is not to say that it is, finally, *significant.* And purists of both film and literature who argue for the autonomy and (implicitly) the preeminence of one mode or the other seriously misunderstand the nature of both. I return, as I shall often do in this book, to Keats. The *imagination,* he says, may be compared to Adam's dream. And his use of the word I have italicized marks another important turning point in the history of literature and the literary idea. Until the very late eighteenth century, the word "imagination" was not a very serious one for the description of literary genius at all: it meant precisely what its etymology suggests—the image-making or image-forming faculty of the mind—and as such was considered, at the most, a picturesque adjunct to the more important moral, educative force of poetry. It is one of our chief legacies from the romantic period—and particularly from the prose of Coleridge and Keats—that for us the word "imagination" implies the highest creative power of art, including the moral force to which classical rhetorical theory largely opposed it. Once again, while the romantic poet wishes to awake and find his dream true, he characteristically insists that the dream's truth is a function of its dramatic, visual specificity, of the image-making or image-generating power which Coleridge, in the *Biographia Literaria*, termed "esemplastic" (i.e., shaping into Oneness) and likened to the creative force of God.

E. H. Gombrich, in his monumental *Art and Illusion*, suggests that the whole tradition of realism in Western painting (perspective, lifelike shading and postures, and so on) derives from the immense influence on Western thought of the narrative poem, particularly the Homeric epics. For Gombrich, that is, in the beginning was neither the word nor the image, but the imaged fable. And at least in the history of romantic and postromantic art, we can see the terms of Gombrich's arguments startlingly realized. Writing since the romantic revolution has been, for better and worse, an attempt to think and argue philosophically through images. And if this apotheosis of the imagination has produced, on the one hand, the iconic symbolism of Hopkins, Yeats, and Mallarmé, it has also produced, as the fullest realization of its myth, the art of the film, of images that actually move, actually tell a story, and therefore actuate the poetry of romanticism as language can perhaps never hope to do. Classical criticism and poetic theory played with the Horatian formula, *ut pictura poesis* ("a poem is like a picture"). But romantic theory—and, by extension, film practice—makes the more problematic assertion *poesis est pictura*—"a poem is a picture," even a *moving* picture.

Nowadays, it is a fairly common but still instructive practice to find in romantic narrative poems or in nineteenth-century novels "cinematic" passages and scenes—passages in which the romantic emphasis upon the power of the image gives to the details the kind of significance we are accustomed to look for in serious films. It is not my concern in this book to catalogue or to explicate such direct literary anticipations of film technique; but it is hard to resist citing two such passages, from major and very early modern writers.

Wordsworth, at a climactic moment of his confessional epic, *The Prelude*, speaks of "spots of time," privileged and enigmatic moments of vision which shape and direct our psychic destiny. He then describes one such "spot of time":

> I remember well,
> That once, while yet my inexperienced hand
> Could scarcely hold a bridle, with proud hopes
> I mounted, and we journeyed towards the hills:
> An ancient servant of my father's house
> Was with me, my encourager and guide;
> We had not traveled long, ere some mischance
> Disjoined me from my comrade; and, through fear
> Dismounting, down the rough and stony moor
> I led my horse, and, stumbling on, at length
> Came to a bottom, where in former times
> A murderer had been hung in iron chains.
> The gibbet-mast had moldered down, the bones
> And iron case were gone; but on the turf,
> Hard by, soon after that fell deed was wrought,
> Some unknown hand had carved the murderer's name.
> The monumental letters were inscribed
> In times long past; but still, from year to year
> By superstition of the neighborhood,
> The grass is cleared away, and to this hour
> The characters are fresh and visible. . . .

It is a splendid passage, and if we force ourselves to read it without our inherited prejudgments about the "literariness" of Wordsworth, it is even more striking. The dreary, dusky landscape, the forbidding gibbet, and especially the freshly tended letters spelling out the murderer's name—all could easily be details, with much the same force and grim beauty, in a scene by Lang, Murnau, or James Whale at his best.

In a very different but equally "cinematic" fashion, Byron climaxes *The Bride of Abydos*. The tale narrates the love of Selim for the Turkish Pacha's daughter Zuleika and his attempt to elope with her. But in the final battle against the Pacha's soldiers, Selim is mortally wounded:

> A broken torch, an oarless boat;
> And tangled on the weeds that heap
> The beach where shelving to the deep
>   There lies a white capote!
> 'Tis rent in twain—one dark-red stain
> The wave yet ripples o'er in vain;

But where is he who wore?
Ye! who would o'er his relics weep,
Go, seek them where the surges sweep
Their burden round Sigaeum's steep
    And cast on Lemnos' shore:
The sea-birds shriek above the prey,
O'er which their hungry beaks delay,
As shaken on his restless pillow,
His head heaves with the heaving billow;
That hand, whose motion is not life,
Yet feebly seems to menace strife,
Flung by the tossing tide on high,
    Then levell'd with the wave—
What recks it, though that corse shall lie
Within a living grave?

This great passage involves all the characteristic ambiguities of Byron's best verse: the dead Selim, though now become simply another bit of unconscious matter in a nonconscious universe, continues ironically his warlike gesture of heroic defiance, thanks to the very mechanism of the forbidding, circumambient, inhuman cosmos. And if the passage from Wordsworth reminds us of Lang or Murnau, the lines from *The Bride of Abydos*, with their carefully haphazard montage, should surely bring to mind the materialist ironies of Eisenstein or Hitchcock.

It is not my concern in this study, however, to trace literary analogues to cinematic scenes—and even less so, of course, to discuss some putative (and largely chimerical) "influence" of literary narrative on the film. What interests me is the more general, and more elusive, problem of the fundamental isomorphism of two major strains of the modern imagination, that of postromantic writing and that of the film. And, in this respect, one of the most fascinating preliminary versions of our subject is neither in film nor in literature, but in early nineteenth-century painting.

If romanticism tends to redefine the Word as the Image, to place upon the language arts the responsibility of becoming the incarnational art of truth made flesh, romantic painting correspondingly tends to become fictive, in the sense that it increasingly attempts to represent, not things in their static, posed reality, but things in *process*— that is, as Gombrich would perhaps argue it, things as *becoming*, as elements of narrative. The works of David, Caspar David Friedrich, Constable, and Turner present varied but equally compelling examples of romantic paintings that are intended to represent things-in-motion, which is to say things-as-they-are-perceived. But perhaps the most important aspect of this phenomenon—one of which Bazin, apparently, had not heard, but which is a startling validation of his thesis about the myth of total cinema—is the case of Philippe Jacques de Loutherbourg.

De Loutherbourg (1740–1812) is hardly among the best-known Romantic painters today. Yet in the late eighteenth century he was a widely celebrated, innovative, and highly influential talent. Migrating to England from the Continent early in life, he became a member of the Royal Academy and an intimate of most of the established artists of London. A lover of storms, shipwrecks, and general meteorological violence, de Loutherbourg's special genius as a painter, according to his contemporaries, was in the representation of weather and cloud formations—in other words, states of becoming—with peculiar and dramatic lifelikeness. The tag "dramatic" is especially appropriate for him: for years he held the lucrative position of set designer for David Garrick's productions at the Drury Lane Theater, and his sets were well known for their intense realism.

He is most significant for our discussion, though, not because of his landscapes or his stage work, but for an odd and quite successful experiment that he conducted midway through his mature career. The *Dictionary of National Biography* describes this experiment as follows:

> In 1782 he planned and constructed an ingenious system of moving pictures within a proscenium, which, by a clever disposition of lights, coloured gauzes, and the like, imitated atmospheric effects at different times of the day. This, which he called "Eidophusikon," he exhibited with music to accompany the movements of the pictures, and the display attracted a numerous audience. The painter Gainsborough was deeply impressed by it. So popular was the exhibition that when De Loutherbourg was prosecuted for exhibiting his system without a musical license, the justices before whom the case came at once granted him the license without inflicting any penalty.

De Loutherbourg's judges, we may conclude, showed great critical sense in effectively dismissing the case against him for exhibiting a performance without a musical license. For what they were confronted with in the Eidophusikon was not a performance—at least, not as the eighteenth century understood the term—but rather a primitive version of an art that would take another century and more to grow to maturity, the art of the film.

In fact, there were three or four vignettes presented at separate performances of the Eidophusikon. And, although the *DNB* does not indicate it, each performance of the Eidophusikon was a dramatic narrative; besides the effects of clouds, sunlight, and landscape, there was the movement of small puppets representing human actors and at least a minimal plot. One of the original presentations of the Eidophusikon has been carefully reconstructed by the museum at Kenwood House, Hampstead Heath, London (which also contains an impressive selection of de Loutherbourg's stormy landscape paintings). It is a version of Book I of *Paradise Lost*, the meeting of the fallen angels in Hell and their construction of the devil's palace, Pandaemonium; and, as in the original production, it includes not only musical accompaniment but an offstage reading of the appropriate lines from Milton's poem. There is, to be sure, an inevitably comic quality to this reconstruction: as we watch it unfold, we are aware how crudely engineered are some of the special effects with which de Loutherbourg tries to realize the Miltonic narrative. But despite this unavoidable historical snobbery, it is impossible not to be moved, and even awed, by the power of de Loutherbourg's conception. "Moving pictures within a proscenium," as the *DNB* puts it, does not adequately convey the genius of the experiment. For it is precinema, brilliantly realized as a total art and intimately involved with the movements of aesthetics, metaphysics, and poetics which were, in a century, to generate the technology that would fully articulate de Loutherbourg's own manifest dream of a perfectly representational and mysteriously symbolic re-creation of the real world.

De Loutherbourg's Eidophusikon is the first of a number of examples of the precinema to which I shall refer in this book. Other examples will include Plato, Lucretius, and of course the Romantic poets. But the aim, in locating such ancestry for the film, has not been to diminish or to underplay the radical originality of the art itself; I have not tried to use history to sap the autonomy of the form. Rather, the discovery of precinematic art forms and philosophical concepts should remind us—as, I hope, will the whole book—of the deep implication of the art of the film in our most permanent and most perennially vital concerns of life and thought.

Clumsily pedantic formation though it is, the term "Eidophusikon" may have two complementary and equally important meanings. We may construe the Greek roots to mean either "a view of nature" or, more actively, "a seeing into nature"; and, of course, we need to bear in mind that (whether with a Greek or a Latin root) "nature" for the early romantics had a much stronger connotation of process, of becoming, than it has come to have for our own era. Both interpretations can be useful in describing the art of the film. For whether we wish to regard it as a view of or as a special insight into nature, film seems to make the most sense to us and the most sense of our condition as an especially powerful, iconic version of the epistemological and imaginative problems which also beset our poetry, fiction, and indeed, our attempts to lead fully conscious, fully human lives. That, at least, is the assumption of the following pages, which seek to describe "film *and* the literary imagination" as if the two arts were not mutually exclusive or engaged in some sort of intellectual warfare, but rather, as if they were mutually supportive descriptions of the modern consciousness.

I begin, then, with the assumption that a truly accurate description of the art of film must include a sense of the two hundred years of imaginatively revolutionary thinking and writing that precede and parallel its own development. And my discussion of film attempts to deal with the art in terms defined, in one way or another, by the tradition of modern writing as well as by filmmaking. Following the hints of the Keats letter, I begin by discussing the curious and ambiguous sense of reality which film gives us, a sense of reality including the alternative extremes of animated cartoon "reality" and photographic, frozen "reality." This double realism suggests, on a higher level of abstraction, the problem of automata and of artificial intelligence which has obsessed philosophers, poets, and filmmakers for three hundred years. And if automata—artificial humans—are a possibility raised with peculiar immediacy by film, so is the problem of language itself, the human art of signifying, which may be either a deception (we may not know, after all, that the words we use really name the world we live in) or our only salvation from the inarticulate world of matter. Language, however, is a social as well as a phenomenological event; and to talk about talking is also to talk about our ways of talking to each other, of articulating a grammar which can mediate between the claims of the individual and the claims of the mass to which the individual belongs in some organized, humanizing fashion. And at this level of the argument, we confront the specifically artistic problem of narrative genre: that is, the problem of describing the preestablished, mythic forms of significant action that largely determine our possibilities of intelligent response to the situations in which we find ourselves. But the description of literary or filmic genre also implies—at least for our postromantic sensibility—

the description of the ways in which the individual personality rises above the concerns of tradition and inherited meaning to create a meaning and reality of its own.

These, in highly allusive and sketchy form, are the phases of my discussion of film. The reader who, like myself, shares an affection for (or addiction to) diagrams may be guided by this *esquisse* of the following chapters:

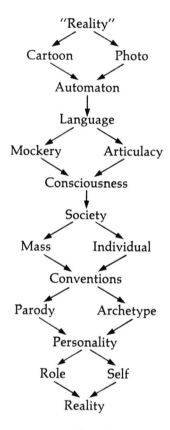

The outward-slanting arrows may be taken to mean "fragments into"; the inward-slanting arrows, to mean "unites into (at a higher level of abstraction)"; and the vertical arrow to mean "leads us to the problem and discussion of." This is not, of course, to be taken as an exhaustive outline of the argument, but simply as a guide to the way in which I think the individual chapters make progressive sense of film art and of its relations to the literary imagination.

The reader will notice that at some points in this book I have occasion to quarrel with the established, formalist, or *auteur* school of film criticism which has, over the last two decades, more or less dominated serious discussions of the art. As the derivation of my fundamental premise from Bazin indicates, I hold the auteur approach in great regard as a theory which has made possible, for perhaps the first time, a serious, critical, academic appreciation of film. But, like all formalist theories—of any art—the auteur school tends toward a dehumanization of the artwork, a translation of the primal experience of the work into abstractions and formulas, which I feel needs to be disciplined and chastened by the constant reminder that we are, after all, discussing an art that affects *us*—and not some alembicated idea of what we might like to be. Indeed, this quarrel is part of my attempt, throughout this book, to remain faithful to the insight of Keats: to discuss film and literature in terms that avoid the technicalities of a "critical" vocabulary, and to bear constantly in mind the deep relevance of these matters of art to our most elemental experience. Thus, too, the diagram I have provided of the book's argument begins with the term "reality" in quotes and ends with the same word, denuded of its inverted commas. It is, in its way, an attempt to describe what it means to "wake and find our dream truth," what it means to turn our backs on the darkened screen and walk out of the theatre. But if the quotation marks are successfully removed from the word "reality," it is done only by the film—or the poem or the novel —itself. I have merely tried to describe how, and how totally, that curative amputation may be carried out. We begin, then, with the first transition film imposes upon us, a transition from one sense of the "real" world to another, stranger sense of that reality.

2

THE REEL WORLD: TRAVELS WITH MY SON

"Roll away the reel world, the reel world, the reel world," says the dreamer HCE in Joyce's *Finnegans Wake*, making the inevitable pun his own. We have, by now, heard it made so often and in so many contexts— newspaper reviews, excruciatingly witty classroom lectures—that we are likely to forget that, like most puns, it masks an underlying seriousness. For film does have a curious relation to the world we call real, more curious, perhaps, than does any other art form. It is seductively real, the world that film gives us; and, as with most seductions, part of the pleasure of our yielding to it is the suspicion that the yielding is somehow—we don't quite see how, and that too is a pleasure—dangerous. It is no accident that guardians of our public morality like *Time* and *Newsweek* worry more about sex and violence in the film than in any other medium. Their journalistic ancestors have been doing so ever since that bandit fired a gun point-blank at the screen in *The Great Train Robbery* and Theda Bara gave the vampire its distinctively erotic and abbreviated twentieth-century reincarnation as the "vamp." In the spate of film theories, aesthetics, and critiques that have appeared in recent years—and in the strong resistance to that movement by literary humanists—this subtle sense of the possible sinfulness of film is a constant, if largely unacknowledged, undertone to the debate. "Sinfulness," of course, is usually translated in critical discourse as "aesthetic poverty," "dependency upon other media," or some such criterion. But I think we deceive ourselves, and lose a valuable insight into the real nature of film, if we fail to recognize the essentially moral terms in which the discussion of this, like any, art properly resonates.

What I am suggesting is that our first, preanalytical reaction to the art is also our most accurate one and the one upon which any further analysis needs to be consciously founded. The hangdog expressions of the men you see lined up outside a 42nd Street X-house are, in this way, a true and suggestive analogue to the shrilly defensive statements about the "autonomy of the art" uttered by professional film people, as well as to the attacks upon film as the death of the imagination which come from our more conservative academic intellectuals. Perhaps our culture still retains some deeply embedded moral distrust of the making of graven images—especially when the images are graven with such preternatural accuracy. Or perhaps, as Parker Tyler suggested long ago in *The Hollywood Hallucination*, the film reminds us of the unhappier aspects of the myth of Pygmalion: a simulacrum so "real" that we fall in love with it at the expense of our own relationship to reality. At any rate, there is a continuum from the guilty titillation of the most minimally critical pornobuff to the discourse of the most cerebral semiologist of film, and that continuum of response is probably the first, and most important, aspect of the art. Film is almost *too* real. Not by accident did Siegfried Kracauer subtitle his important *Theory of Film* "The Redemption of Physical Reality," in an attempt, something like infant baptism, to "save" the hyper-reality he sees as the essence of filmic truth. Edy Williams (the former Mrs. Russ Meyer) articulates the same phenomenological problem at the other end of the theoretical scale when she describes her forthcoming movie to *Esquire* (July 1973): "There'll be all sorts of frontal nudity and sex, and I'm going to make everyone in the audience *come*."

What is the "reel world," that verbal pun which in fact describes precisely the technological, artistic, and representational pun which is the film? It is an art that seems at once absolutely artificial and absolutely realistic: the reel on which those incredibly convincing hallcinations are wound and stored is so mechanical, so remote from our inherited prejudices about the comparative "naturalness" of oil on canvas, wind forced through an oboe, or words on the page. Indeed, in its combination of artificiality and compulsiveness, film as a medium reaches almost the level of tension that thinkers have discovered in language itself, that first of perceptual machines, at once an arbitrary system of rules and interfaces and at the same time all we can or shall ever know of the "real." Recent theorists like Peter Wollen and Robin Wood have, in fact, made some progress toward a linguistic description of film, utilizing the tools and methods of structural analysis to explore the complexities of film as language.

One problem with such semiological approaches, though, is their innocence. As with the structural description of language, the structural description of film tends to assume a rather constricted, alembicated delimitation of the subject before the analysis can even begin. Everything Saussure says about language, that is, is startlingly, brilliantly right; but he does not say everything there is to say, and much less do his disciples (particularly the American Bloomfieldian structuralists), who erect his concision of viewpoint into dogma. In the same way, even as interesting a study as Wollen's *Signs and Meaning in the Cinema* can at times give us the impression that we have been intellectually cold-decked. In his important third chapter, Wollen discusses the various kinds of signs that language and film are capable of producing in an attempt to get at the distinctive (i.e., nonliterary) quality of film language. Here is his conclusion: "Unlike verbal language, primarily symbolic, the cinema is, as we have seen, primarily indexical and iconic. It is the symbolic which is the submerged dimension. We should therefore expect that in the 'poetry' of the cinema, this aspect will be manifested more palpably."

The conclusion is analytically sound and, under the right circumstances, highly suggestive for the study of film. But surely many readers can be forgiven for finding this juggling of "iconic," "indexical," and "symbolic" signs a little impoverished, a little arid, if it is to account for the actuality of the films we see. It is a fact of some sociological importance (at least, for that little society called "the academy") that as film critics are beginning to achieve their deserved but hard-won franchise in humanistic studies, they seem to feel more and more compelled to imitate the solemn, deadening formalism that distinguishes so many of their established neighbors in literary and fine arts criticism. The outsider who finally makes it to the suburbs usually tends to imitate suburban styles—even if the the wallpaper *is* awful.

But this need not happen. Part of the excitement surrounding the entry of film studies into academic legitimacy is that of letting a gust of fresh air into a stuffy room. Film, as art and as subject matter for criticism, represents a challenge not only to our accepted ideas of fine art but also to our concepts of what art criticism should be. This does not mean that film theory should be the kind of pseudo-swinging, gaping "pop" appreciation which it has quite often become—particularly, I suspect, in courses taught by literary men bored with their own specialties. But it does mean that film should impel us to reexamine the nature of that reality we think we encounter on the street and think we have located and mounted, specimen fashion, on the printed page. Thus, in discussing the idea of a film language and its relationship to other, older kinds of linguistic artifacts, I want to begin with some considerations whose chief characteristic is their simplicity— a simplicity we too often edit out of our response to art. Fortunately, I have a guide.

I begin with what I have come to think of as McConnell's Theorem on Film: not my own, but one formulated by my son, Christopher. When Christopher was four, I took him to a showing of Walt Disney's *Song of the South*. Already an accomplished film watcher from hours of television, he was fascinated and delighted by the mixture of live actors and animation in the Disney film. As we picked our way out of the noisy, crowded, candy-wrapper-strewn children's matinee, we began talking about films in general and monster movies (another common affection) in particular. Trying to be a good, reassuring parent, I reminded him that he shouldn't let them frighten him, since of course the monsters—e.g., *The Son of Godzilla*, which we had seen a few days before—weren't real. Christopher thought a moment and said, "Well, the ones in *real* movies aren't, but the ones in cartoons are, you know."

I hadn't thought about it before, but he was absolutely right. The monsters in cartoons—all the characters in cartoons—are the only real things to be seen in films. That is, when you watch a cartoon, you are seeing, exactly and absolutely, what is in front of you: a projection of variously colored shapes and lines moving at calculated, eye-fooling speed. "Real"-"reel" is not a pun applicable to cartoons, since the cartoon allows no space, no epistemological gap, between the two words: the reality is what is on the reel and what exists nowhere else.

What Christopher called "*real* movies," however—films of "live action" (and only the film could have forced us to invent that tautology)—are unreal, fallacious in a relatively complex way. The living, breathing reality they record is, unlike the elemental presence of the animated cartoon, a sham: it is an elaborately encoded transcription of light that deceives us because it so intimately resembles the decoding process through which we normally perceive the world. But however complete the deception, no one—not Godzilla, Olivier, or Steve McQueen—is ever *there*.

It is important to realize that some of the basic principles of the cinema are among the most ancient conundrums in Western thought and most deeply imbued with the problems of reality and knowledge. Lucretius, writing *De natura rerum* around 50 B.C., was concerned with demonstrating the truth of Epicurean materialism: that all reality, mental as well as physical, is nothing more than variously shaped atoms colliding and rebounding in infinite combinations. In arguing this atomism from the evidence of ordinary experience, he gives us a rich description of the precinema:

> Again, *our shadow in the sunlight seems to us to move* and keep step with us and imitate our gestures, incredible though it is that unillumined air should walk about in conformity with a man's movements and gestures. For what we commonly call a shadow can be nothing but air deprived of light. Actually the earth is robbed of sunlight in a definite succession of places whenever it is obstructed by us in our progression, and that part we have left is correspondingly replenished with it. That is why the successive shadows of our body seem to be the same shadow following us along steadily step by step.

This is the phenomenon we know as the "persistence of vision." But Lucretius' earlier and less familiar presentation helps us to see its importance afresh. For this simple, long-known peculiarity of the human eye is the indispensable foundation of the art of the film. Without this frailty, the eye could not be deceived into translating a succession of still pictures into a moving picture. And if it could not be so deceived, it could never see the "real" world founded on that lie. For what the eye sees is not a world "out there," but, in a special and obsessive manner, its own operation and its own creative fallibility. The film is projected onto the screen, but it takes place somewhere in the brain cage of each spectator. To the dichotomies of "reel"-"real" and "cartoon"-"live" we add another paradox of the film experience: the experience of the movie theatre, of crowds sitting in darkness waiting for the screen to be illuminated, is at once the most public and most private experience of art to which we have access.

To return to Christopher's observation, it is the live action film, as opposed to the cartoon, which we naturally call the "realistic" movie. As he enters treatment to rid him of his antisocial tendencies, Alex, the violent antihero of Anthony Burgess's *A Clockwork Orange*,

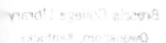

observes that blood never looks as much like the real thing in life as it does when it is spilled on the screen. And his treatment, which will establish in him a conditioned antiviolent response by associating the effects of nauseating drugs with films of bloodshed, bears out his point in terrifying fashion. (Stanley Kubrick's problematic film of *A Clockwork Orange* maintains and cleverly inverts this relationship: the only blood we see actually spilled in the film is *in the films* shown Alex during his treatment.)

Sociologists have been making hay for some time now out of the movie-ridden nature of our culture, the indisputable fact that many of our dearest fantasies are manufactured out of celluloid. More elegantly, critics like Dwight MacDonald and Parker Tyler point out how the most ancient and perennial yearnings of the psyche find their clearest modern manifestation in the hyperworld of the film. Theorists like Kracauer and Bazin make of the filmic image something very like a totem or sacrament, more intimately and mystically allied with reality than is any other human technology. Bazin argues that the picture is not only artifact, but itself a "natural object": in photography, "for the first time, between the originating object and its reproduction there intervenes only the instrumentality of a nonliving agent." The film obliterates the artist, in his traditional role as recorder of reality, and therefore frees him for a more abstract, more delicate kind of art, that of organizing the impartial, mechanical registrations of the camera into some kind of unity.

We may, in fact, regard Bazin's ideal of the film artist—the *auteur*, in his now-famous phrase—as a rather Lucretian conception. His is an artist whose only exercise of creative will is the organization of an immutable—and immutably *other*—physical reality. At any rate, it is interesting to notice the points at which Bazin and Kracauer, two of the most influential theorists of the film, sound much like the epic poet of atomism defending the reality of his universe by argument from the deceptive and yet somehow truthful interplay of shadow and light.

But any filmgoer knows as much, and a good deal more, about the ultimate reality of film, although perhaps not consciously. He knows, indeed, the central fact that the realism of the photographic image is only part of the technical and epistemological subtlety of the film, and that that realism is constantly complemented and undermined, in our viewing of a film, by another element. The combination of photographic, "live" reality and cartoon animation in *Song of the South* or (even more elaborately) in *Mary Poppins* pleases us, not simply because of its ingenuity, but because it is in its way a history of the cinema itself, a sophisticated recognition of the dual origins of the art.

This twofold origin remains a tension-charged, unresolved mix to the present day. For it represents two kinds of reality, two ways of suggesting and creating a world, which do not necessarily coincide or even tolerate each other at all points. We may call them the "cartoon" and the "photographic" elements. But to discover really efficient and suggestive names for them we must reexamine the technological history of the cinema.

As a survey like Kenneth MacGowan's *Behind the Screen* makes clear, the cinema is a hybrid form sprung from the parallel development, during the nineteenth century, of the magic-lantern show and the camera. The former is a shadowgraph, or series of silhouettes which appear to move when spun rapidly before a light source. The latter is the elaborate process, about which Bazin and others have so much to say, of recording light impulses. It is crucial to realize that initially these two developments had nothing whatever to do with each other.

The art of the shadowgraph is a representation of reality purely in terms of process and time. The constituent drawings, or silhouettes, of the series mean nothing in themselves and are only the crudest approximations of their subject (a horse running, a clown jumping, etc.). It is only in process that their truth becomes manifest, that one actually sees, not a horse or a clown, but the fact of a horse running, and so on: it is a kind of abstraction of time into its own profile.

The art of the camera, on the other hand, is that of the frozen moment, the annihilation of time as process. No one, surely, has failed to notice the posed stiffness of old daguerreotypes, the now almost legendary artificiality of the family photographs of our grandfathers (a stiffness parodied in recent nostalgic films like *Butch Cassidy and the Sundance Kid, Bonnie and Clyde,* and *The Godfather*). Normally, we assign this posed quality to the oldtimers' confusion between photograph and painting. But, in fact, the stiffness was primarily dictated by the comparative slowness of shutter and film in older cameras. And this is a practical indication of the true function of the machine, which is to catch time and translate it into subtle gradations of shadow and light, a spatial configuration of high points which might preserve, and transcend by preserving, the atomic moment. In their discussions of photographic reality, film critics do not normally pay close enough attention to this ineluctably frozen quality of the photograph. Far from being the precinema which Kracauer, Bazin, and the film semiologists think it, the photograph, divorced from its stormy union with the shadowgraph-process, is really an anticinema. In his essay "The Work of Art in the Age of Mechanical Reproduction," the Marxist critic Walter Benjamin comes much closer to the truth of the matter when he remarks on the inexpressible melancholy of the photograph, the "snap-shot," which is a record not only of a moment of human life but also of the moment's sad *pastness*.

Is it merely capricious to see in the conflict of these two technologies a reflection of the duality of the persistence of vision itself —that is, of the fundamental perceptive tension between the dynamic and the fixed, between our desire to move forward and our equally strong desire to stay where we are? It may well be that one of the reasons for film's arrival and for its present indisputable dominance over the other arts is precisely its combination of these two primal dimensions of human consciousness—its combination, in unique and stark interrelationship, of the quest for permanence and the quest for the future.

I have mentioned *Mary Poppins* as an example of the dual nature of film. By no means a major film, it nevertheless underscores—and, indeed, beautifully incarnates—many of the points we have been discussing. Like some minor but rich Elizabethan pastorals or Victorian novels, it unselfconsciously, but not naïvely, incorporates the central conventions of its art and thus can illuminate the nature of the art itself more directly than many greater works.

In the most famous sequence of the film, governess Mary Poppins (Julie Andrews) takes her two charges, the Banks children, to visit Bert (Dick Van Dyke), street artist and benevolent *fainéant*. Bert has just completed an elaborate pastel pastoral, a drawing of a rolling English countryside, sketched on the concrete outside the gate to Hyde Park, that "real" pastoral imported into the heart of London. Mary was to have taken the children to the park, but at their and Bert's urging she opens her magic parasol and they parachute into the drawing. What follows is a "jolly holiday with Mary" in which the four "live" characters mount a cartoon carousel, finally ride the horses off the carousel and down the road, and lunch at a restaurant operated by cartoon penguins. It is all what we have been carefully taught to sneer at as classic Disney—soft-line sentimentality, the apocalypse of the childish. But it is also immensely moving, for throughout the sequence, the film (not *Mary Poppins*) speaks of its origins and potentialities.

Permanence and process, photograph and magic lantern, spatial and temporal reality enter into complex transactions in the sequence. Significantly, it is a *drawing* of Bert's which becomes real (i.e., animated) by Mary's magic. Like the Prospero of Shakespeare's *Tempest*, she is a pastoral sorceress whose power is allied with and limited by the magic of the art which creates her. The magic lantern, which in the nineteenth century finally gave to drawings the power of movement, is counterpointed by the photograph, which carried to its ultimate the instantaneous nature of the picture. Both technologies, that is, define themselves in contrast to the conventional idea of art, as extensions of that notion into new and adventurous realms of perception. Which is real—the photographic images of Julie Andrews and Dick Van Dyke (light-ghosts of actors playing roles), or the tap-dancing penguins who serve them (projections of shapes that are really there, but which have no existence off the reel on which they are printed or the screen on which they are cast)? Both, of course, but in interestingly different ways.

This is the point, not only of the jolly holiday sequence, but of the plot of *Mary Poppins*. For if the magic of the art is its balance between permanence and process—a balance of philosophies having their metabolic root in the way we actually see the world—the magic of Mary Poppins herself is to initiate her charges into a saner reality, a more expansive childhood. She is the fairy-tale good mother who compensates for the children's vague, conventional real mother and who, through her vision (the vision of cinematic possibilities), cures the unhealthy impersonality of the Banks family. She is a saver of children: that is, a preserver of the balance between present and future, reality and growth, which is the romantic, metaphysical significance of the archetype of the child. And in the film, she performs this service *through* the film, through the enchanted passage into and out of the moving picture Bert (the fantasy good father) has made, the cross-pollination of the realities of perception. The jolly holiday ends when rain begins to wash away the sidewalk drawing and the adults and children must jump back onto the pavement outside Hyde Park. But the return to "reality" is not a cancellation of the enchanted world of the holiday, but rather a solidification of its gift—precisely, the gift to put "reality" between inverted commas.

It is unfortunate that the phrase "Mary Poppins" has become almost a synonym for childish sentimentality and irresponsible optimism. For though these elements may be present in the film (as they are in much greater works, including all of Dickens and most of Shakespeare), much more is present also. I have spoken of the seductive quality of the film experience. The image of the jolly holiday is, surely, an immensely seductive—and hence embarrassing—allurement, including as it does the invitation to surrender to all those impulses and wishes which the adult in us makes a lifelong job of suppressing. But *Mary Poppins*, and perhaps film in general, is nowhere so valuable as in the case it makes *for* that surrender; a self-conscious resuscitation of the latent child can finally attain, not childishness or childlikeness, but the visionary infantilism that, as the last two centuries have taught us, is perhaps the most efficient viaticum to real human maturity and civilization. For an adult to watch and enjoy *Mary Poppins* should, at least, require a tough-minded act of self-recognition and self-forgiveness. Christopher's capsule review, as we recently left his first (my third) viewing, was, "I know it's just a movie, but wouldn't it be nice if there *really* was a Mary Poppins?" That subjunctive—wouldn't it be nice?—that sense of reality in quotes, is largely what the film is about (as in *As You Like It*, where the Fool Touchstone epitomizes pastoral fantasy in the phrase "Much virtue in *if*"). And, indeed, it would.

Often, as with any art, one finds a relatively minor work like *Mary Poppins* exhibiting particularly resonant and striking details. But the real value of such resonance is its implication for the central concerns of major works. Taking *Mary Poppins* as a kind of ground bass of simplicity, we can see the counterpoint between our two senses of cinematic reality elaborated in a series of films of much greater stature.

Let us turn to another children's film, perhaps the best ever made. Victor Fleming's 1939 *The Wizard of Oz* is, among many other things, an extended essay on the nature of the fantastic, and on the sham, the lie, at the heart of poetic (and filmic) truth. So many clichés have grown up about the film that it is by now difficult to recognize its full brilliance. Like some of the greatest romantic lyrics, it has become virtually invisible through overexposure.

Indeed, it *is* a romantic lyric—a meditation on the landscape of perception which alters the landscape by altering perception itself. Unlike the complacencies of a jolly holiday with nurse Mary, Dorothy's journey to see the Wizard is as dangerous and as truly terrifying as Keat's journey to the center of the Nightingale's song or Alice's to the Red Queen's court. For, once the nature of "holiday"—of escape into artifice—has been absorbed into the conscious structure of the artifice itself, that escape becomes the much more serious business of the night journey, the underworld voyage at the heart of myth and of human experience.

Over the Rainbow, "Where troubles melt like lemon drops / Away, above the chimney tops," is a world adequate to desire, adequate to Dorothy's Kansas-bound, color-starved nostalgia for the future. The shift from black and white in Kansas to color in the dream world of Oz is blatantly obvious allegory, but it is the blatancy of genius. Through historical accident, we tend to associate color film with spectacle and fantasy and black and white with documentary realism. Of course, this habit of association is a mirror-reversal of our perception of daily, nonfilmic reality: in the movie theatre, colorblindness is the norm. But *The Wizard of Oz* deliberately utilizes this common association, raising it to the level of a perception in which we are asked to participate. Oz is not real: the color film tells us it is only a dream from the beginning. And yet it also reminds us that we really see things in color, that whatever happens over the rainbow is not simply fantasy, but fantasy whose innermost structure is a transformation, a distortion, and therefore a model of the truth of our lives.

I reinvoke Keats: "The Imagination may be compared to Adam's dream—he awoke and found it truth." The manipulation and counterpointing of realities in a film like *The Wizard of Oz* is Adam's dream in the most explicit, since metabolic, terms. We awake, leave the theatre, and walk into less-than-technicolor daylight, to discover that our fantasies—not those of the film, but those which the film forces us to recapitulate and recognize—are the truest things about our mental lives.

"Was it a vision, or a waking dream? / Fled is that music:—Do I wake or sleep?" Thus Keats concludes his own dream-odyssey to the center of the nightingale's song. And Dorothy's rather more banal comment on awaking back in Kansas—"Oh, Auntie Em, there's no place like home!"—loses its banality in the context of the film it concludes. There is, literally, no *place* like home. For all of us home is not a place but precisely the perceptual field of vision that allows us to inhabit and humanize "places," imprinting them with the varied shapes of our own reality. We simultaneously wake and sleep, observe and dream, in our unending business of living in and harmonizing the two universes, those inside and outside the head.

The Wizard of Oz is one of a number of important films—*The Cabinet of Doctor Caligari, The Woman in the Window, Repulsion,* and others—involving the mechanism of dreaming not simply as a plot device but as a central aspect of their structure. Indeed, the undeniably dreamlike quality of film viewing itself, and the kind of perceptual self-consciousness we have been noting in the medium, make the dream plot a natural resource of film narrative. Edwin S. Porter, the early director whose *Great Train Robbery* and *Life of an American Fireman* established the possibilities of the art for recording action and narrative continuity, also established the relationship of film to fantasy in his lesser-known *Dream of a Rarebit Fiend*. But the ancestry of the motif goes back far beyond Porter.

I imagine that by this point, at least some readers are disturbed by my association of *Mary Poppins* with *The Tempest* or of *The Wizard of Oz* with the "Ode to a Nightingale." If such disturbance has been generated, I assume that it is either because of the evident absurdity of comparing the sublime to the ridiculous or because of the evident pretentiousness of trying to dignify film with literary flummery. For this is precisely the crux, the central "scandal" of film as art to which I alluded at the beginning of this discussion: it forces us, like any good dream, to take it more seriously than its own terms seem to support. Elliott Sirkin, writing in *Film Comment*, takes a healthy sideswipe at the "ponderous, self-ignorantly deranged flights of mock-erudite ecstasy, launched by lumpen philosophy and English majors who sincerely believe in the affinities between Thomas Hobbes and Robert Aldrich and the relevance of G. W. F. Hegel to D. W. Griffith." Despite the Agnewesque accumulation of dyslogistic adjectives, it is a fairly clear statement of what is most annoying and offensive about a good deal of humanistic film theory. And yet, one wants to ask Sirkin, what are we to do? For scandalous as the fact may be, Hobbes and Aldrich, and Hegel and Griffith, *do* make larger sense of each other than either set makes by itself alone. The reel world is a distinctly literary world, a narrative world which constantly converts—in Kenneth Burke's phraseology—"terms for narrative" into "terms for order," and which therefore forces us back, again and again, to find literary, philosophical, and linguistic analogues for the moving images we witness and which so strangely move us. The difficulty, I think, has largely been that critics who have understood the literary nature of film have, as literary men, tended to assume that this means that film is, at best, an adjunct or an interesting technological footnote to older, more established modes of novelistic, lyrical, and dramatic meaning. What I am trying to argue here is that film, in its essence, represents a new *kind* of "literature" —and one which, in its radical opposition to accepted notions about literature, requires us to revise our ideas of literature itself.

But the origins of such radical revisionism are found in literature before the advent of the film. The well-known critic of English romanticism M. H. Abrams has written a highly suggestive essay on the structure of what he calls the "greater romantic ode." According to Abrams, the romantic lyric at its most typical and most powerful involves a tripartite movement. The romantic poet first witnesses a given landscape (Mont Blanc, the River Wye above Tintern Abbey, etc.), then finds that landscape transformed by his own perception of it into a visionary model of human consciousness and perception, and finally returns to the original, quotidian and "realistic" landscape with which he began, but which has been irrevocably changed through his lyrical elaboration of it. Abrams's terms describe not only Shelley's "Mont Blanc" and Keats's "Ode to a Nightingale," but, point-for-point, a film like *The Wizard of Oz.* For Dorothy also undergoes the tripartite evolution of consciousness which the major romantic poets discovered as the key to human perception. But the crucial difference—not just from Romantic lyricism, but also from L. Frank Baum's original *Oz* novel—is that the film *The Wizard of Oz* not only suggests but enforces the transformations involved in the romantic lyric. The figure of the archetypal poet, suffering and perceiving on behalf of all mankind, disappears from the world of the film (how many films, even including those of Cocteau, successfully incarnate the figure of the poet?), and what is left to replace the void of his disappearance is the audience itself. An interesting and profound question which no one, to my knowledge, but children ask of *The Wizard of Oz* is this: does *Dorothy* see only black and white in Kansas and color in Oz, or do *we*? At one level, of course, it is a rude and absurd question, like asking how Shelley can say to a skylark, which he *knows* is a bird, "Bird thou never wert." But at a rather more complicated—which is, in this case, to say a more childlike— level, the two questions make a great deal of sense indeed. Both questions go to the center of the redefinition of awareness their respective subjects demand, and both, in their innocence, underscore for us the degree of credibility which our "sophisticated" reading is prepared to grant its texts in order to preserve their truth. Shelley says that his symbolic bird is not a bird just so that we can question his reasons for saying so and thus move into the visionary landscape of the romantic ode. And in Oz Dorothy sees colors which she does not see in Kansas just so that we ourselves can collaborate in the creation of a visionary world, making each of us a participant in the construction of an ode to failed chances, lost visions, which are, finally, *not* lost and *not* failed.

The quarrel of romanticism with reality was that reality had become, through the development of nineteenth-century science and technology, too *other* to man; it had become too much a secretion of his intelligence, which had, fundamentally, nothing to do with his most primal and perennial needs. And this quarrel led the romantic movement, in its phase of maximum exhaustion, into the twin traps of symbolism and naturalism. The first alternative (as exemplified in Wilde, Yeats, Beerbohm) was an attempt to locate the imaginative impulse in an absolutely nontechnological, nonmechanical myth of consciousness—to insist, in fact, that the personality of the artist had no more than an *ideal* connection with the production of the artwork. Carrying to an extreme the aesthetics of Shelley and Browning, the symbolist movement could believe (or make believe) that the artistic activity was inevitably betrayed and diminished whenever it came in contact with the sordid business of machine production, and hence that (as with the aesthetics of William Morris) only a return to enlightened amateurism, to the totalitarian handcrafting of artifacts, could save the world or consciousness from mechanization. (This attitude still survives in the cult of the underground—i.e., badly made— film, as witness the work of Stan Brakhage or the criticism of Gene Youngblood.)

Naturalism, on the other hand, may be seen as an attempt by the romantic movement to reconcile itself with the myth of the machine, the myth of technology triumphant. Zola, Dreiser, and even Hemingway give us a vision of romantic prophecy defeated: the ideal of the autonomous intelligence cognizant of and complicit in the capitulation of mind to the mechanization of the human world. In this phase of its career, romanticism turned upon itself, denying, in a paroxysm of self-contempt, not only the validity of the prophetic vision of the world, but also the vision of the world as a unified entity. It insisted instead upon a disjunctive, slow-motion sense of reality which not even film could adequately, or with quite the same sense of deprivation, represent. Witness the great first paragraph of *A Farewell to Arms*:

> In the late summer of that year we lived in a village that looked across the river and the plain to the mountains. In the bed of the river there were pebbles and boulders, dry and white in the sun, and the water was clear and swiftly moving and blue in the channels. Troops went by the house and down the road and the dust they raised powdered the leaves of the trees. The trunks of the trees too were dusty and the leaves fell early that year and we saw the troops marching along the road and the dust rising and leaves, stirred by the breeze, falling and the soldiers marching and afterward the road bare and white except for the leaves.

This is language imitating the supposed impartiality of the camera, but also language annihilating itself in a hyper-real self-cancellation. We learn, as we read *A Farewell to Arms*, that Frederick Henry, the narrator, has lost both his sense of identity and his sense of human community in the First World War; that he has deserted the war in disgust, only to find a deeper disgust, in his retreat, with the inevitable nihilism of life itself. His narrative, then, will be that of a sleepwalker, that of a man trying not to remember the traumatic reality of his experience. And here, as so often in Hemingway's work, that deliberate denial of memory and stylization (and therefore evasion) of reality is articulated in terms of the perennial present, the atomization of time into discrete instants which denies, as it alludes to, the reality described by Lucretius and by the art of the film.

Between the alternatives of symbolism and of naturalism, however, the romantic quest for an efficient human consciousness continued, and that quest was incarnated in the early movie. And here, once again, we see the wisdom of André Bazin's observation that the film was an invention of the nineteenth century even before the nineteenth century had invented it. For if romanticism had succeeded in dividing the universe into the organized world inside the head and the chaotic world outside the head, the universe of human order and the universe of natural disorder, then film and the new sense of reality which the film brought with it succeeded in proposing a new way to map those disparate realities onto each other. "Reality" itself, in the context of film, is no longer an absolute to be discussed, described, or denied: it is a variable to be defined by the performance of the camera, for the first time a function—not a condition—of creativity.

We have all become acclimatized to the "reality" of the film experience, so much so, that it is difficult to comprehend precisely what that experience represents in the history of consciousness (it is almost as difficult, indeed, to comprehend what the experience of reading means in the history of civilization). But it was a long while before the film decided what sort of reality was its proper sphere. That length of time itself should suggest the difficulty of the decision. In other words, Hemingway's realism and that of most naturalistic novelists of this century depends upon a choice basically conditioned by film, a choice having almost nothing to do with the "real" state of affairs and everything to do with the particular sort of reality bequeathed by romantic tradition and filmic development.

We have examined *Mary Poppins* and *The Wizard of Oz*. Now let us turn to a work where the certitudes of these fantasy films are very uncertain indeed, both in terms of the story told by the film and the era of film history which the work initiates. I am referring to *The Cabinet of Doctor Caligari* (1919). Here, the disjunctive worlds of the romantic ode are present, not merely as an overtone, but as the central subject.

The film opens with an old man, seated on what appears to be a park bench, telling a young man, "There are spirits in the air around us—I myself have seen them." The young man then points to a woman walking through the park. "That is my fiancée," he says. "What has happened to us is stranger than any tale I know." He proceeds to tell his tale, how a strange mesmerist—Dr. Caligari—came to his hometown fair advertising the display of the "somnambulist" Cesare; thwarted by local officials, Caligari sends his automaton-like sleepwalker on a series of missions of murder and violence until he is found out by the narrator and tracked to his home, a sanitarium of which he is the director. The film seems to end with the arrest and confinement in a straitjacket of the mad doctor. But after this scene, we cut back to the park bench of the opening, only to discover that it is the *narrator* who is mad, in fact a deluded, paranoid patient in the asylum run by the kindly doctor who is the villain of his tale. It is probably the most famous and most controversial dream-ending in the history of film. Even from the brief summary I have given, it is at once apparent that the central structure of *Caligari* is the tripartite structure of vision described by Abrams as definitive of romantic lyricism. Here, again, it is the viewing audience which is asked to play the transforming role of the romantic poet: both the youthful narrator and the ambiguous doctor (acted to perfection by Werner Krauss) are unreliable consciousnesses, and it is *we* who make the transition from "real" world to fantasy world (the "Caligari" plot) back to "real" world transformed. In this respect, however, *Caligari* raises more problems than it clarifies, and goes far beyond the other two films we have discussed in its vision of the "reel world" and the "real world."

Let me, once again, refer to my authority: when Christopher and I watched *Caligari* on television one Sunday afternoon, he was excited by the prospect of seeing a famous monster movie, bored by the first third of the film, frightened by the middle, and by the end had gone off to play with the little boy across the street. Most commentators on the film have had the same sort of reaction. The framing narrative of *Caligari* has been almost universally condemned as a loss of nerve, an act of bad faith, on the part of the producers and director. We know, indeed, that Carl Mayer and Hans Janowitz, the scriptwriters, were incensed when the frame was added to their original screenplay, in which the Caligari story was taken at face value, as the true or real story. And, of course, it is the middle section of the film, accounting for approximately 90 percent of its running time, which we remember and upon which *Caligari's* reputation is based.

But the frame-tale is not only necessary to *Caligari* but is in fact the true source of its genius. There is corroboration for this position. Fritz Lang was originally offered the direction of *Caligari*, but because of other commitments finally had to abandon the project, leaving it to the less famous director Robert Wiene. But, as Lang tells Peter Bogdanovich in the series of interviews collected as *Fritz Lang in America*, he himself had intended to use a framing device for the central, "mad" story. Lang is not a director many would accuse of moral cowardice or of capitulation to considerations of censorship or box office. And with his authority, we may ask if the frame in *Caligari* does not tell us something important not only about the particular film but about the medium itself.

The analogy I have suggested to film reality, that of the tripartite romantic ode, would of course demand some such device as the frame, some establishment of a "natural" landscape at beginning and end of the story against which the central, visionary part of the story could be counterpointed. But I think the exigency goes deeper than simply that. *Caligari* is perhaps one of the few films ever to be conceived originally in terms of its décor. And the painted, expressionist sets of the middle section are among the best-known, most unmistakable sets in the history of the film. Nothing is real, nothing is even natural: all lines are out of perpendicular, all angles are sharp and jagged, even the doors open and shut at a bias. It is only in the opening and closing frame-scenes that we see a realistic set, a convincing representation of an out-of-doors park bench. Looking at the film from the dual vantage of the romantic analogy and of what we have seen about film fantasy in *Mary Poppins* and *The Wizard of Oz*, we can begin to revise our sense of it. The middle section—whose whole point is terror and whose whole original conception is that of the painted scenery—is, in fact, as terrifying as it is because it is a *frozen cartoon*. As in the jolly holiday of the painted penguins and the nightmare-vacation of colored, animated Oz, the nightmare-scape of *Caligari* is film taking cognizance of its origins in the magic-lantern show; but, in this case, it is also film deliberately isolating and paralyzing that aspect of its genesis. Real (live) actors scuttle across painted, obviously and absurdly artificial scenes; and what the eye notices and the mind remembers is, preeminently, the artificiality of the sets.

No critic, I think, has mentioned the powerful effect of the opening shot of the middle, "mad" sequence of *Caligari*. The narrator is beginning his tale; the printed title reads, "Our town. The Fair." And we see for the first time the painted scenery which is the landscape of a madman's vision. But our very first sight of this landscape (after an initial and obviously "painterly" painting to show the overview of "our town") is of a painted carousel revolving against a painted backdrop. Now, a carousel is a mechanical device whose original intent is to reproduce the "real" feeling of riding a horse. It is, in other words, a direct nineteenth-century relative of the magic lantern (which also involved a "carousel," a circular set of painted silhouettes held against the light), a machine designed to counterfeit reality, a technologically manufactured experience—a version of precinema. Indeed, the makers of *Caligari*, sixty years closer to the origins of the phenomenon than are we, were certain to be aware of it all the more strongly. And while a mechanical representation of real experience may, to the innocent, be convincing on an elemental level, the mechanical representation *of* a mechanical representation cannot help but arouse the most profound, instinctive suspicions about the nature of what, precisely, is being presented. The entire central section of the film may, indeed, be extrapolated from the ridiculously unreal carousel that is our initial vision of its world. What you are about to witness, that first shot says, is a series of images which are not only highly artificial, but which include artificiality and illusion as part of their central content—which will ask you, as spectator, to decide for yourself how far you are prepared to trust their artificiality, and therefore how much belief in your own real world you are willing to sacrifice in order to sustain and preserve your enjoyment of the story about to be played out.

Du musst ein Caligari werden, "You must become a Caligari." This was the slogan used in the advance publicity for *The Cabinet of Dr. Caligari*, and it became—like all successful advertising slogans— a common in-joke, in this case, among cultured Germans of the early twenties (more or less like the "offer you can't refuse" in seventies America, following the success of *The Godfather*). But *Du musst ein Caligari werden* is also the slogan which Dr. Caligari, *in* the film, sees written (in neon) across his world at the moment when his mind snaps and he decides to become a psychopathic villain. That moment is one of the most powerful in the film: the mad doctor does, indeed, decide upon his madness, chooses it, in the same way that film allows us to choose our belief or disbelief in the photographic fiction being played out for us. The original Caligari, the film tells us, was a famous medieval savant and magician who displayed, in his travels, a somnambulist which mindlessly performed his evil bidding. The mad doctor, as the "mad" section of the film narrates, becomes obsessed with the figure of the ancient Caligari, until finally, upon discovering a contemporary case of somnambulism, he is forced to assimilate the identity of his medieval archetype: *Du musst ein Caligari werden.*

Not many films are as perceptive as *Caligari* about the relationship between the art of the film and the art of writing, between movies and fiction. It is a written text, after all, which drives the Caligari of the central narrative mad; and, like Quixote, he is already a man whose imagination has been warped by the black-letter volumes over which his life has been spent poring. We have, in fact, not simply a frame-tale and a fiction within that frame, but at least three tales embedded within one another: the mad narrator, his mad story, and the equally mad fixation upon historical texts which is the downfall of the antihero of the madman's tale. "You must become a Caligari," the film's advertising argues and its crucial scene tells us, and much of the energy of the film is directed toward underscoring that imperative. Writing and books, those artificial "cartoons" of reality, and photography, an apparently naturalistic reflection of the real world, cancel and comment upon each other in *Caligari.* The film remains as intelligent and as deeply disturbing today as when it was first made, two world wars ago.

Caligari is an unrealistic film, but part of its lack of realism is precisely because it is deeply involved with matters of realism and fantasy as qualities which film, as art or artifice, calls into question. Like the jolly holiday sequence of *Mary Poppins*, but much more subtly, *Caligari* reminds us that once we have made the initial decision to watch the film—i.e., to give some sort of credence to its series of patently fallacious images—we have thereby sacrificed our comfortable, everyday assumptions about the separation of fantasy and reality. Coleridge, writing a century before *Caligari* and out of the context of the romantic ode, could speak of the "willing suspension of disbelief" which it is the poet's right to demand of his audience. It was not until the development of film, however, that we could comprehend how dangerous that suspension of disbelief could become. As we ask of *The Wizard of Oz*, though more securely, we may also ask of *The Cabinet of Dr. Caligari*: What is more "real," the fantasy or the unrelenting reality framing the fantasy? the transformation of the landscape into apocalyptic vision, or the "real" landscape with which we begin and end? Or, when do we most truly wake, and when most truly sleep? The final scene of *Caligari* returns us to the sane world of the asylum (the world, that is, where insane fantasies are kept under restraints, at a distance from the normal people). But the final shot is of Werner Krauss's face, as he muses to himself, "So he thinks I am the madman Caligari. Now I see how I can cure his delusion." If this is a happy ending, it is one singularly devoid of comfort or reassurance. We do not, of course, know what the Doctor's curative treatment will be—and we need not be familiar with recent developments in behaviorist psychotherapy to fear that the remedy may be as bad as, or worse than, the disease. But more centrally, we are disturbed by the sight of Krauss's face itself, that face which the fantasy-center of the film has taught us to associate with malevolent, irrational destructiveness. We *remember*, in other words, what the explicit story of the film has told us to forget: the potential evil and dehumanization of official authority. And it is this tension between memory and forgetfulness, between the reality of the film's images conceived on two different levels, that constitutes its lasting horror.

Indeed, the idea of memory—at once the prime constituent and most problematic element of a truly human personality—is crucial to all the films we have discussed and, I believe, crucial to the nature of film reality itself. At the most basic level, returning to Lucretius and the persistence of vision, we may say that we *see* moving pictures through a kind of deceptive physiological "memory" of the optic nerve itself: the series of still photographs moves for us because our eyes "remember" the gap, the continuity between $photo_1$, $photo_2$, $photo_3$, . . ., $photo_n$, even when it does not exist. And the most fantastic films in our history are fantastic, not because they deny, but rather because they reassert and raise to the conscious level of plot, action, and image the curious double heritage of film technology, at once a lie and a higher truth.

It is no accident, in this respect, that the most memorable horror of *The Cabinet of Dr. Caligari* is the figure of Cesare the somnambulist, the role which was to make Conrad Veidt internationally famous. Cesare, in his movements and in his makeup, is the progenitor of film's most successful monster, Boris Karloff's Frankenstein. But he is perhaps even more significant than Karloff's creature. As the agent of Caligari's malevolence, Cesare is not quite the problematic automaton of Dr. Frankenstein, but rather an ambiguous "creation," a sleepwalker, definitively human but deprived of the definitive quality of human life, its self-consciousness. Indeed, if film, as we have been examining it in terms of romantic sensibility, is a carefully engineered "waking dream" of reality, then the figure of Cesare may well represent one of the most authentic monstrosities of the art, since he represents the horror of forgetfulness, of being forever lost in a dream, which is so central to our lived experience of the film-*as*-dream. The problem of the automaton, or of the evolution of human speech and consciousness out of a seemingly mechanistic physiognomy and anatomy, has of course been at the heart of many of the greatest romantic myths—"The Rime of the Ancient Mariner," Mary Shelley's *Frankenstein*, Byron's *Manfred*—and many of the greatest romantic films—Fritz Lang's *Metropolis*, James Whale's *Frankenstein*, Stanley Kubrick's *2001: A Space Odyssey*. And to examine the image of the automaton even partially is to venture into the complex nature of film language, indeed of language itself as it is regarded by contemporary linguists. But here we may note, at least, that Cesare in *Caligari* has a special permanence and persistence. The other two main characters, the demented narrator and the ambiguous doctor, change their roles and their behavior between the sane and the mad parts of the narrative, but Cesare, the eternal dreamer lost in a trance from which he cannot extricate himself, appears in both the mad village and the antiseptic asylum with precisely the same gestures, the same fixed, pathetic stare. We think of Dorothy not able to escape from Oz, of Keats if he could not ask, "Do I wake or sleep?"

The art of the narrative film, V. F. Perkins observes in *Film as Film*, is to force the observer to put a false construction upon a set of true images. It is a fine observation and one which Perkins means to explain our most elementary manner of "reading" a movie: we are shown a close-up of a hand holding a pistol; the gun fires; we are shown a full-length shot of a man clutching his chest and falling to the floor; we believe (or part of us believes, at least) that we have just seen a man shot dead. I think, though, that we may take Perkins's insight to an even more elementary level: not that at which we reconstruct the action of a film, but that at which we, as viewers, make the *initial decision* to view the action at all. General theories of film tend to divide between those which regard it as a free-floating, dreamlike series of associative images (such theories overvalue the abstract, underground film) and those which regard it as a preternaturally clear, truthful image of the real world (these, naturally, tend to overvalue documentary styles). But the formula "false construction of true images"—like the idea of Adam's dream, which he awoke to find true—helps us see that film is actually a much more complex experience than such elephantine theories manage to account for. For film is a dream—but a dream whose inescapable content is the dreamlike nature of its own reality. Most people have had that particularly curious feeling during a dream of knowing that they are dreaming and of even being able "consciously" to manipulate the unfolding of the dream in which they are caught. It is the achievement of film—and, indeed, of romantic and modern literature—to raise this confusing experience of mirrored dream and reality to the deliberate, stylized level of a major art and a major epistemological, phenomenological problem. Even the most innocently popular movie, in other words, viewed by even the most unselfconscious, uncritical movie buff, involves at an elemental level the questions of memory, perception, identity, and reality that *Caligari*, *The Wizard of Oz*, and *Mary Poppins* incorporate at the surface level of their style.

A remarkable number of celebrated films, in fact, employ techniques which, though more abstract than the dream-narrative itself, have much the same effect. Carl Dreyer's *Vampyr* (alternatively titled *The Strange Adventures of David Gray*) is not a dream film, although its celebrated photography renders the story of David Gray more eerie and dreamlike than the story itself, perhaps, justifies. David Gray, in the all but nonexistent plotline, finds himself in a strange countryside inhabited by a female vampire; her agent, a nefarious doctor; and two beautiful young women, one of whom has fallen prey to the vampire and one of whom is in the process of being preyed upon by her. As the action develops, Gray manages to destroy the vampire and escape with the young woman; in the famous and puzzling last scene, the doctor falls into the giant hopper of a flour mill, where he is slowly buried alive in flour falling from the massive grinder above him. Perhaps the most common interpretation for the ending is in terms of the abstract, purely cinematic value of light, with which Dreyer experiments in *Vampyr*. (Like many great early films, *Vampyr* is inconceivable in color.) Virtually the whole film is shot through a gauze filter, giving the action and the landscape an unusual, threatening paleness—a paleness we are, possibly, meant to associate with the anemic condition of the vampire's victims. In fact, the whiteness of the film increases throughout the action until, in our last sight of Gray and his lover escaping through a forest, it is all but impossible to distinguish the figures at all. The image of burial in flour, actual suffocation by whiteness, can then be regarded as the terminal triumph of style over content in *Vampyr*, the final assertion of the elegant ballet of black and white which, much more subtly and intimately than cartoon drawings or painted sets, affirms the identity of the film as an artificially constructed "magic-lantern" fantasy. Dreyer himself, of course, wrote frequently of cinematic form as an artistic balance of shapes, masses, and colors, so this reading has some justification; he confessed, indeed, that his inspiration for the flour-mill scene was the striking aesthetic effect of seeing white-coated workers in a plaster works.

But the magic lantern, here as elsewhere, is paradoxically wedded to the photograph: the two realities of artifice and nature continue their creative warfare. For our very last sight of *Vampyr*, after the doctor has been buried in flour, is of the monstrous gears of the grinding machine turning slowly to a full stop. And it is inevitable that we associate those turning gears which have just killed the doctor with the turning gears, the sprockets, and the wheels of the motion-picture projector itself, the machine that has just elaborated the abstract, mystical fantasy of David Gray's strange adventures. It is one of the most self-conscious and successful visual puns in all cinema—especially since the pun is made on the dual reality of the very medium of cinema. And to underscore the pun, Dreyer, for the first time in *Vampyr*, removes the filter from his camera: we see the gears in a sharply etched, realistic chiaroscuro that is literally shocking after the long march into mist of the rest of the film. As a way out of the unresolved delirium of the story, it reasserts the mechanical, physical bases of film's dreamlike reality (or unreality), deliberately reminding us, in fact, that all film succeeds in capturing us by making us forget our normal, everyday memory of who, what, and where we are. Dreyer's ending was borrowed recently by another Nordic film-maker, Ingmar Bergman. His *Persona* narrates the mysterious, perhaps mad love-hate of two women isolated in a country house. At the film's conclusion, after a series of rapid, time-distorting quick cuts, we are shown a final shot of the terminals of a motion-picture projector arc light separating and growing cool and dark. Bergman's image is not as successful as Dreyer's because the realism of the arc light violates our experience of the film's photographic realism: if the arc light *were* turned off, we could not see the footage of the arc light *being* turned off. Because Dreyer employs the unstated metaphor of the gears for the mechanical process of projection, he more power-fully indicates the technological foundation of his fantasy while remaining within the reality of our actual experience of viewing the film.

Given this essential duality between magic lantern and photograph, cartoon and icon in the film's presentation of reality, we may hazard a generalization about the history of film technique—a generalization remarkably parallel to the history of romantic and post-romantic writing. In earlier filmmaking and film viewing, the potentialities of the camera as a recorder of live, photographed action seem to have far outweighed—or, at least, to have been more comfortably and naturally assumed—than its possibilities as projector of fantasy. Films tended to assume photographic reality as their epistemological, narrative basis and to strive toward developing their elements of fantasy and high artifice *out of* that basis. The hallucinatory sets of *Caligari*, for example, are painted sets simply photographed by the recording camera; the hazy effect of *Vampyr* is a distortion achieved by tampering with the camera; the extreme camera angles and expressionistic lighting of James Whale's *Frankenstein* are distorting because they assume, as their ground bass, the straightforward, natural techniques of the film's village festival and marriage scenes. Even so celebrated—and overcelebrated—an intellectualization of cinema as Eisenstein's theory of montage depends upon this proportion: the montage, a rapid series of shots which manifests concepts through the collision of images, is after all simply a rebus, a puzzle whose clues are things—and things recorded with unquestioning and unquestioned faithfulness.

Curiously, though, with the evolution of film technique, film's realism seems at last to have become so efficient and complex that it actually transforms itself into a kind of higher-level fantasy, an art whose ostensible artifice comes to predominate over its realism in the minds of filmmaker and viewer alike. It is difficult and probably foolhardy to try to identify the moment of this transition, but it may be useful to associate the moment—like so much else in the history of film—with 1941 and *Citizen Kane*. For in *Kane*, all the pyrotechnics of earlier film fantasy—extreme camera angles, erratic camera movements, disorienting cuts, unusual lighting—are present, but present as the *basis* of the film's undeniable realism. It is, in the classic sense of the word, baroque art: it converts the filigree and decoration of earlier art into its own fundamental structural principle. Photographic realism has become fantastic—an encoding of the complexities of Kane's own mind—and through the very development of photographic technique. If, as the cliché goes, you can do anything with a camera, then it becomes problematic and difficult to do one special thing with it: catch the "truth." Thus Thompson, the "camera eye" reporter searching for "Rosebud," may be an almost elegiac reminiscence of a realist camera whose day has passed. We shall have more to say about *Kane* and "Rosebud" in the next chapter. But for now we may observe that, in contrast to the realist aesthetics of Eisenstein, *Kane* (and most of the major films that have succeeded it) is in fact a montage in reverse, a potentially endless set of explanations, reminiscences, and personal fantasies in search of a single object to which they might attach themselves.

I do not, of course, mean to suggest that these alternatives describe the whole range of film possibilities, nor that the history of film ideas they indicate is an exhaustively accurate one. But the two formulas do help us to locate most films on an axis of realistic tendencies: films may be regarded either as photographic icons straining toward the condition of fantasy or as fantastic dream-shows straining toward the condition of photographic iconicity.

Most of the major "intellectual's films" of the years since *Kane*, surely, constellate themselves around the second of these formulas. Whether we think of Bergman, Godard, Fellini, Resnais, or Antonioni, we are struck by the way in which the recording camera functions as a problematic truth-teller, a principle of realistic narrative whose very realism leaves a great void in the middle of our intelligence of the world—a void which can only be filled, these filmmakers suggest, by the discovery of the relativity of all truths, the dreamlike fluidity toward which all reality perpetually surges.

The ambience of these films strongly resembles that of modern postromantic fiction. The resemblance is substantiated by such facts as Antonioni's use of Julio Cortazár's story "Blow-Up," by Resnais's collaborations with Alain Robbe-Grillet, and by Visconti's concentration upon novelists like Lampedusa, Camus, and Mann for the matter of his films. Modern fiction, at least since Joyce, has become increasingly obsessed with the fictiveness of all life and all truths and with the difficulty of writing a tale that can somehow break through that inevitable fictiveness to the central, existential truth behind the numerous masks of reality. And though many critics still choose to regard such fiction as the "death of the novel," as an escape into irresponsibly aestheticized dream worlds, we can view it otherwise. The course of modern fiction, like that of film, can represent an increasingly difficult, challenging essay upon the proportions of internal fantasy and external constraint in our experiences of life, and an attempt, perennially disappointed and perennially renewed, to establish through narrative form a stable reality in which self-consciousness may come to rest. In this respect, the fictions of Thomas Pynchon or John Gardner and those of Visconti or Bertolucci are much more fundamentally similar than they are disjunctive; and the differences of medium (if, indeed, such differences are as great as literary and film specialists believe) do not affect a primary identity of quest.

The quest of film fantasy for film reality, however, is not limited to the austere works of the Viscontis and Bertoluccis. The contemporary American film, even in its most popular manifestations, appears to share the same dilemma. I began this chapter by observing the peculiarly violent nature of the contemporary American film and the strong moral critiques levied against that violence in some circles. Let me return to Edy William's theory of film reality, a theory which is especially appropriate to the current situation, and really a rather profound bit of film history. If Ms. Williams really did expect, as she indicated to *Esquire*, to make "everybody in the audience . . . *come*" in her forthcoming opus, that expectation signals a strange development indeed in the growth of popular film. For the recording techniques of the film have become so hyper-real that for the average viewer film has reached the status of personal fantasy—e.g., fantasies of masturbation or revenge. And in this situation, the narrative film must strain harder and harder for a measure of sexual excitation or of violence that will break through the solipsism of the technologized daydream. To return to our romantic model: what saves Adam's dream from being just another wet dream is that he awakes to find it true—that somehow it connects his waking and sleeping life to the life of the world around him. And in films of the last decade, we have been treated to an escalation of violent or sexual "reality" (more blood, longer moans) whose chief justification seems to be the hopelessness of breaking out of their status as "cartoons" of a desired consummation and into the reality of a real one. Pornography and porno-violence, in film as in literature, are interesting but ultimately unsuccessful alternatives for art because they are betrayed by their own idealism: they attempt to employ the means of the art self-consciously, not to transcend or to revalue, but to obliterate the means themselves as mediators between form and reality.

One technical facet of the new violence in particular relates to the point we have been making about film reality, and that is the prevalence, in recent films and television productions, of slow-motion photography and of the peculiar device of the freeze-frame. The slow-motion killing has become a trademark of Sam Peckinpah's work (*The Wild Bunch, Straw Dogs,* etc.) but has grown common enough elsewhere that we may call it one of the distinctive techniques of the sixties. Always employed at moments of maximum violence (or, in some films, maximum sexual passion), slow-motion photography is an explicit case of the formula we have been describing: the film literally retards its magic-lantern movement and calls attention to itself as a series of photographs. The freeze-frame is an even more violent assertion of the photographic nature of the motion-picture sequence.

I have mentioned the nostalgic use of old daguerreotype tints and groupings in films like *Butch Cassidy and the Sundance Kid;* but however simply nostalgic the technique might be, the actual freeze-frame has a much more striking effect. At the end of *Butch Cassidy,* Butch and Sundance are surrounded in an adobe hut by hundreds of South American police; and as they rush out of the hut in their final attempt at escape, we hear a roar of gunfire, but see the figures of the two outlaws first freeze into a photo, and then gradually shade from color into brown-and-black tint as the gunfire reverberates on the sound track. It is the most brilliant moment of that much under-rated film, for at that moment our nostalgia (for the old West that never was, for our own youth, for the photos of our grandparents) merges with the nostalgia of film itself for one of its two major origins. When you die, you become the *record* of your life: you become a photograph, all your photographs. This simple and shattering fact, incarnated in the film process itself, actually does manage something like the transition from fantasy to icon, inner to outer vision of which we have been speaking. An even more profoundly disturbing use of the freeze-frame is Hitchcock's. In both *Psycho* and *Frenzy* he shows us photos—literally, still lifes—of the two female victims of sexual murder.

But I have, at this point, left my guide Christopher rather far behind the terms of the argument, and the argument itself has, correspondingly, exhausted the usefulness of its terms. The concepts of "reality," "fantasy," "cartoon," and "photograph" are important for understanding our response to films, but they are ideas whose imprecision and, sometimes, interchangeability cannot take us past a certain point. We are not honest in our response to films—or to romantic poetry—if we deny that a large part of their attraction for us is precisely that they reawaken in us doubts, confusions, and even a certain delightful anarchism about the boundaries between make-believe and reality. These doubts and confusions are characteristic of childhood but are repressed or sublimated after maturity.

It is not enough, however, to say that romanticism, postromanticism, or film simply liberate the child within us and return us to the oceanic perceptions of the prerational. That, too, is a distortion of our experience, though one which seems to be gaining in popularity as more and more cultural critics celebrate the "new sentimentalism" of untrammelled, liberated emotion. I want to suggest that art is much closer to an old sentimentalism—to the "sentimental," in fact, as Schiller distinguishes it from the "naïve" as a universal type of poetry. The naïve perceptions of a child—or, for Schiller, of the

THE REEL WORLD

childhood of poetry and culture, the archaic masterpieces—are forever closed to us, readers and viewers of a later day. Sentimental art, the art of the romantic imagination, recognizes both the necessity of recapturing those naïve perceptions for the sake of a fully human, fully conscious life and the impossibility of recapturing that life without the aid of the sophistication, the intelligence, and the techniques of artifice which separate it from us so irrevocably. We are never, in other words, taken out of ourselves: we read the poem, view the film, as mature men and women; and the gift of the poem or film is not a cancellation of that maturity, but an enrichment of it. "Reality," "fantasy," "dream," even "consciousness" itself are terms which, in order for us efficiently to understand and control them, require another term, another gift of mind.

That gift is language—but language, as we can now see, in a much wider, more difficult sense than the "language" taken so seriously by contemporary semiologists. For whether we are dealing with poetry or film, semiology and structuralist approaches to meaning are relevant only within the highly general, aesthetically urgent problem underlying any specific description of the process of meaning: the problem of meaning as a human act at once necessary to the life of the mind and yet subject to question by its very necessity. The question is not simply, *How* do we mean? but rather, *Why* do we mean? and Why do we mean the exact meanings which seem so important to us? Adam in the Garden gave names to all the creatures. But we, heirs to his Fall as much as to his language, are faced with the more dangerous task of trying to name Adam himself—which is to say, trying to name ourselves.

Marcel Proust articulates these matters in the overture to *Remembrance of Things Past*. The overture was written before any of the films we have thus far discussed; but as Proust reexamines his memories of childhood and his means for recapturing those memories in fiction, he discusses exactly the tension between magic lantern and photograph, internal and external reality that has been the subject of this chapter. Lying awake, trying to revisit the lost Eden of his vulnerable, neurotic childhood, Proust remembers the magic-lantern slides of the hero Golo with which his mother and great-aunt had tried to divert him:

If the lantern were moved I could still distinguish Golo's horse advancing across the window-curtains, swelling out with the curves and diving into their folds. The body of Golo himself, being of the same supernatural substance as his steed's, overcame all material obstacles

—everything that seemed to bar his way—by taking each as it might be a skeleton and embodying it in himself: the door-handle, for instance, over which, adapting itself at once, would float invincibly his red cloak or his pale face, never losing its nobility or its melancholy, never shewing any sign of trouble at such a transubstantiation.

The word "transubstantiation," heavily weighted as it is with associations of eucharistic, sacramental power, is a deliberately scandalous one for Proust to employ about an insignificant toy like the magic lantern. But the images of the lantern and of the cartoon character Golo will reappear again and again in his novel and always with such overtones. For the magic lantern, and its "transubstantiating" power of converting a real, ordinary bedroom into the stuff of fantasy and saving fiction, is one of Proust's most important images for his own work, his own massive attempt to convert the memory of the ordinary into a sacramental fiction which may guarantee him the only eternity in which he chooses to believe.

Another important Proustian image, which stands in counterpoint to the magic lantern, appears later in the overture. Proust remembers his grandmother's desire that his childhood be surrounded with scenes of "natural" sublimity:

> She would have liked me to have in my room photographs of ancient buildings or of beautiful places. But at the moment of buying them, and for all that the subject of the picture had an aesthetic value of its own, she would find that vulgarity and utility had too prominent a part in them, through the mechanical nature of their reproduction by photography. She attempted a subterfuge, if not to eliminate altogether their commercial banality, at least to minimise it . . . she would inquire of Swann whether some great painter had not made pictures of them, and preferred to give me photographs of 'Chartres Cathedral' after Corot, of the 'Fountains of Saint-Cloud' after Hubert Robert.

Proust, to be sure, does not share his grandmother's curious sense of the relationship between art and photography but only because Proust's own sense of that relationship is even more curious. Throughout his book, the image of the photograph, or of photographic reality, is associated with the most intense problems of life and fiction, the relationships between the world we re-create through memory and narrative and the world as it would appear to us were our memories and narratives accurate.

Both these processes—the transubstantiating magic lantern and the vulgarizing photograph—are transcended in *Remembrance of*

Things Past by the coming-into-being of the novel itself, by Proust's arduous creation of a new language, a new system of signification that can adequately contain and revivify the warring alternatives of reality and dream which the child lost and the man needs to regain. And, we may suggest, film—insofar as it is heir to the same romantic urgencies of the self which created Proust, the magic lantern show, and the photograph—is involved in the same enterprise, the creation of another such language to contain our inner and outer universes. The scene with which *Remembrance of Things Past* begins and concludes is that of a man waking from troubled sleep to possess, to utter his dreams. And as we move from the dreamers and somnambulists of film's quizzical "reality" (Cesare, David Gray, Dorothy, ourselves under the spell of the darkened theatre) toward an examination of the film as a conscious language, a distinctively modern speech, we also move toward a grammar which may aid us in containing and preserving the curious experience of this most real, unreal of the arts.

3

ADAM AND THE AUTOMATON: THE LANGUAGE OF FILM

The "language of film" is a concept —some might call it a cliché—of film criticism about which we have already heard a great deal; and as film establishes itself increasingly as a serious academic subject, we are likely to hear yet more. In the classics of cinema theory, notably Sergei Eisenstein and André Bazin, the phrase has a primarily metaphoric value. By the "language of film" they mean either the "syntax" of editing (Eisenstein) or the "semantics" of the single shot (Bazin), but for them the word "language" is really only convenient shorthand for a set of more or less traditional aesthetic techniques. Thus, Eisenstein's indebtedness to the "editing" of Dickens and Balzac, and thus also Bazin's emphasis, after Renoir *père* and *fils*, upon the painterly aspects of the *mise-en-scène*. More recent writers, however, have taken the idea of film language at the highly complex face value that the phrase really implies. Partly, of course, this development is based upon a misreading of the usage of the older critics, but it is, after all, to such concerted misprision that the art of criticism usually owes its impetus. It is hard to imagine what dramatic theory would be like without its millennia-old confusion over Aristotle's chance phrase for tragic emotion, *Katharsis;* or what we should think of modern poetry had we not grown unduly exercised over Coleridge's "Imagination," primary and secondary.

At any rate, critics like Raymond Durgnat, Andrew Sarris, Peter Wollen, and Stanley Cavell have written eloquently and suggestively about film as language. And though no two of them, surely, would agree about what language really is, they all take as their point of departure the assumption that film *is* a language, not only in an analogical, but in a precise sense of that maddeningly imprecise word. They view film as a new and unprecedented system of signification which needs to be interpreted and codified along entirely new avenues of exegesis. And in spite of their mutual disagreements and contradictions, we should not understand—or, more important, enjoy— films as much as we do without the insights into the art given us by these writers.

My concern, however, is not with the various appropriations of the idea of film language, but with the idea itself and with the ways in which we may take it even more seriously than has yet been done. We have discovered that concepts and modes of analysis properly belonging to linguistic study may be applied fruitfully to the study of film. But what if film *is* a language? And not only that, but a language whose very appearance was somehow made inevitable by the history of Western culture and Western self-consciousness? What if film, like the best of modern literature, represents what the linguists call a "metalanguage"—that is, a language whose direct referent is not the real world, but the possibility of meaning wrested by the human mind from that putative reality? To suggest this is, I think, to suggest not only how films mean, but why they mean—and, especially, why they do, and should, mean so much to us.

Bazin suggested that the idea of total cinema has its origin, not in the technological developments that made film possible, but in the romantic myth (or ideal) of representative, transfiguring art that made the technology inevitable. Under Bazin's aegis, I want to take this argument even farther back, to the figure who may be the ultimate father of modern linguistic philosophy, of romanticism, and also of the cinema: the Descartes of the *Discourse on Method* (1637).

This masterpiece, more than any of Descartes's other works, presents the full import of his epochal distinction between matter and spirit, *res extensa* and *res cogitans*. Yet the *Discourse* is the least methodical of philosophical texts. It is psychic autobiography, secular religious confession, in which Descartes tells us, with charming indirection, not what he believes, but how he came to believe it. Life-story and metaphysics parallel each other: and as the philosopher works his way toward his division of the universe between thought and thing, the infinity of space and the infinity of the mind turned in on itself, we see the man working toward the same delicate poise in the loneliness of his own existence.

Loneliness, indeed, is the key factor in Descartes's philosophy, as his modern commentators have increasingly discovered. And that loneliness is his most powerful legacy to the centuries which follow him: it can be seen in the loneliness of Milton facing the exploded universe of the late seventeenth century, of Shelley meeting Mont Blanc, and of Kubrick's Jupiter ship in *2001*, and, in general, in the nostalgia for a human cosmos which is so deeply embedded in the language and imagery of post-Cartesian man.

The central autobiographical passage in the *Discourse*, at the end of the third section, has a striking relevance to the art of the film. There, immediately before launching into his famous restructuring of the world from the central principle of *cogito, ergo sum*, Descartes narrates how, looking for a *scene* in which to conduct his intense and isolated experiments in introspection, he settled upon that definitive landscape of modern privacy and isolating materialism, the city: "It is exactly eight years since this wish made me decide to leave all those places where I had acquaintance, and to withdraw here to a country where . . . in the midst of a great crowd of busy people, more concerned with their own business than curious about that of others, without lacking any of the conveniences offered by the most populous cities, I have been able to live as solitary and withdrawn as I would be in the most remote of deserts."

In this passage, I suggest, we are witnessing the emergence of the modern city from the holy site, the god's shrine of antiquity, and the trading center, market town of the Middle Ages. But it is an emergence that took almost three hundred years to complete and was not, in fact, complete until the development of the crowd scenes in Lumière and Méliès or the mass-man celebrated equally in *Birth of a Nation* and *Battleship Potemkin*. Note that Descartes seeks, as much as he flees from, loneliness, for only through isolation with himself will he be able to transcend his terrible isolation in a world of mute, mindless things. That isolation—which his predecessors, the saints and mystics of the Christian centuries, found in the desert places of their world—Descartes finds in the populous core of modern technology, the city. "As . . . withdrawn as I would be in the most remote

ADAM AND THE AUTOMATON

of deserts"—in this phrase we can see the watershed between two epochs and hear the faint premonitory echo of Eliot's wasteland, Blake's London, Fellini's Rome, and Godard's Paris.

We can also see here the first intimation of modern linguistics. For in a cosmos whose absolute denominator is loneliness, the possibility of language becomes a crucial test of the mind's chances for salvation, for communion with others—that is, for love. The problem of other minds is perhaps the most crucial problem of modern philosophy, and Descartes raises it in the *Discourse*. For if each mind is indeed alone, if each mind constructs its own reality out of the originating abyss of its doubt and raw sensations, then what guarantee have we that there *are* other minds—that each of us is not a unique myth of self-consciousness, projecting our own shapes on an absolutely alien universe, devoid even of brothers or lovers? Language is the fragile net connecting humans to each other, the one ambiguous contract which seems to ally my pain and my joy to yours, even though language itself is a bundle of misunderstandings, mistranslations, badly decoded or undecoded messages. The present eminence of linguistic study among the human sciences is surely a late—and significant—aspect of the Cartesian Revolution in thought, for it is an exercise in the possibility of human connections, in the possibility of belief in other minds. This is the way Noam Chomsky views the heritage of Cartesian linguistics: "Language, in its essential properties and the manner of its use, provides the basic criterion for determining that another organism is a being with a human mind and the human capacity for free thought and self-expression, and with the essential human need for freedom from the external constraints of repressive authority." But as the Chomsky passage also makes clear, the urgent importance of language for contemporary humanism is still intimately bound up with its impingement by the "external restraints of repressive authority," that is, by the "most remote of deserts," which is the modern, depersonalizing city.

The proposition is simple: in a world overfull of people, we all need someone to talk to. And the fuller the world gets, the more desperate the need. If life forces us to live closer and closer to each other, to surrender more and more of our private needs for the survival of the mass, then the word itself—the word in the collapsed, claustrophobic space of the city—is in danger of losing its *human* connection, its primal power of linking *I* and *you*.

No other art—not even the novel or the drama—is quite as capable of registering this peculiar danger and triumph of the world as is film. For no other art is able to register with quite the same immediacy the solidity and the clutter of the human universe, and at the same time the awful fragility of the words we speak to each other amid that clutter. Two very subtle stories, *Top Hat* and *The Passion of Anna*, make this point in complementary ways.

In *Top Hat*, Ginger Rogers and Fred Astaire fall in love, as always, through dancing together ("Isn't This a Lovely Day to Be Caught in the Rain?"); but their speeches to each other throughout the film are a mixture of contempt and distaste on her part and flippancy on his. She, in fact, thinks that he is her best friend's husband, so that every time their language approaches courtship it is filled with double meanings and—from her point of view—with shockingly unselfconscious immorality. The whole plot, of course, hinges on the absurd chance that she never hears him speak his name. But in the context we are describing, that chance is not so much absurd as absolutely appropriate. For *Top Hat* is a romance whose main function is to celebrate the gradual coalescence of speech and celebration, the spoken and the danced declaration of love. When the inevitable explanation finally takes place, it occurs among the gaudily cluttered sets of a back-lot "Venice," and through either supreme taste or happy accident, the explanation itself is not shown. Rather, it is celebrated in a final dance ("The Piccolino"). The word—the saving *name*—for Fred and Ginger's love has been spoken, but the film immediately transcends that delicate adjustment of information storage to return to the wordless, choreographed vision of their connection with which it began.

The Passion of Anna, on the other hand, is a tragic vision of the comic, celebratory world of *Top Hat*. Liv Ullman and Max von Sydow do love and make love; but as their life together becomes fuller of languages, public and private (confessions of guilt, TV reports of the Vietnam War), it loses the unspoken connection that makes language bearable. In the final scene, after a bitter quarrel, she picks him up in her car. As she drives, he delivers perhaps the most bitter, hateful condemnation of another human being in all of film (the word turned curse), and then asks her why she came to him anyway. She replies, "I came to ask your forgiveness," stops the car, and lets him out. It is the word spoken too late, after the unspeakable has already been spoken, the word coming, unlike that in *Top Hat*, after the very last moment. In the highly Dreyeresque last shot of the film, von Sydow paces back and forth in a whitening landscape which finally engulfs him. After the failure of the word, there is nothing left but assimilation by the white noise of the universe.

In both these films—and, of course, in countless others—the word in space, the tension between language and the rocky, inhuman universe out of which language arises, takes on the dimensions of necessity and fragility imagined for it by the isolated, monologizing philosopher of the *Discourse*. Language in the desert becomes a new, endangered pastoral, a human oasis, a vision of the chances for alien flesh to be made word.

One of the concepts at work here, surely, is what Siegfried Kracauer calls, as subtitle to his *Theory of Film*, "The Redemption of Physical Reality." And, in fact, Dr. Kracauer was responsible for a good deal more, and a good deal more valuable, film theory than his opponents have given him credit for. His fundamental perception of the affinity of film for the crowd scene, the photography of masses in movement, comes close to the sort of Cartesian theory of film we are here proposing. The antagonism between neo-realism and fantasy in film is not really the issue—*pace* Dr. Kracauer himself. The camera's affinity for the crowd—for the true Cartesian and modern desert—is a function neither of its realism nor of its magic but, rather, the *cause* of its preternatural, magical level of reality. It gives us the world of our own isolation, but multiplied a hundredfold and clarified.

We need not think of Rossellini or De Sica here; even so classic a director as Hitchcock embodies this materialist linguistics. From *The 39 Steps* to *North by Northwest*, and again with *Frenzy*, Hitchcock's cameras and characters inhabit a world which is incomprehensible, not through its mystery, but through its overwhelmingly weary weight of *fact*. The Hitchcockian trapped man struggles against a world of confusingly alien details—sinister McGuffins—and suspicious people, a world whose labyrinth he must both thread and name if he is to save his life. The trapped man is always either *seen* in the wrong context (*39 Steps, North by Northwest*) or *seeing* a universe which to know is to fear (*The Man Who Knew Too Much, Rear Window*): that is, Hitchcock need not show us the crowd or the city, since its pressure is implicit in the very structure of his films. It is Sartre, another late-blooming Cartesian, who defines the true hell of our age as "other people." But for Sartre, as for Hitchcock, that public hell is also our best and only chance for the vision of an articulate and humanized paradise. And for both men, again, the real paradise of the contemporary imagination is its vision of the material impingements upon its freedom, its saving realization of the bars of its cage.

In one of the most famous instances in which Hitchcock does show us the crowd surrounding his characters, he also defines one of the perennial alternatives for film's transaction with masses and with the "language" of human action. The climactic scene of the second version of *The Man Who Knew Too Much* takes place in the Albert Hall. Doris Day and James Stewart play an American couple who have stumbled onto a plot to assassinate a foreign dignitary and whose son is being held hostage by the assassins in an attempt to buy the couple's silence. Day and Stewart know that the murder will take place during the concert in progress. They do not know—but we do, having seen it carefully rehearsed by the conspirators—that the shot will be fired at a precise moment in the music (the *Storm Cantata*, by veteran movie composer Bernard Herrmann) when a cymbal crash will mask the sound of the gun. They rush into the hall after the *Storm Cantata* has begun, Stewart frantically trying to get into the dignitary's private box, Day standing in an aisle and scanning the audience for the assassin. Throughout the sequence, as the music builds in intensity and dissonance, we see a series of extremely rapid cuts: Stewart rushing up the stairs, being intercepted by security guards, Day's anxious face, the complacent audience who do not know what is about to occur, the dignitary listening comfortably to the performance, the assassin's gun slowly edging out from behind a curtain, the percussionist getting his cymbals ready. Finally, just before the fateful moment in the cantata, Day catches sight of the gun and screams, spoiling the assassin's timing and aim: the intended victim is only wounded in the shoulder, the assassination plot exposed and, ultimately, defeated.

The use of rapid intercutting to increase tension and give a sense of urgency to the action has been a cliché of film technique at least since the days of D. W. Griffith. But the intercutting in the sequence from *The Man Who Knew Too Much* is not simply a device of narrative style: it goes deeper than that, to a vision of the very basis of one type of narrative style in film. Hitchcock has, on many occasions and in many interviews, drawn a distinction between mystery and suspense. Suspense, in Hitchcock's view, involves, not our curiosity about the causes or motives for a particular action or crime, but our anxiety about whether an action or crime will or will not take place. The example he usually gives is that of seeing a man driving his car, knowing that he has to get to the airport through traffic to prevent something from occurring. In other words, Hitchcock's kind of suspense involves the obstruction of things, of space, their intrusion upon possibilities of free action. In an article originally published in 1937, he makes explicit the narrative ramifications of this attitude: "So you gradually build up the psychological situation, piece by piece, using the camera to emphasize first one detail, then another. The point is to draw the audience right inside the situation instead of leaving them to watch it from outside, from a distance. And you can do this only by breaking the action up into details and cutting from one to the other, so that each detail is forced in turn on the attention of the audience and reveals its psychological meaning."

There could be no clearer anticipation or justification of the sequence from *The Man Who Knew Too Much*. But the sequence itself goes far beyond the sort of psychological pressure Hitchcock described in 1937. Significantly, Hitchcock speaks of "inside" and "outside" in his description of suspense techniques. And the "outside" is present in our sequence in the most imposing fashion: the setting is a public place, a concert hall—to an American, *the* English concert hall—filled with not only Sartre's "other people," but other people in the jealous complacency of a ceremonial occasion. The Albert Hall, furthermore, is filled with sound, with music. But here the music itself is alien, *other* to the anxiety of Day, Stewart, and the film's audience. Hitchcock has made sure that we have heard the relevant, fatal section of the composition at least twice before in the film, so that when we hear it again performed in the actual concert, we perceive it not so much as a piece of music moving and developing through time but as yet another impingement upon the characters' freedom of action; the music is a limit to time, moving toward a single fateful sound, the cymbal crash.

If film as language is a Cartesian art of the word in space, then the Hitchcock sequence gives us an especially austere version of the endangered status of human utterance in a world of other things and other people. For Doris Day knows, and we know, that there is really only one way to stop the assassination: that is, to scream aloud in the middle of a concert in the Albert Hall and alert the thousands of listeners that something is amiss. Hitchcock's characteristic genius has always been to concentrate, in moments of maximum stress, upon the impossibility or the very great difficulty of performing certain simple, "natural" human acts. He shows us, in other words, how things force themselves upon our freedom and retard that freedom. The rapid cutting preceding the scream, then, is not simply a device to heighten tension—or even, as Hitchcock's own theory has it, to reveal the "psychological meaning" of the various aspects, objects, and circumstances of which the situation is composed. It is, rather, a deliberate fragmentation of the space surrounding the central, crucial figure of Doris Day, the effect of which is to magnify, by a kind of spatial-temporal foreshortening, the inhibitions *against* her saving utterance, her scream. Each detail, each cut occupies its own space, like the pieces of a non-Euclidean puzzle; and only the scream—it is tempting to call it the primal scream, the originating, organizing voice response—unites the hall, the assassin, the victim, and the ominous music in a single act of meaning.

It is difficult, in this connection, not to think of the technique of Joyce's *Ulysses*. In both instances, a single, unified action (the assassination attempt, Bloom's wanderings through Dublin) is fragmented and foreshortened by rapid shifts of perspective and concentration. And in both works, the miracle of human speech is that it can occur at all amid the din of an inhospitable universe, in the midst of space viewed as inimical to, mocking the scale of, human effort. Stephen Dedalus muses to himself, in that great novel, "I hear the wreck of all space, and time one livid final flame." And, whatever else we might wish to say about the Joycean vision, it is—like Hitchcock's, like that of much post-Cartesian thought and poetry—a vision of the space surrounding us as threatening, dangerous for language.

There is, however, an alternative technique for filmic and literary narrative which suggests quite another relationship among crowds, space, and action. The opening sequence of Orson Welles's *Touch of Evil*, released two years after *The Man Who Knew Too Much*, is an uncannily complete example of this alternative, involving as it does so many structural similarities to the Hitchcock sequence.

Touch of Evil begins with what may well be one of the most breathtaking, virtuoso shots in film history: three minutes shot from a moving camera on a twenty-foot boom, without a single cut. But it is not simply the length of the sequence, of course, that makes it so brilliant. In a small, shabby Mexican border town (Venice, California) a time bomb has been planted in a gangster's car by a rival. The gangster and his girlfriend drive across the Mexican-American border, passing the strolling figures of the hero, Detective Vargas, and his new wife (Charlton Heston and Janet Leigh). The car crosses into the American zone; Vargas turns to his wife and says, "Do you realize I haven't kissed you in over an hour"; and the car explodes. Welles and his cameraman, Russell Metty, convert this action into virtually a fugue of spatial configurations, groupings, and dynamics. The camera first reveals the hands of the anonymous assassin setting the timer on the bomb and placing it in the trunk of the car; as the car pulls off, the camera draws back and up in the first of a startling series of withdrawals from and approaches to the movement of the characters;

ADAM AND THE AUTOMATON

Heston and Leigh pass in front of the car, and the camera follows them for part of their walk, picking up the car again when all four reach the border; and all the while we are watching the two human groups weave and unweave their separate courses, the landscape, storefronts, and population of the little town are being established in a fluid, almost musical structure.

As in the Hitchcock sequence, Welles shows us a mass of people —with the focus upon two main characters, a married couple— in whose midst an explosion is about to take place. And, as with Hitchcock, a large part of the genius of this sequence is the way it fills in the space and time of expectation, as we wait for the blast. But in the opening of *Touch of Evil*, none of the characters in the action are aware of what is about to happen: space and time for them, if not for the audience, are a comfortable habitation, and the fluid movement of the camera, the uninterrupted movement of characters toward and away from each other, not only emphasizes but incarnates on film the image of space—the Cartesian city—as liveable, as a place where ordinary human impulses and concerns may play themselves out without danger of impingement. Most viewers of *Touch of Evil* catch the dark humor of the climax of the opening sequence: Heston bends to kiss Janet Leigh, and the first interruption of free-flowing sequence in the film occurs, in the cut to the exploding, burning car in which two other lovers have just died. Lest we find the assertion of the camera too consoling, too pastoral—that is to say, too pre-Cartesian—the cut to the exploding automobile reminds us of the imperiled status of the human city.

There is, however, a subtle but essential difference between the techniques and visions of Hitchcock and Welles. The distinction between, on the one hand, cutting or "editing" in the most Eisensteinian sense (Hitchcock) and, on the other, camera movement, *mis-en-scène*, and "deep focus" has been, of course, celebrated and by now institutionalized in the theory of the *Cahiers du Cinéma* school of film criticism; but in the two instances of those respective techniques suggested here, we can see, I think, that they define radically different and complementary attitudes toward the presence and power of language—human meaning-making—in the narrative film. Editing, as I have suggested, is a syntax of film language, a making of meaning by collocations of words or images; single-shot deep focus, on the other hand, is fundamentally semantic, depending for its manifestation of meaning upon the signification and complexity of a single image, a single utterance. But depending upon whether we assume a "syntactic" or a "semantic" orientation toward reality and toward the possibilities of wresting some sort of human meaning from reality, we develop two quite different attitudes toward human freedom—which is to say, toward the nature of narrative.

Chomsky has been concerned with this problem since the publication of his book *Syntactic Structures* in 1957. We do not need to describe transformational-generative grammar exhaustively to understand its implications in this respect. If language—human significance—may be described adequately and efficiently in terms of the rules generating the syntax of utterances, then the meaning, or semantics, of the individual members of any utterance are largely irrelevant to the interpretation of a sentence, a book, or a film. Such a triumph of syntax, though, raises serious problems about the relationship between our utterances about the world—about space, time, and, ultimately, death—and the reality toward which those utterances presumably point. Given a syntactic view of reality, then, it is perfectly possible to imagine that human meaning is self-contained, significant—and totally unrelated to the structure of a "real" world out there (like a legal document, the most fully syntactic variety of literature our culture has produced). We are not happy with such a vision, of course: the mind, no matter how comfortably it establishes its own closure, wants to believe that it is not closed off from the universe it inhabits and tries to interpret.

Yet a semantic vision raises problems in another way. Semantics concerns itself with the way our utterances have meaning and, finally, is based upon the faith that such meaning does, in some way, exist. If syntax finds itself most fully manifested in the self-referential organization of a legal document, semantics finds its most complete realization in the rituals and spells of magic. But if legalism is continually endangered by its isolation from the presumed reality of experience (as anyone who has ever tried to read an auto insurance policy has discovered), magic is endangered by its own failure to incorporate the whole of experience into its system, by the moment at which the spell does not work, by the moment at which the word no longer adequately signifies the thing. Thus, in the heavily edited climax of *The Man Who Knew Too Much*, our anxiety is that the scream, the human word, may not occur in time to preserve the syntactic isolation of civilization from the disruptive reality of death and the gunshot. In *Touch of Evil*, however, our attention is concentrated upon the triviality of the word ("Do you realize I haven't kissed you in over an hour?") when weighed against the literally explosive reality it seeks to name and control. In other words, the peculiar terror at-

ADAM AND THE AUTOMATON

tending language as syntax is that it will cease to utter; the terror of language as semantics is that its utterance will be stopped by a world that no longer tolerates its arrogant impositions of meaning.

I have devoted so much space to these two examples because of their intrinsic brilliance as varieties of film narrative and also because of the strange pressure of machinery—the myth of machinery—upon them both. A prearranged, musically timed gunshot and a time bomb —in both Hitchcock's vision of violence as an eruption into society and Welles's vision of violence as an interruption of that society, the violence itself is imagined as especially artificial, technological, as a human product. Man, romantic and postromantic literature tells us, is the creature who imagines and voices his own death. But the articulation of his death is also its technologization: to say a thing is to make a model for a thing and to open the possibility of more, and more efficient, models.

Indeed, only in the human sphere can we speak of violence at all, for (as far as we know) only man imagines violence as an interruption of his normal concerns, as a denial of the universal web of significance and intelligibility which the mind spins out. And if film gives us our most problematic version of the existence of other minds (the creator imposing significance upon, the viewer extracting significance from, a series of mechanically produced phenomena), film also gives us our most disturbing version of the violent denial of mind (creator and viewer alike trapped in a monstrous set of technologized phenomena, all of which are simply images of the delusory, ineffective "intelligence" of the human robot). The word and the explosion, rational life and the death of reason, are obverse and reverse of the same coin.

Hitchcock, again, helps us to see the deep connections among film, language, violence, and the idea of automaton. At the beginning of *The 39 Steps*, a shot is fired in a crowded theatre; the same shot will echo at the end of the film to kill Mr. Memory, the robot-like, vaudeville reciter of trivial and unconnected facts who had opened the action. And Mr. Memory, dying, will rattle off the information which solves the mystery of the "39 Steps," without himself understanding that his last speech is making sense of the world of the hero and heroine, clarifying their confusion. Speech, the crowd, and the disruptive act of murder—all three elements implicate each other in the film, and for good reasons. For speech, if it is to work at all in the universe of blankly material things—the only universe which film or modern philosophy will let us inhabit—is *itself* an act of violence.

It is a primal bridging of the abyss between mind and not-mind, the universe inside and the universe outside the head, the universe which film perhaps gives us in all its scandalous brutality better than does writing itself. It is human, artificial, and betrays the silence of the cosmos: like a gunshot, like a word.

Here, too, Descartes is our best guide. The problem of other minds, of the word as the human connection, is crucial to his thought and invokes almost inevitably the problem of the automaton. The simulacrum of a human being—which is, in spite of all its human-seeming, not human, not conscious as we are conscious—is a figure that has, in one form or another, haunted much modern thought. For if consciousness can be created out of inarticulate matter, then the last basis for the illusion of human centrality has been lost. Man would, in some sense, have become God—but his achievement would also reduce his own sense of the uniqueness, the *otherness* of his humanity. And from Descartes down to contemporary linguistics and cybernetics, the test of consciousness for an automaton is the test of its ability to use language, the ability of matter to evolve speech.

This is why, in fact, Descartes insists so strongly in the *Discourse* on the impossibility of making a perfect automaton. He has posited that the mind is capable of constructing a perfect—we might say a "photographic"—replica of the world as it already exists, and comes to the crucial question, Can the mind then also make itself, make man—that is, become a competitor with the creative power of God himself? Might the robot, that unvoiced sacrilege at the heart of ancient magic and alchemy, really be possible? No, Descartes answers piously, for however perfect a human imitation of the human form might be, it would inevitably lack the quintessentially human power of speech, by which we recognize the true and divine spark of consciousness in the world. It is not an argument; it is an assertion, and one which indicates how deeply Descartes fears the disappearance of language, of consciousness itself, into the atomic necessitarianism of the physical universe.

Later writers, of course—particularly since the advent of computer technology—have not been able to be quite as sanguine as Descartes about the inimitability of language. But the terms of the problem remain as serious and as central as they were for him. If consciousness is real (i.e., something other than a name for mere reflex behavior), then it is intimately bound up with the forms of language. But if language itself is capable of being created artificially in an artificial entity, then the structure and very nature of consciousness is in danger of being defined as a complex kind of reflex behavior.

ADAM AND THE AUTOMATON

Speech has become, then, a function of inarticulate matter, of space: both halves of the function define themselves and each other through their mutual tension. We have spoken of the word as "bridging a gap" between mind and matter. But, of course, the gap can be bridged by language only because language has first established the very existence of the gap. It raises the problems it tries to solve. For Descartes, language is the collision point between inner and outer, between the autonomy of the human will-to-meaning and the universe of physical chance (or necessity) which seems, at times, to render that will supererogatory. It is an insight which contemporary linguistics has borne out, for whether we read Saussure or Chomsky, Lévi-Strauss or Wittgenstein, we are struck by the degree to which language, for our best thinkers, represents not only a prime form, but a prime *condition* of consciousness: a delicate interchange between mind and world, it is also the highly problematic hypothesis which allows us to posit, if at all, the existence of either mind or world. The question of the automaton, that is, invariably raises the more general question of a human creation in the human void.

Our technology and mythology, of course, have grown increasingly full of such visions—visions of the terror inhering in the triumph of cybernetics. Film itself—moving pictures, a mechanism that gives us a simulacrum of life and speech—is poised delicately between the positive and negative aspects of this epistemological riddle. It is supremely appropriate, in this regard, that one of the most popular and best films of all time should be a version of Mary Shelley's *Frankenstein*. For Mary Shelley's automaton is a terminal, romantic, and modern version of the problem of language and automatism. Most of the monster's long, central speech in the original novel is concerned with his discovery of language, the ways in which learning the power of the word was, for him, learning the irrefutable fact of his own ugliness and his exclusion from that word and that human world. This is the real brilliance of James Whale's 1935 sequel to his original film, for in *The Bride of Frankenstein* he endows Karloff as the monster with the power of speech. And the monster's first words— "Friend *good*"—in their deep pathos are as moving and as grim as any monologue I know of in the film.

Tarzan, too, had to wait till the sound era for his definitive reincarnation on the screen. For at the center of Edgar Rice Burroughs's original novel is an optimistic version of the negatively Cartesian myth of Frankenstein. How much, asks Burroughs, can you take away from man and still call him man? Almost everything, is his answer. Like *Frankenstein*, a large portion of *Tarzan of the Apes* is dedicated to describing the process through which its hero learns to read and speak. But here, unlike Mary Shelley's version of the problem, the acquisition of speech is an earnest of triumph. A true Adam of the post-Gutenberg garden, Tarzan first discovers language in the written, not the spoken, word. It is the spoken word, the word in space, which is his most difficult and rewarding assimilation. This is why the popular mind remembers, not Elmo Lincoln's silent Tarzan, but Johnny Weissmuller as the great type of the role. For Tarzan represents a victory over silence, a fundamentally epistemological victory of the human mind over the mute universe of things, the primal tropic jungle. And for the representation of *that* victory the Tarzan films need sound. Weissmuller's famous guttural—so like Karloff's speech in *The Bride*—is among the most eloquent of screen utterances. No less than the anthropology of Lévi-Strauss, it reminds us how short is the leap between "primitive" and "sophisticated" language, and how immeasurable the abyss between both of them and the circumjacent wilderness of *res extensa*.

The ape-man and the mechanical man, those qualified visions of the truly human, belong irrevocably in the locales where film has placed them, either in the "realistic" set of the world as jungle, or in the expressionistic (and technological) one of the world as laboratory —as, perhaps, cutting room. They are two indelible names for the fate of the word in space. But two others more often used by "serious" historians of film are those of Méliès and the brothers Lumière. They are most generally associated with the traditions of fantasy and realism in the history of the art. But I suggest that this association is partly a mistake. The proto-documentaries of the Lumières were received as—and *were*—no less magical than the *Trip to the Moon* or *Journey to the Pole* of Méliès; and the great charm of Méliès, even today, is largely because of his contrived innocence, his insistence upon the materiality of his settings (e.g., the cardboard Moon's eye put out by the rocketship).

Much more important than their relative proportions of fantasy and realism is the way these great early filmmakers represent alternative visions of the language of animate-matter-in-space. For the Lumières, our first "Frankensteinians," the space of the screen is contained by the space of the "real" world: the screen is a recorder of events in "real"—i.e., nonhuman—space, and as such, an explorer of the impingements of space on human meaning. The train arriving in the crowded station, the busy Paris street—these are legitimately unsettling spectacles, since they intimate the negative aspect of the Cartesian city, of Cartesian space. *Watering the Gardener*, one of the

     ADAM AND THE AUTOMATON

oldest and most durable bits of film slapstick, is in this respect a crucial comment upon the fate of the mind in the universe of post-seventeenth-century epistemology. Since the gardener cannot see the boy standing on his hose, he will, naturally, look into the nozzle—with predictable results when the boy moves on.

For Méliès, on the other hand, film space contains the space of the real world, and he is thus able to manipulate the putative "reality." Mélès is the first "Tarzanian" of the film, at least in the terms we have imposed upon the history of the art. One indication of this is the manner in which most of Méliès' great scenes are shot from a staged, proscenium-arch point of view, as if there were only two dimensions in the world. For Georges the magician, there *are* only two dimensions to the real world, and the film, the manipulation of the possibilities of that reality, supplies the third. It is not that he believes in the authority of the proscenium arch but, rather, that the reality of the proscenium arch is a necessary condition for his own reshaping of the world's structure. If the art of the brothers Lumière represents the cinema as exploration, that of Méliès represents the complementary concept of the cinema as analysis: the one seeks to use the camera to discover what of interest or terror might be found in the world as it stands, while the other seeks to use the camera to make explicit what the world as it stands might, according to our concept of it, contain of the interesting or the terrible. For the former, the language of our idea of reality is a *donnée* to be catalogued; for the latter, it is a phenomenon of the mind's transaction with whatever is *not* the mind, a phenomenon capable of reconstruction.

These are not mutually exclusive traditions of cinema, of course, any more than they are mutually exclusive traditions of linguistic philosophy. Far from it, they depend upon each other, in a kind of perpetual adversary relationship, for their respective powers. John Lyons, in his *Introduction to Theoretical Linguistics* traces these two attitudes to the sources of linguistic thought itself. Lyons's names for them are, respectively, the "anomalist" and the "analogic" traditions of language study. Anomalism—that is, our "Frankenstein-Lumière" school—tends to insist that language is radically disorderly, not self-structured, since it depends for its organization upon the prior organization or lack of organization in the real world it describes. Analogism—the "Tarzan-Méliès" side of the argument—insists that language is radically orderly, that it is structured according to its own rules without the necessity of referring to the reality which its speakers inhabit.

The terms of the argument, according to Lyons, have not significantly changed since the grammarians of late-classical Alexandria first laid down their version of it. But in the history of the film, one can see an especially exciting and complicated development of its implications. I have already alluded to the strong relationship in the film between concerns of language and concerns of violence: film brings home to us the violent, disruptive self-assertion implicit in the very fact of language. This is one of the reasons why slapstick, from the earliest two-reelers to Woody Allen and Peter Bogdanovich, has been one of the central plot resources of the art. Slapstick is, more than simply a comic *kind* of violence, violence itself, purified and schematized as only the film is capable of doing. Bergson's famous discussion of the comic as the warfare of human will and the encrustations of the material and automatic helps indicate to us the involvement with serious linguistic matters of the violently, absurdly comic. It is appropriate, in this respect, that Antonin Artaud, whose "theatre of cruelty" is a visionary art aimed at rediscovering the primitive roots of the Word, sees in the films of the Marx Brothers the fullest realization of his own complex aesthetic.

It is in the masterpieces of film slapstick itself, however, that we find the most valuable explorations of this double linguistic inheritance. The word—the human presence—in space is at once endangered and conditioned by the world, or absurdly free and dangerously independent from the world, as soon as it is uttered. Chaplin and Keaton, two masters of film language and schematic violence, are our most indispensable poets of these complementary ways of Being-There.

Much has already been written of the uncanny ways in which Chaplin and Keaton seem to divide so much of the world, so precisely, between them. Charlie the sentimentalist and Buster the ironist, the dancer and the acrobat, the critic of capitalist society and the deviser of happy-ending Edens outside of society—all these distinctions are well known and important. But the most richly creative difference between these geniuses is in their language—not the language *in* their films (how wonderful it is that they are forever silent) but the language that their films make real. For Chaplin, the space of the world is always and insidiously dangerous, perhaps even murderous. For Keaton, that same space is, breathtakingly, his toy.

Key images abound. In *Modern Times* Charlie, showing off for Paulette Goddard, roller-skates blindfolded through a deserted department store. He cannot see the central shaft, plummeting down many stories, whose edge he again and again skirts. But as soon as he takes the blindfold off and *sees* the abyss, he is drawn to it, almost as

ADAM AND THE AUTOMATON

into a whirlpool. Flailing his arms, frantically backpedaling, he cannot keep away from the edge. Surely there has never been—not in Descartes, not in Milton, not in Blake—a more powerful imagination of the impingements of matter upon the human will, of our panicky awareness that the void, sheer space, once we see it for what it is, can kill. And surely there has never been a wittier vision of the alternative possibility, the autonomy of mind within the void, than in the climax to Keaton's *Balloonatics*. Buster and his girl sit, staring fondly at each other, in a canoe floating down a river. Neither notices that they are approaching a waterfall; and instead of crashing down it, they simply float straight off its edge, into thin air. A sentimental, metaphoric celebration of airy love? Of course not, for, as the camera draws back, we see that the canoe is attached to their balloon. Keaton's insight is unimpeachable: it is we, the viewers, who have been blindfolded by the camera, obsessed with the dangerous abyss, and Keaton, resourceful master of space, who reassures us that the mind can articulate its own reality, even in the world of fact.

The opening sequence of Chaplin's best film, *City Lights*, is in fact very nearly an essay upon the Cartesian city we have described earlier. As the pretentious monument to progress is unveiled by the mayor, we see the immortal tramp, man as cosmic vagrant, asleep in the stone lap of a titanic figure. And as he attempts to get away, he is literally imprisoned in a world of stone, now slipping on a monstrous statuary breast, now being goosed by a monolithic sword. That *City Lights* was made in 1931—that is, that it is a silent film by choice—only underscores the poignancy, perhaps even despair, of its language myth. In the universe of the slapstick abyss, for Chaplin at least, the human word is defeated almost before it is born. Conversely, the word in Keaton need not be spoken, since its triumph over space is almost of the nature of divine grace. The hurricane sequence in *Steamboat Bill, Jr.*, is a good case of this: Buster stands before a house whose entire front façade falls upon him. But he is positioned exactly so that the open attic window falls over him, and since he is looking for his girl, he hardly notices what has happened. Closer to Shelley or to the Shakespeare of the late romances than to any other filmmaker, Keaton insists in his great period that the will cannot be destroyed, cannot be daunted, even by the abyss itself.

The reader will have noticed that for my two principal illustrations of the linguistics of the word in space I have gone to classics of the silent film. And for the discussion so far, the distinction between "sound" and "silent" is in many ways a trivial one. But we may now see that the development of the sound film, if anything, deepens and makes more critical the imaginative problems raised by the film—not by what a particular film might say, but by the existence of the art itself.

Alexandre Astruc, in a well-known essay, invented the phrase *caméra-stylo* to allude to the idea of film as a new kind of writing. Henceforth, Astruc suggested in 1948, the film would free itself of the elephantine techniques of narration characterizing its primitive period and achieve a subtlety of register and expression approximating the accomplishments of the modern novel. In a passage rich with implications for our discussion, Astruc writes: "A Descartes of today would already have shut himself up in his bedroom with a 16 mm camera and some film, and would be writing his philosophy on film: for his *Discours de la Méthode* would today be of such a kind that only the cinema could express it satisfactorily."

Astruc's idea of film as writing is more accurate, in fact, than he himself indicates. For writing, essentially, is the translation of speech into a medium (the written character) that bears only a formal, structural—i.e., arbitrary—relationship to the original spoken word. The relationship, that is, between the sound "cat" and the representation *c-a-t* is one which calls into operation the entire technological, grammatological history of the civilization and the speakers who write *c-a-t*. And it is the same with film. Though the film may give us compelling images of the real world of facts, things, and processes, nevertheless, if its subject is, as we are suggesting, the existence of human language and human meaning among those details, it is a translation of speech into precisely the desert (or ruined garden) of the physical world that is the modern world's only landscape. Not drama, painting, or music operates on precisely the same disjunction of levels, the same distinction of primary from secondary level of signification.

Like writing, then—and unlike any of the other, and we may well say less revolutionary, arts—film is a semiotic technology; and to the revolutionary, history-making fissure between spoken and written language it adds a second fissure, the fissure between language as words and language as the collision between words and inarticulate matter. This is largely the point of Peter Wollen's *Signs and Meanings in the Cinema*. But, going beyond Wollen, we may now observe that film as "writing" is the *writing of Cartesian space itself*. Far from being a non- or anti-literary medium, it becomes the most radical of literatures, since its universal subject is meaning-in-space, the word in space, a language reduced or expanded to the absolute purity of the origins of linguistic meaning, of the possibility of meaning.

This is to say that film *is* the "supreme fiction" envisioned by Wallace Stevens; or at least a particularly acute, challenging version of that supreme fiction. And the growth of the sound film—the integration of the spoken and recorded word into its Cartesian spatial coordinates—is a brilliant parallel to the development of contemporary poetry and fiction. Modern writing, from Joyce and Eliot through Beckett and Stevens, has increasingly tested the validity, the humanizing power, of written language in a world that seems more and more to challenge the power of that language to establish a secure human place in the universe of inarticulate extension. Film, in its evolution from Keaton and Chaplin through Welles to Kubrick, performs a similar test from the opposite direction: assuming extension, Cartesian space as its *donnée*, it attempts to locate a space in that threatening universe for speech, for human pretensions to meaning, organization, and civilization.

Images of this coalescence and parallelism abound. Stevens's poem "The Idea of Order at Key West" is one of our fullest disquisitions upon the primal word, the word within, tested by the space of its utterance. Hearing an unseen girl singing as he strolls beside the bobbing lights of anchored fishing boats, Stevens discovers that her sung words impose order upon and humanize a random arrangement of lights without ever participating in or even touching the lights' absolute randomness:

The sea was not a mask. No more was she.
The song and water were not medleyed sound
Even if what she sang was what she heard,
Since what she sang was uttered word by word.
It may be that in all her phrases stirred
The grinding water and the gasping wind;
But it was she and not the sea we heard.

The Word is here tested against the aural and visual locale which generates and impinges upon it: we must call the poem, in the deepest sense, cinematic.

But in a film as important as *Citizen Kane*, the same testing goes on in a perhaps even more desperate frame. *Kane* is the first full triumph of the sound film: its unfolding, in fact, may be seen— and heard—as a witty and grim three-part dissonance of speech, writing, and vision. We begin with the spoken word "Rosebud" mouthed by aged lips in obscene close-up; we then shift to the ramshackle furniture of a burned-out life, to Xanadu as the Cartesian city imploded upon itself, now an impossible, looming clutter of *things*.

And all this wreckage centers on the iron gate-initial *K*, i.e., writing as transaction between the rocklike thinghood of the world and the vulnerable, transitory structuring of the human word. The newsreel life of Charles Foster Kane that follows, with its archaic printed captions and its annoyingly loud "March of Time" voiceover, is one of the most brilliant parables of the art of the film ever recorded *by* the film: it is the transposition of a life into the public technologies of word-and-image, a cinematic emptying-out of Charles Kane's life which foreshadows the real emptying-out, the psychic suicide which in fact his life was. After the preliminary screening of the newsreel, we are confronted with an alternate version of the word in space, as the film moves from the stentorian certainties of the narrative voice to the confused, contrapuntal, intractable wilderness of the newsmen trying to make sense out of, give meaning to what they have just seen. The impetus of the plot for the rest of the film—photojournalist Thompson's quest for the "human interest" of the word "Rosebud" —defines *Citizen Kane* as a search for the signs and meaning of the cinema, an attempt to ascertain the chances that this newest of the arts will tell us something of the survival value of meaning in a meaningless world. And if the life itself of Charles Foster Kane is a disaster of abdication, of the self's capitulation before the exigencies of public image, the film is an assertion of the meaning it calls into question— in despite of, in contradiction of the spoken narration of which it consists. After so many stories about Kane, so many contradictory words about the nature and meaning of his career, we end again with the written word, the word "ROSEBUD" painted on a burning sleigh, the enigmatic mediation between things in their dumb eternity and mind in its mortality, the triumph or the transfiguration of the universe that surrounds our attempts to make sense of, to *speak* our lives.

Kane may have drowned himself in a sea of material possessions, but—the film insists—it was him and not the sea we heard. Stanley Kubrick's *2001: A Space Odyssey* is a very different film. It is perhaps the next most important film after *Steamboat Bill, Jr.*, and *Citizen Kane* in that it represents the voice of the void, of the sea, of the primal *res extensa* that surrounds and threatens the human word. If *Kane* is a film about language, void, and writing, *2001* is a film about language, void, writing, and God. Its theme is simultaneously Paradise Lost and Paradise Regained, and we read it as one or the other of these myths, depending upon what we bring to it. We may also read the film as a parable of the history of cinema; for cinema, as we are now discussing it, is also a parable of the Fall.

It begins in silence, but not the silence of the films of Keaton or Chaplin, nor even the deliberate and die-hard silence of *City Lights;* rather, it is a silence that is the *absence* of speech, the deliberately engineered and deliberately maintained nonpresence of the spoken word. If Welles in *Kane* is fond of newsreel captions as anachronism, Kubrick in *2001* uses them as reversions to and metaphors of the paralinguistic nature of his art: "The Dawn of Man," "Jupiter—And Beyond the Infinite." Words, the *prima materia* of concepts, are tools. And *2001* is a movie about the invention of tools, the development of techniques that separate man from his savage environment and yet give him an increased vulnerability to that environment. Many critics have noted the utter banality of the dialogue in the film. But that banality, whether through genius or inadvertence, makes it the most eloquent of sound films: it is about sound, about the word in space and in Space. Pennies dropped hopefully into the abyss, each cliché in *2001* gives back a tinny echo which is unmistakably inadequate, unmistakably human. Even the computer, HAL (a metaphor for the film itself?), that artificial representation of consciousness-through-language, raises the fundamental question of the Fall into time, into space, into history. For HAL goes insane because he has been taught to lie—i.e., to use language as something other than an absolutely accurate realization of the real status of consciousness in space. And HAL's death, like the exile of Adam from the Garden, is one of the most moving of myths precisely because it is so deeply entwined in the condition of consciousness itself, in the very act of speaking.

John Simon, in a rather silly review, called *2001* a "shaggy God story." But Simon is correct: as the film itself makes clear, it is a case of language reaching profundity through its own inaccuracy and stupidity. Or, better, it is the slapstick of Keaton and Chaplin infinitely slowed down, the pratfall transposed into cosmic time; the newsreel sensibility of *Citizen Kane* grown articulate and metaphysical. An odyssey is a journey *home,* as Kubrick and Clarke obviously mean us to understand. For the starchild whose strange birth ends the film, is ambiguously, either a monster designed to destroy human habitation of the cosmos or a messiah ushering in an era of true at-homeness in infinite extension: either an interplanetary Frankenstein monster or a stellar Tarzan.

But the end of *2001* is not so much a solution of the problems of language, film, and space as it is a transformation of those problems into a yet more complicated—and more quintessentially human—

sphere. The starchild gazes on Earth with an enigmatic smile that suggests to us that the real meaning of the film lies in whatever happens *after* the film has ended. In *2001*, in other words, as in *Kane* and perhaps in *Potemkin*, film succeeds so wonderfully because it succeeds in imagining its own genesis—the moment before speech, out of which speech is born, the situation of consciousness afloat on the void of the material universe just before it begins to organize that universe into the stuff of words, meanings, and politics. For politics, too, is part of the imaginative aura surrounding the advent of the film as art. And at this point in our discussion we need to examine the ways in which film, as a postromantic dream of humanized technology, manages to incarnate that most ancient of human concerns, the organization of people into societies which can live and speak together without bloodshed.

Indeed, returning to our generative models of Frankenstein and Tarzan, we can see that everything so far said about the "grammar" of film is insufficient to describe a satisfactory artistic grammar. What is lacking, simply, is the sense of community, of a civilization of other people to whom one may speak and from whom one may hear things of more than trivial interest. It is the Cartesian paradox with which we began, that our contemporary sense of the value and nature of language arises out of our urbanized sense of loneliness, of our all but immitigable isolation from each other. And the word in space, the language we evolve to cure that mutual isolation, has only partially succeeded when it solves the relationship between the individual mind and the universe of matter; there remains the more vexing problem of the individual mind and the existence of other human, nonautomatic minds.

The novels *Frankenstein* and *Tarzan of the Apes* devote a great many pages to describing how their respective heroes learn language; and in both novels (surprisingly, for anyone who has only seen the films), the heroes speak fluently and articulately—like nineteenth-century English gentlemen, in fact. Hollywood's demotion of both characters, in Karloff and Weissmuller, to the limits of articulacy is a fascinating phenomenon of filmmaking. The grunts and gutterals are more meaningful for us than full-length speeches would be because we see in them an especially self-conscious, acute quest by film for its origins as romantic, visionary linguistics. But such a linguistics is, finally, a failure until it achieves relevance to the universe of ordinary discourse: until, that is, it manages to tell us something valuable about our crowded, urban, desperately lonely existence side by side with each other.

Both the Frankenstein and Tarzan motifs have found their way into a number of films that are largely antipolitical and pessimistic about the chances for human survival in a deeply disturbing and perhaps nihilistic way. The series of films based upon Pierre Boulle's novel *Planet of the Apes* represents an especially curious transformation of the motif.

The thesis of the "*Ape* cycle," as enthusiasts have christened the series, is that at some future time, after man has obliterated his civilization through atomic warfare, the lower primates have come to take possession of the world, developing a language and culture of their own. A motley assortment of human time-travelers from our century and human, radiation-scarred survivors of the atomic holocaust confront the now-ascendant ape culture, eventually achieving, in the last film—*Battle for the Planet of the Apes*—an uneasily civilized detente. Apologists for the series have no doubt overstressed the political subtlety of its allegory, but the allegory is undeniably there and helps explain the immense popularity and very real fascination of this relatively low-budget set of films. The central irony of the story, of course, remains that of Boulle's original novel: the "planet of the apes," that apparently alien world where normal assumptions of human supremacy are crazily inverted, is Earth itself. And, as we realize watching the films, Earth is, even now, the planet of the apes, of those naked apes gifted with speech, ourselves, about whom writers like Desmond Morris have recently created such a large noise. Particularly in the first of the series, though—*Planet of the Apes*— we learn how full an atmosphere of political cynicism has developed, not only through, but within the film, since the heyday of the Tarzan films. The shipwrecked astronaut Charlton Heston, like the castaway Lord Greystoke of Burroughs' novels, is in the position of becoming a Tarzan, a triumphant assertion of the human word's victory over space. But his ape captors are more articulate than he (he has been wounded in his capture and cannot speak for the first third of the film). They are, in fact, more human than Heston. In a brilliant bit of casting—and one that persists throughout the whole series, in different but isomorphic roles—the part of the most sympathetic, moral, and civilized ape is played by Roddy McDowall, whose soft, faintly British speech and the whole range of whose previous performances (feckless aesthete to maniacal aesthete) underscore the ironic humanity of his ape character. Heston, the technological man whose clichés are parodied in *2001*, the machine-man, cyborg and lord of the mathematical universe, is in fact both Tarzan and Frankenstein monster here—at once a beast trying to speak and assert his humanity, and a machine (or mechanical man) trying to forget his technologically implanted responses and recover his humanity.

The implications of *Planet of the Apes* for the prophets of racial and cultural prejudice are obvious: the apes call the humans beasts, the humans call the apes beasts. In this vein, *Battle for the Planet of the Apes* contains a moment of particularly rich comedy when Mc-Dowall, playing as usual a particularly gentle ape, urges his beleagured and surrounded co-simians to "fight likes apes!" The whole cycle may be viewed as a bitter ecological fable, a long recognition that if we do not manage to understand our brotherhood with all that lives and grows on our planet, we shall eventually destroy our own racial life—and perhaps that of others—through the arrogance of our rationality. But somehow, the bitterness of the *Ape* cycle finally rings false: the very division of the warring elements of present humanity into warring *species* evades the real problems of politics and of film language. It is, in terms familiar to science-fiction readers, an inverted invasion story: not a tale of man being invaded by aliens from outside, but a tale of man himself as the invader, the intruder upon a balanced world-system which his intelligence and his prejudices tend to destroy. But it is bad science fiction. For the aliens, the apes, are either too close or too far from the conventions of ordinary civilized humanity fully to test its claim to lordship over creation.

The same sort of situation obtains in a more recent film, Mike Nichols' *Day of the Dolphin*. Building upon facts already established about the intelligence of dolphins, the film posits a dolphin who has actually learned to speak—a submarine Tarzan of the fish, as it were —and who is lied to by conniving humans in an attempt to have the president of the United States assassinated. In an obvious reminiscence of the intelligent computer of *2001*, *The Day of the Dolphin* assumes that the gift of language inevitably carries with it the curse of the lie, of isolation both in the universe of insensate matter and in the more terrifying universe of ambiguity and half-truths. The talking dolphin, of course, does not assassinate the president, and the film ends with an assertion of the purity of free instinct, of the ecstatic life of impulse which is the dolphin's mode of existence. But as a parable of language and, specifically, of the language of modern technology (which is to say, the language of film) it is an unrelievedly cynical tale. For the humans—the scientists, the naturalists, the plotting politicians and the secret agents—who have capitalized upon the dolphin's power of speech have thereby reduced themselves to a less than bestial level.

Such pessimism is highly fashionable, of course—not only "these days," but perennially. But the dilemma of language, whether filmic or literary, questioning its own possibilities is not necessarily the cynically reductive mythology that has become enshrined in the popular mind as definitively modern. For a *political* version of the motifs we have been discussing so far—that is, a version allowing us to imagine a social, fully human resolution of the dilemmas of the word in space—we must examine, as a sort of prelude to the concerns of the following chapter, a film like François Truffaut's *The Wild Child*.

The Wild Child is, as its opening credit assures us, based on an actual occurrence. In 1798, in the French countryside, peasants discovered a naked, wild boy who had apparently been abandoned by his parents in infancy and who had, miraculously, survived the abandonment to become, literally, a human animal. Incapable of speech—in fact, incapable of walking erect—the boy (later christened Victor) was adopted by a Doctor Itard, who, concerned with the problem of the origin and nature of human intelligence and language, spent years trying to train Victor to speak, reason, and behave as a normally civilized human being. The boy never did learn to use language except in an exclamatory, Pavlovian-reactive way, although he was trained to behave in socially acceptable ways and ultimately showed a recognizably human propensity for creativity, invention, and wit.

Truffaut's film is an extraordinarily faithful record of Victor's initial capture and of his early days in the house of Dr. Itard. Out of this material Truffaut creates a compelling, complex vision of the ambiguous nature of intellect and art. The date itself, 1798, is an important one, perhaps even more so for an English audience than a French. Set in the heart of the French Revolution, that great, foredoomed era of romantic optimism and rationalistic self-confidence, the discovery of the wild child also occurs in the year in which Wordsworth and Coleridge, with the publication of *Lyrical Ballads*, initiated the romantic era in England. The figures of Descartes and Rousseau brood behind the film, just as they brood behind the whole history of thought since the beginnings of the modern era: for the obsession of the doctor with Victor's educability is a particularly romantic rephrasing of Descartes' concern over the automaton as a potential threat to human centrality, or of Rousseau's ideal of the noble savage, raised free of the crippling and deforming influence of civilized prejudice. Victor's chances for learning to speak, for learning to become fully human, hold out the possibility of a final answer to the question of man's uniqueness in the universe, and of the validity of his consciousness to organize a truly rational society and politics.

Truffaut repeatedly invokes and underscores the philosophical background of Victor's adventure. The continual voiceover narration from Dr. Itard's journal relates each stage of Victor's capture and education to the cultural, epistemological prejudices of the late eighteenth-century intelligentsia: indeed, the centermost irony of this highly ironic tale is that Itard thinks of, and refers to, Victor as an "experiment" or an "opportunity" for discovery long after the boy has manifested his own pathetic and compelling humanity. Filmically, too, Truffaut invokes an atmosphere of innocence (or dated simplicity) by his use of the iris technique at crucial moments of the plot development. The identification between the classical period of Western philosophy and the "classical" period of Western filmmaking is one which Truffaut has previously traded upon, but never more appropriately than here. The iris, with its concentration of screen space into the bright circle-in-darkness of artificially established space, is a direct equivalent of the assumptions of romantic rationalism about the power of mind to abstract, classify, and highlight the true nature of the phenomenal universe.

Only the doctor, of course, wishes—obsessively and, finally, cruelly—to force Victor to use language. And the techniques of *The Wild Child* teach us, as we watch the sad story unfold, that the doctor's idea of language is itself a highly artificial, limited one, and one which directly impinges upon the modern, technological assumptions of film language by which we are conditioned. For Victor—at once Tarzan, child of nature, and Frankenstein, artificially educated and conditioned monstrosity in civilized society—does speak in the film, though not with words. He speaks, and speaks to us, through the very pathos of his situation, trapped between the alternatives of a nature to which he cannot return and a civilization which can never fully assimilate him. His physical presence, in other words, bespeaks him human, and that presence serves to refute each of the experimenting doctor's assumptions and conclusions about the so-called progress of the wild child toward the Enlightenment ideal of humanity.

But if it were as simple as that, the film would not be the triumph it is. For while our sympathies and identification are much more with the wild child than with his coolly empirical warden, the film never allows us to forget that we ourselves, both existentially and as viewers of the film, participate more in the doctor's consciousness than we do in the child's. François Truffaut can hardly be accused of being an unselfconscious director: one of the founders of the *auteur* theory of cinema, he chooses to make his acting debut in *The Wild Child*, in the subtly distasteful role of Dr. Itard. As the doctor-director's penetration of Victor's mind develops, we realize, with that immense melancholy which so many of Truffaut's films produce, that

ADAM AND THE AUTOMATON

we are witnessing the confrontation not of man with nature or with the wild, but of man with the innocence and unsophisticated, elemental life he has forever lost. If *2001* made a subtle point about language as the first of human tools, the first technologized mediacy between man and the environment, *The Wild Child* carries the point further. As the doctor attempts to communicate with Victor, he literally reduces words to the level of tools, training him to fetch a hammer, a saw, an awl, etc., after he has been shown the appropriate pictures, or training him to arrange an alphabet of wooden characters in correct order. The tools are impossibly crude, impossibly inadequate to the boy's own, pre- or sub-conscious vitality. Yet, they are all the doctor has to work with; and they are all we have. Like the written word, like the filmic image, like the complex politics of the Cartesian city, they are at once the triumph of our domestication of the world and the price we pay—in energy, in instinct, perhaps in freedom—for that triumph. Truffaut's film is truly humanizing, truly political because it refuses to opt for either politics or nature, but insists, rather, that only through the language of our civilized, mediated world can we even begin to imagine or articulate the value of the Eden we have left to build our cities.

Perhaps the most compelling single scene in *The Wild Child* occurs near the beginning, when the doctor and a colleague examine Victor for the first time. As Victor wanders wonderingly around the eighteenth-century scientist's library (which reminds us of the famous Louis Quinze room at the end of *2001*), he happens upon a full-length mirror. Amazed at the strange figure, himself, who moves as he moves and yet whom he cannot touch, he stares into the glass as, behind him, we watch the two scientists staring at him. In a long moment which is one of the finest parables recorded on film, civilized man beholds the face of the Adam whose myth he needs so desperately to preserve; and beholds that face, not in the flesh, but as an image, an "automaton" projected by the surface of artificially-polished glass. The rationalist doctors are ourselves; the wild child, the dawnman, is the image of ourselves who marks our progress and our fall; the glass is cinema and, indeed, all the arts which give us a reproduction of the word in space, of consciousness in its struggle with unyielding matter. But the total image, in which all—including the mirror—are caught by Truffaut's camera is the image of film as a political art, a new language for politics and a new politics of language.

1   The dream of evil: Werner
Krauss and Conrad Veidt in *The
Cabinet of Dr. Caligari*. Caligari, the
nefarious hypnotist and manipulator,
and his victim-instrument, the
somnambulist Cesare, present one
of the richest and most perennial
paradoxes of film. Whose dream—or
whose nightmare—do these figures,
of waking but malevolent reason
and dreaming but murderous
unconsciousness, act out? And which
force, the waking or the dreaming
mind, is finally in control of the
world the film projects? Note the
heavy, perhaps circus-inspired, eye
shadow on Cesare—a standard
feature of early film make-up,
exaggerated here to contribute to
the artificial, "cartoon" atmosphere
of *Caligari's* mad world.

Decla-Bioscop, 1919

Metro-Goldwyn Mayer, 1939. Courtesy of Films Incorporated.

2 The dream of the garden: Ray
Bolger, Judy Garland, Bert Lahr, and
Jack Haley in *The Wizard of Oz*.
Here is the romantic garden imagined
as fully as film—or poetry—has
attained. The landscape, even more
than in Disney cartoons, is
humanized, pastoral even in its
hazards, a transformation and
transfiguration of the real. The
Scarecrow and the Tin Man may
appear frightened by the Lion; but
when the Lion looks like Bert Lahr,
we know that the danger can only
be a benevolent, educative one.
Dorothy, the dreamer (is she a
pastoral Caligari, Cesare, or both?)
is delicately placed outside the
triangle of imaginary beings here.
For as their creator as well as
their companion, she both shares
and directs their journey—a journey
into the heart of the magic garden
and thence, of course, home.

73

Metro-Goldwyn-Mayer, 1932. Courtesy of Films Incorporated.

3 The master of the garden:
Johnny Weissmuller in *Tarzan, the
Ape-Man*. The garden here, despite
its obvious sound-stage artificiality,
is not the pastoral of Oz. It is the
jungle, and Tarzan is its master, not
its complacent dreamer and pilgrim.
One is tempted to call this a picture
of *homo cartesianus*. The
implication of Tarzan's alert but
assured stance is that he is lord of
the jungle through his Promethean,
innately civilized consciousness. (We
might even note that the triumphant
civilization of this Tarzan extends to
wearing some rather improbable
slippers.)

4 Unaccommodated man: Boris Karloff in *Frankenstein*. At the other end of the mythic scale from Tarzan, the Frankenstein monster is the victim of the natural landscape, the isolated sufferer. His ironically supreme "civilization"—he is himself a *construct*—alienates him visually as well as narratively from the trees among which he wanders; the real garden is, for him at least, a nightmare of otherness, a madness that has been forced upon him. It is all the more appropriate, then, that Karloff's make-up here is so obviously derived from that of the sleepwalker Cesare in *Caligari*.

Universal Studios, 1932

5 Tarzan bound: Charlton Heston in *Planet of the Apes.* As a children's riddle might put it, How many monsters are in this picture? A possible answer, and the one suggested by the film, is, One: the chained human in the center of the court. The contrary myths of Tarzan and Frankenstein are here inverted, merged, and made ironic. As the only intelligent human on a planet of intelligent apes, astronaut Heston finds his assumptions about human primacy in the universe undermined, if not abrogated; even Descartes would have been upset by a culture of such unsimple simians. But behind the irony of the film lies the classically Cartesian assumption that "humanity" is a value defined through behavior rather than through some shadowy, metaphysical concept of essence.

Twentieth Century-Fox, 1968. Courtesy of Films Incorporated.

United Artists, 1931

Metro Corporation, 1921

6 Hell is other people: Charlie Chaplin in *City Lights*. Charlie is about to enter a prize fight to win money for the woman he loves. But it is unlikely any contestant ever looked less at home in a locker room; we might call this part of the film "Planet (or City) of the Gorillas." Charlie's hat, his clodhopper shoes, and above all his perfectly embarrassed posture and smile indicate how acutely unhappy he is having to go without his clothes—in other words, facing the naked facts underlying the structures and amenities of the Cartesian city. Indeed, Chaplin's particular comic genius, throughout *City Lights* and elsewhere, is in raising to the level of poetry the feeling of being *not at home*. His Tramp is, in a quite serious way, the laughing version of Frankenstein's monster.

7 The state of grace: Buster Keaton in *The Boat*. Tarzan may assert his mastery over circumambient space in the lordly stance of alert control, but Keaton can establish a comic version of the same mastery even in the posture of befuddlement. Keaton was perhaps the most beautiful of comedians, as is evident in this particularly beautiful still. Compare the almost philosophical bemusement of the stationary Keaton with the frantic embarrassment of Chaplin. Chaplin's derby is an absurdity, a shocking irrelevance atop his bare torso. Keaton's hat, on the other hand, is the compositional center of the tableau; as he scratches his head in uncertainty, he holds the hat in such a way that the line of his arm completes the stable triangle that defines his pose. And even as he puzzles over the compass, his right hand already grasps the wheel firmly and with assurance; his body, one feels, knows better than his head. One senses that, as is usual for Keaton, he will triumph over space, not through Promethean assertion, but through the wiser— perhaps saintlier—virtues of acquiescence, quiet, and resignation.

8 Drowning in a room: Dorothy Comingore and Orson Welles in *Citizen Kane*. Comingore's pose of tension and discomfort, at the uneasy center of the "living room" (most ironic of misnomers), is reminiscent of Chaplin's pose of unease in *City Lights*; but here it is no longer funny. Hell is other people; or, as *Kane* grimly insists, *one* other person whom you have lost the knack of loving. Kane himself, drained and dehumanized by the massive, superhuman statuary of his home, takes on the deathly repose (emphasized by the lighting) of the simulacra of life with which he has surrounded himself.

9 Living in space: Stanley Kubrick's *2001: A Space Odyssey*. The spacecraft *Aries* has just landed at Moonbase Clavius. If the human figures in *Kane* were dwarfed by the relics of past art, here they are even more severely dwarfed by the visions of future technology. But the effect is different. The film will finally affirm that man needs to transcend his tools, his dependence upon technology, in order to realize his full humanity. But *2001* is neither contemptuous nor suspicious of mechanical complexity, regarding it, rather, as a necessary stage in the evolution of the imperial intellect. Indeed, stunning scenes like the one here assert, not only the baroque grandeur of science-fiction technologies, but the even stronger brilliance of film technology itself, which can achieve such a complete illusion of a "reality" no man has seen. Kubrick's so-called "visionary" film is visionary precisely as a film and as a film about filmmaking.

RKO, 1941. Courtesy of Films Incorporated.

Metro-Goldwyn-Mayer, 1968. Courtesy of Films Incorporated.

10 The sea of fertility: Julie Adams,
as Kay, in *The Creature from the
Black Lagoon*. In this remarkable
underwater ballet sequence, the
Creature first sees Kay, swimming
luxuriantly above him. Few scenes
capture more successfully the sexual
ambiguity of the film, especially in
the rapturous, graceful position of
the Creature's arms, contrasted with
the unmistakably suggestive shape of
his head.

Copyright © *Universal Pictures, 1954*

Twentieth Century-Fox, 1959. Courtesy of Films Incorporated.

11 Shaman and priest: Henry
Fonda and Richard Widmark in
Warlock. The magical, fetishistic
qualities of the gunman-as-shaman
and the stable, ritual character of the
sheriff-as-priest are articulated in
Warlock even by the clothing and
postures of the actors. Fonda (left),
as Clay Blaisdell, dresses in what might
be called high gunman fashion, a
distinctly ornamental and
"legendary" outfit, and can be caught
in hieratic poses like the one shown
here. Widmark, as John Gannon, is
cut—literally—of more common
cloth. Dressed more ordinarily than
his antagonist (his vest is
unbuttoned; his hat is out of shape
and has a hole worn in the crown),
he is not the magical incarnation
but the ritualistic agent of the Law.
His postures and expressions are,
fittingly, those of concentration and
concern, not—like Fonda's—of icy calm
or trancelike exhilaration.

12 Archetype into parody: Yul Brynner and James Brolin in *Westworld*. Compare Brynner's poised, archetypal gunfighter stance with that of Henry Fonda in the scene from *Warlock*. Here the pose is a deliberate parody of the myth it incarnates, for Brynner is a computerized robot in the elaborate amusement park Westworld, and Brolin, a paying customer, is, at this point, simply playing at the danger Brynner seems to present. Things get out of hand, of course, and Brolin will learn to his cost that there is life—or death—in the old archetypes yet. But more interesting than the plot is Brynner's performance. He is dressed, to the thread, in the costume he wore in *The Magnificent Seven*, one of the most famous and most powerful of recent incarnations of the myth of the gunfighter. His performance in *Westworld*, then, is a witty and self-conscious comment on his own stardom and on the complex technology of screen myth and screen personality.

13 Archetype as muse: Woody Allen and Jerry Lacey in *Play It Again, Sam*. Allen plays a feckless movie critic haunted by the specter of Bogart with his self-confident virility. Lacey, with near-perfect mimicry, plays the specter. The film makes a stronger and subtler point about the idea of film personality than does Brynner's self-parody in *Westworld*. For Allen recognizes— and a scene like the one shown here beautifully visualizes—the reality of the star, the film persona, as a central feature of our mental landscape, one of our most intimate myths of possibility. It is worth noting that, in this scene, while Allen's normal, everyday-type face appears simply caught in half-shadow, the same shadow, on Lacey-as-Bogart, inevitably recalls the baroque lighting effects of the forties' film noir, that richest and most melodramatic of film subgenres. Our mental conception of Bogart transforms even our interpretation of the physical details around him.

Warner Brothers, 1941

Warner Brothers, 1942. Courtesy of Stuart Kaminsky.

14 Hell is other people, part two: Humphrey Bogart, Mary Astor, Barton MacLane, Peter Lorre, and Ward Bond in *The Maltese Falcon*. I have said that we remember Bogart, most typically, seated, watching the world fly apart around him. In this scene, from perhaps his most definitive film, his posture and his tense but bemused expression present almost a visual metaphor for the term and concept "cool." Compositionally and psychologically, his single poised figure counterbalances the quartet of conmen, murderers, and police who act out their mutual violence under his gaze. But, as the scene suggests, Bogart is not simply disengaged from their dance of death. Like Sam Spade, the detective he portrays, he is part of the hellish world he seeks to control. And Bogart's characteristic raised eyebrow and sardonic cast of mouth are, like Chaplin's lunatic grin in the scene from *City Lights*, as much a shield as a weapon against the other people in his room.

15 The state of grace, part two: James Cagney in *Yankee Doodle Dandy*. Cagney's performance as George M. Cohan is a tour de force —he almost singlehandedly raises the banal plot of the film to the level of genius. But, more importantly, *Yankee Doodle* is perhaps Cagney's definitive film, as *The Maltese Falcon* is Bogart's, for it gives him the chance to dance, or, more properly, to move. Cagney is no Fred Astaire or Gene Kelly, but he is something larger, an incarnation of motion itself. Here, while the other human figures are at rigid attention, he is posed in a shuffle that aligns perfectly with the slant of the flags —but gives that angle a raffish, human force. It is a vital, good-humored geometry, and, as such, surely one of the most valuable gifts film or any art can offer us.

4

CAVE AND CITY: THE POLITICS OF FILM

"It is a strange picture, and a strange sort of prisoners." This is the response of Socrates' interlocutor to the allegory of the cave (chapter 25 of Plato's *Republic*). Of all the versions we have, philosophical and artistic, of the precinema, it is by far the most remarkable, and perhaps the most revealing about cinema itself. In the midst of a dialogue about the nature of justice and the means by which a truly just state may be imagined and constructed, Socrates proposes an allegory, a model for the relationship of the mass of mankind to the truth of life. The allegory must be quoted at length; Socrates is the speaker:

Next, said I, here is a parable to illustrate the degrees in which our nature may be enlightened or unenlightened. Imagine the condition of men living in a sort of cavernous chamber underground, with an entrance open to the light and a long passage all down the cave. Here they have been from childhood, chained by the leg and also by the neck, so that they cannot move and can see only what is in front of them, because the chains will not let them turn their heads. At some distance higher up is the light of a fire burning behind them; and between the prisoners and the fire is a track with a parapet built along it, like the screen at a pup-pet-show, which hides the performers while they show their puppets over the top. . . . Now behind this parapet imagine persons carrying along various artificial objects, including figures of men and animals in wood or stone or other materials, which project above the parapet. Naturally, some of these persons will be talking, others silent.

A strange picture, indeed, and strange the prisoners held captive by it. Francis MacDonald Cornford, whose translation I have quoted, observes in a footnote to this passage that "a modern Plato would compare his Cave to an underground cinema, where the audience watch the play of shadows thrown by the film passing before a light at their backs. The film itself is only an image of 'real' things and events in the world outside the cinema." Cornford's insight seems unimpeachably correct: most of the concerns of film we have so far raised are implicit and precisely imagined in Plato's metaphor. The tension between "reality" and the copy, the simulacrum of reality, is central to the vision. So is the duality of language and space, the word as artifact and the word as sacrament of the real, speech as at once "spirit" and tool: "Behind this parapet imagine persons carry-ing along various artificial objects, including figures of men." But what is added to our sense of film by this passage is the significant *situation* of the viewers of the spectacle. The impoverished dwellers in Plato's cave have no choice but to watch and to believe in the show being played out before them. They are a civilization of cinéastes who can never leave the theatre. But the point of the allegory is to specu-late what would happen if one man should break free, ascend out of the cave of images to the sunlight of truth, and return to tell his brothers what he has learned. Socrates' conclusion about their re-sponse is a gloomy one: "If they could lay hands on the man who was trying to set them free and lead them up, they would kill him." He entertains this conclusion only tentatively (his freed cave-dweller will become, after all, his model of the philosopher-king), but it is a question the difficulty of which involves, for us as for Socrates, the deepest concerns of politics, civilization, and artifice.

It is surprising and disturbing that Plato should have imagined the phenomenology of the cinema so accurately (within the limits of his own technology) and that the invention should have been prompted by the desire to formulate an image of human knowledge —and especially of social and political knowledge. It is a vision, in other words, of a socially mediated metaphysics, of a metaphysics of media. The most poignant detail of the passage, surely, is that the citizens of the cave are chained by leg and neck, so that they can see only what is in front of them: they cannot, that is, see each other, so that their sense of the "reality" behind the screen is also the prime—indeed the only—constituent of their sense of themselves. Sociologists of the film and media critics like Marshall McLuhan have for some time been either complaining or rhapsodizing about the ways contemporary public media provide a "reality" for society that predominates over and even redefines the more physical reality of everyday experience. But Plato's allegory is more precise than most of their theories, for it shows us the absurd situation which is our first political experience of filmviewing: hundreds of people, gathered for an occasion which is partly social, partly ritual, partly aesthetic, gather in air-conditioned darkness to look straight ahead, taking care not to interfere with each other. We may laugh if the film is funny —but not so long that we drown out the next line. We may weep if it is sad—but silently. Laughter and weeping, however, are essentially private responses: how often do we applaud? Parker Tyler long ago observed that the basic irony of film is that for all the passion, action, and wit on the screen, no one is really there. No one, that is, but ourselves; and we are there not as a group (as we are at a play), but as atomic individuals whose collectivity, if any, will be re-created and reconstituted only upon our exit from the curious, self-enforced privacy of the film experience.

Once again, then, the idea of the cave itself seems brilliantly suggestive for an examination of film as a political art. Plato did not need to be an anticipatory Darwinist to imagine the cave as a convenient locale for the technology of shadow projection, as well as the originating, primitive unit of civilized life. Indeed, the inhabitants of his cave are prepolitical men, waiting to be politicized, socialized by the very fiction, the very shadow play, which presently holds them in thrall. We are reminded of E. M. Forster who, in *Aspects of the Novel,* suggests that all fictive technique, all the great narrative works of man begin with the demand from one primitive troglodyte to another, "Tell me a story." Or we are reminded of the "Dawn of Man" in *2001,* which may also be the dawn of fiction and the dawn of film as a tool to transmit myth: shaggy half-humans crouched together fearfully, gnattering incoherently to each other to ward off the fall of night.

The cave, after all, is man's first domestication of the landscape, his first *homely* space. Gaston Bachelard, in *The Poetics of Space,* observes that most of us when we think of "space" tend to think of the infinite, chilling vectors of Cartesian extension—the space against which we posed the human word in the last chapter. But, Bachelard insists, there is another space, the enclosed space of the home, the mother's encircling arm, the space which is ours; and it is perennially from this space that we emerge to wrestle with the larger space, only again to return to the smaller space, or an abstracted version of it, for sustenance and regeneration. The Platonic cave and the Cartesian city, then, are not in opposition: rather, their eternal warfare and tension serve to re-create and sustain them both.

In discussing the politics of film, we shall reexamine many of the concerns that have already occupied us, but with the difference that now we shall be seeing these concerns as features, not of the "reality" or "language" of the film, but of the crucial and complex relationship between film, viewers, and filmmakers. We shall be discussing film, in other words, as itself a Platonic cave, whose multifaceted, inchoate human relationships both exemplify and create a society of creators and consumers which may, indeed, be the fundamental political entity of our era. As a beginning, we return to another version of Plato.

In the middle of Bernardo Bertolucci's disturbing film *The Conformist*, there occurs an interview between the "conformist" Fascist agent and his former teacher, an expatriate intellectual he has been sent to assassinate. "If you had not left Italy, I should not have become a Fascist," says the conformist. Particularly, they discuss his lecture on the myth of the cave in Plato's *Republic*: men living a subterranean life and forced to see not things as they really are, but the shadows and simulacra of events cast by the light of the real world. But if these men should ever be exposed to the real light, observes the professor, the shadowy forms of things would vanish like a dream. As he says this, he closes the blinds of his room, and the shadow of the conformist which the sun has been casting on the wall behind him vanishes.

It is a complex moment that enriches the whole film. For if the liberal professor's "light" is meant to disperse, momentarily, the conformist's shadowy confusion, we also realize that the professor's own life (he is deformed, perhaps impotent, and married to a lesbian) is a "shadow" of life on another level. The very gesture through which he "kills" the conformist's tormenting shadow—his fear of his own latent homosexuality—is *not*, as in Plato's myth, by letting in, but by shutting out the light; just as the omnisexual society of the expatriate intellectuals is finally, through an access of "darkness," to goad the conformist into committing the murder he has been postponing through bad conscience.

I know of few scenes in recent films where dialogue and image more deftly comment on each other, or where the fundamental ambiguity of the film process is more efficiently imagined. What is at work in this scene, as in the whole of *The Conformist*, is not so much the antagonism between so-called literary and filmic ideas of cinema as a subtle, self-conscious, and highly suggestive complementarity between such ideas within the wider problem of the possibility of a truly political cinema.

For if we ask, What are the chances for a political cinema? we must also be prepared to ask, What are the chances for a verbal cinema? and, beyond that, What are the chances for a human language at all in this age of the West? Bertolucci's acuity in *The Conformist* is to realize that these questions are inextricably related by a rigorous, if not logical, necessity.

A good deal of stylized and stylish nonsense has been written— and by many of our best critics and directors—about the autonomy of film language, its independence of the traditional concerns of mere storytelling or discourse, and its radically subversive, liberating import for a civilization on the verge of total verbal and social bankruptcy. Specifically, one thinks of the article on and interview with Bertolucci published by Amos Vogel in the Fall 1971 issue of *Film Comment*, where Vogel subtly faults *The Conformist*, invoking "the danger faced by this director in his future work." Since the film has a consistent, comprehensibly literary plot and milieu, the interviewer wonders "whether Bertolucci is to be the staunch revolutionist he aspires to be or the darling of the liberal bourgeoisie." The question itself, in view of Bertolucci's artistic achievement, is inane; but it masks a concern more serious than its own inanity and more cleverly articulated elsewhere than in Vogel's schoolmarmish censoriousness.

The filmic image is assumed by many to have a fundamental, unstructured or self-structuring immediacy that cancels the presumptions of liberal, causally oriented literature and returns the viewer to the primal conviction of his hereness-and-nowness, to a truly revolutionary concern with his own existence denuded of the mediations of State propaganda, a liberation which is or may be the first step toward the construction of a legitimately human, globalized society. So assume journalists like Vogel; so insist counter-cultural cheerleaders like Susan Sontag in *Against Interpretation;* so argue critics like Gene Youngblood in *Expanded Cinema*. And so believe also the self-conscious students of the seventies, heirs to a revolution impotent in its conception, familiars of no films before *Ocean's 11* (except, perhaps,

Citizen Kane or *Stagecoach* on the Late Show) who yet insist that film is, in its novelty and antiformalism, somehow "their" art.

It is a fascinating but shady argument: one would like to believe that there is at least one art, one language available to contemporary man, not corrupted by the real crisis of our own self-consciousness—our conviction, as E. M. Cioran puts it, that consciousness itself is the Fall, a perpetual banishment to the realm of our own facticity, to a land of eternal unlikeness. Film is a tempting candidate for that role, especially film in the realistic Lumière tradition. This tradition, supported by theorists ranging from the reductive Siegfried Kracauer of *Theory of Film* to the phenomenological Stanley Cavell of *The World Viewed*, insists upon the hyper-reality of the film image and upon its transcendence of mediate, verbal modes of presentation. This is not a matter simply of saying that "the camera does not lie." We know, indeed, that the camera cannot help but lie and that the movies, which Jean-Luc Godard has characterized as the "truth twenty-four times a second," are based upon a metabolic lie, a primal *trompe l'oeil*, which is the only possible medium for cinematic meaning. But we also know, or can tell ourselves, that the film image is—however managed and distorted by direction, editing, or projection—a real image, an art not of mediation but of witness by both filmmaker and viewer. It is something to be seen, with the same immediacy and compelling factuality as the sights and sounds of the real world. Not the image transmitted by the film, but the film image itself is a part of the natural world, an indisputable reality, a technological sacrament with all the power to move and enlighten which Western rationalism conventionally assigns to "reality" and "the Word" itself.

So, at least, runs the argument of that most unrevolutionary of critics, André Bazin, in his essay "The Ontology of the Photographic Image." So also, surprisingly enough, runs the implicit argument of the most revolutionary films of Godard, Bazin's disciple during the fifties at *Cahiers du Cinéma* and no less his disciple in *Two or Three Things I Know about Her*, *1 + 1*, and *Wind from the East*. Godard's films, which constitute the most fervent and single-minded attempt at a political cinema we have, are based upon a truly democratic assumption about what actually happens on the screen. Godard does not presume to present a virtual picture of a real world. Instead, he gives us (especially in *Two or Three Things*) films whose ostensive content all but disappears in the self-conscious, self-revealing, immitigably meddling pyrotechnics of the narrator-director. And this, indeed, is the terminal realization of Bazin's ideal of a democratic-aesthetic cinema. The deep focus which Godard's tutor celebrated in *Citizen Kane* and *The Best Years of Our Lives*—allowing the viewer a choice where to look, where to find significance in the screen image —has with Godard widened to include the *fact* of movie-going itself. The viewer's physical and moral option is to decide not only where, but whether to look. The deep focus of his films begins in the brain of the viewer, including in its expanse the screen, the images on the screen, the viewer's sense of his presence in a movie-house, in a country, at a specific time, and so on. Godard returns us to our original metaphor. He tries to make films which, if they do not unchain the necks of the imprisoned cave-dwellers, at least remind them (the Marxist pun is inevitable) that they *can* loose the chains whenever they wish. The crowds who almost invariably leave Godard's films after a half hour or so of what seems to them incomprehensible unstory-telling are the strongest ratification and the strongest limitation of his art. For their boredom affirms, if not his achievement, at least his concentrated attempt at a total cinema where the itch in the viewer's seat and his gasps for a breath of fresh mental air are as much the film's matter as the story told through stuttering light.

Going back beyond Godard and Bazin to their epistemological predecessors, we can reinterpret the crowds who shrieked and ran as the train photographed by the Lumières pulled into the station and "into" the camera. What seems naïve fear and superstition in these audiences can also be seen as a legitimate and deep penetration into the nature of the medium, an awareness that the film, not in what it represents, but in what it *is*, is a threat to and an impingement upon our perception of reality.

In a quite literal way, that is, the onrushing train was a manifestation of the film's intrusion into the cave of the audience's confidence in its everyday, normal perceptions. And the implied collision between train and audience—between each individually perceived train and each perceiver—was one of the birth-throes of the new society of the film theatre. Screams were appropriate.

What I wish to ask, though, is how we can see this breakthrough in artistic form *as* a breakthrough. Given the wit of Godard, the baroque darkness of Visconti, or the radical aestheticism of Bertolucci, are we really justified in claiming for film a more efficient, more immediate, or at least less innately debased political valence than for the older and more battle-scarred medium of literature? In spite of the tendency of most recent film theorizing, I think not—and for the very good reason that film, whatever its pretensions to uniqueness, is irreducibly a literary medium, perhaps the most self-conscious and problematic literature available to our era.

Bazin links the invention of the film to the romantic era, as does his contemporary disciple Cavell. In his essay "The Myth of 'Total Cinema,' " Bazin points out that the *idea* of cinema—including sound, color, and even devices of verisimilitude as yet unrealized (such as 3-D)—can be found, long before its technological development, in the dreams of the nineteenth-century imagination about a truly representative art. The idea of film, in fact, is a natural extension of romantic concerns with art, with language, and particularly with the political implications of language, under whose problematic banners we still labor. Bazin invokes only the tradition of what is now called positive romanticism, with its thrust toward a totally iconic art, where meaning inheres in structure and structure itself inheres in the shared historical existence of artist and audience. But we may also call to account for the birth of cinema that darker, self-doubting negative romanticism which, from Byron and Baudelaire through Mallarmé and Yeats, brings into question the validity of its own imagination of form, dramatizing not so much the imperial control of the mind over reality as the mind's terrible intimation of its bondage to a reality it itself creates.

Harold Bloom has gone so far as to suggest, in his essay "Visionary Cinema in the Romantics," that the dark velleities of landscape in Blake and Wordsworth anticipate and transcend any attempts by filmmakers to deal intelligently with what Shelley called "the everlasting universe of things." This is surely overreaching. But some of the greatest moments of film do underscore the art's resemblance to the self-doubting work of the romantics, trying to negotiate a grammar that allows the human will to live in a world of intractable clutter. We can call to mind the set itself of Babylon in *Intolerance*, Kane's reflection caught infinitely and forever in the mirrors of Xanadu, Marina Vlady walking through the moonscape of modern Paris in *Two or Three Things*, the Jupiter-ship in *2001*, and others.

In his essay "The Intentional Structure of Romantic Imagery," Paul de Man says that the romantic word at its most characteristic is preyed upon by a "nostalgia for the object," a sense of insuperable distance from the purity of the thing-in-itself it seeks to name and transform. Does not the invention of film, as an event in the psychic history of the West, represent, not a rapprochement, but in fact a further recession of things from the grasp of the mind? The train rushing at us, the 3-D rockslide into the orchestra, the oil derrick towering over our puny doubles on the screen—they are all about to touch us but are isolated forever in the fifth dimension which is the space of the screen (even laser holographs only underscore, in attempting to overcome, their ghostliness). Nostalgia for the object, liberated from the mediate word, becomes a keener nostalgia for the present.

In this context, there are few criticisms of film more eloquent or more appropriate than the last stanza of Yeats' "Sailing to Byzantium":

Once out of nature I shall never take
My bodily form from any natural thing,
But such a form as Grecian goldsmiths make
Of hammered gold and gold enamelling
To keep a drowsy Emperor awake;
Or set upon a golden bough to sing
To lords and ladies of Byzantium
Of what is past, or passing, or to come.

The "artifice of eternity" into which the poet has transformed himself through his song turns out to be a machine. But the machine itself is a *verbal* contraption: brilliant image of unmediated experience, of assimilation into the not-self, it nevertheless inevitably evokes memories of fairy tales, myths, traditions of which it is at once the image and the betrayal. And since the machine of immortality can be defined only in terms of a human immortality, its timeless song has no possible theme but the failing mortality the poet has attempted to leave— "Whatever is begotten, born, and dies"—and no possible audience but the sensual, drowsy Emperor who must not sleep but cannot really awake.

We can read the stanza as concerning film since it is about just that possibility of an imaginative and technological metalanguage that so haunted the romantics as both a liberation and an annihilation of the single self. And much more than either Bazin or de Man indicates, this anxiety over structure was and is a political as well as an aesthetic concern. It makes little difference whether we confront Byron's *Don Juan* or Visconti's *The Damned*, Wordsworth's *Prelude* or Chaplin's *City Lights*, Stendhal's *Le Rouge et le Noir* or Renoir's *La Règle du Jeu*. We are confronting the same—and except for the capricious grace of form, insoluble—problem: the evolution of process out of the instantaneous, of sequence and meaning out of series, of reason out of time.

CAVE AND CITY

In our century, the poles of this dilemma have been set out under varied names but with a remarkably consistent urgency. Bultmann's opposition between *geschichtliche* and *historische*, Lévi-Strauss' between "human" and "natural," and Sartre's between the *pour-soi* and the *en-soi* represent, at one level of simplification, the same tension. It is also the tension between Wordsworth the omniscient narrator of *The Prelude* and the "Wordsworth" who lived through the experiences narrated; the warfare between Visconti, opulent and sensual *metteur-en-scène*, and his Martin or von Aschenbach, witnesses and moral victims of that aesthetic riot. "Modern self-consciousness" and "involution" are among the academic charms that have been invoked to lay this ghost, but it persists, in our greatest films and novels no less than in our most shabby ones, as a sensibility beyond the reach of discursive categorization. It is the sense of the *silly*, the nagging intimation in the face of even the greatest and most sustained of artistic inventions that art itself is always, inescapably, *de trop*, a pointless formalization, a vain gesture against the inhospitable rock face which is the world's fullness.

We have already seen how Proust, in the overture to *Remembrance of Things Past*, likens his attempts to consolidate a self from myriad contradictory memories to his childhood sight of the kinetoscope: a parody of movement, a flow which is not a flow, a confusion of discrete facts which in its very confusion hints at a new organization, a new meaning for those facts. The complete texture of the *Remembrance* can be read as a kind of elaboration of this image, not only in terms of its content, but as a primary modality of the Proustian sentence itself, that gigantic period which in its multiplicity of feverish imagery and nervous exuberance always falls just short of a total break with grammar—thus perpetually reasserting the sheerly formal, transhistorical power of grammar.

Proust's fascination with the kinetoscope, or magic lantern, offers another particularly interesting analogy in this connection. For, as a technology for evolving time and movement out of stasis, motion out of individually drawn pictures, the magic lantern is a model of the opposition between individuality and fragmentation, selfhood and otherness, which is at the heart of every individual's attempts to integrate himself into and yet survive the pressures of social existence. The facts of life are that each of us is mortal, finite, and that human society is effectively immortal, will go on after our disappearance from it. And yet a man who lived in constant recognition of those facts would be either a madman or a saint, for it is intolerable knowledge. Most of our language, art, and machines, then, are our attempts to invert the proportions of the facts of life, to insist that we—each one of us—is somehow sempiternal, capable of producing and *being* a meaning that will survive not only our own brief moment but the petty confines of our social, political, historical environment. Human speech itself may be the first manifestation and formal cause of this quest for immortality: it is perhaps true to say that grammar and syntax are our first intimation of godhead. Saint Augustine, in the *Confessions*, likens the relationship between time and eternity to the relationship between the individual words of a sentence and the meaning of the sentence. We hear the words uttered one after another within the time-continuum, he says; but we perceive the meaning of the words as a unity, as something apart from their sequential utterance.

Film, as a grammar of sempiternity, continues and expands the claims of spoken language—and perhaps also raises to a more critical level the attendant threat of mortality, the breaking of sequence, the end of continuity. Certainly, everyone has been struck by the peculiar poignancy of watching a film whose leading actors (Pickford, Barrymore, Bogart, Montgomery Clift) are dead: the syntax of their impersonated passion and action remains, hieratically engraved on light itself, after the living being has ceased.

But at a less speculative level, we may observe that the movement of Ingmar Bergman's *Magician* builds upon and develops the same Proustian-Augustinian point about human artifice, human society, and our terrible thirst for permanence. Bergman's magician, Albert Emmanuel Vogler, is an early-nineteenth-century traveling charlatan who, with his crew of assistants, happens into a provincial Swedish town. Examined by the town's magistrate, Vogler is commanded to give a sample performance of his act—and his sales pitch—for the officials and police before he can be allowed to perform in public. The plot of the film is a narration of the afternoon and evening the Vogler troupe spends at the magistrate's house preparing for their show. We discover that Vogler's very real magic, as total social outsider and deliberate fraud, is to elicit from the comfortably normal people of the town reactions of hatred, love, and jealousy that reveal the terrible anguish underlying normal life. He is a magician in reverse, that is: he is not working a transformation on the everyday, but forcing the everyday to work its own transformation, its own shocked moment of self-discovery, against his ambiguous, problematic presence. In a world of charlatans and deceptive mirrors, the confessed charlatan and mirror-master knows a truth—the truth not behind but within the mask—which is almost a kind of salvation for the society frozen into its fallacious modes of role-playing. The face of Max von Sydow, who plays Vogler, is deliberately Christlike and deliberately artificial, cosmetic; and the original title of *The Magician* —*Ansiktet*, or "The Face"—emphasizes the importance of the rouged artificiality of the magician's presence. For Bergman, here no less than in such later films as *Persona* and *The Passion of Anna*, is constructing a deep allegory of the art of the film itself: a socialized, artificial myth of eternity (the phony Christ of Vogler's "animal magnetism") which tests, as it is necessitated by, the time-bound mortality of a society which *needs* to imagine magic or the transcendent as the basis of its own existence and rationality. And, as with Proust, we are shown only one apparatus of the magician's mysteries: in the central temptation scene, at midnight in the magistrate's house, Vogler and his wife-assistant fiddle with the lenses of a magic lantern, the paradoxical ancestor of the cinema which makes the ironies and the profound political morality of *The Magician* possible.

What I wish to suggest is simply this: that "politics," if it makes sense at all, must signify its most general meaning, "life in time." No sign system, either language or the succession of images which is cinema, can escape from the fundamental contradiction of all sign systems which try to deal with "politics" in our sense—the contradiction being that they are attempting to signify precisely what no system *can* signify, the higher system which is its cause. Ferdinand de Saussure, the father of modern linguistics, suggested this central ambiguity in his distinction between *parole* and *langue*, the radical, willful utterance and the abstract system which makes the utterance possible but of which the utterance is always a betrayal. Heidegger, in his *Introduction to Metaphysics*, written after he had enlisted in the National Socialist Party, converts the same fundamental linguistic distinction into a political ontology. For Heidegger, "Being" in its purity can be approached only through a systematic resistance to the delusions of language in its "normal" spoken or written state, since this state represents the Fall of Being into "Being-There" (the celebrated and overused *Dasein*) or historical, temporal experience. (We might note in passing that Heidegger's Nazified phenomenology, in its perverse brilliance, is a perfect discursive analogue to Leni Riefenstahl's scandalous genius in *Triumph of the Will*.) The Danish structuralist Louis Hjelmslev, in the *Prolegomena to a Theory of Language*, gives us this dichotomy at its most abstract and, paradoxically, most compelling: any language—any "text," as Hjelmslev says—may be described equivalently as *process* (historical act of meaning-making) or *system* (transhistorical, supervenient rules *for* meaning-making).

But the two aspects of the single text, the life-in-time and the higher system that causes life-in-time, are mutually exclusive and require two separate vocabularies of differentiation for all their subordinate aspects. The problem of unifying these two antinomies is the major problem bequeathed to our imaginative and political era by over three centuries of epistemological speculation. And if this dilemma is solved no more by *Battleship Potemkin* than it is by *Remembrance of Things Past*, neither is it less splendidly posed. On the quai at Odessa or the streams of Combray, we and our best guides are in the same boat.

But there is one crucial difference between film language and written language, and it also relates to certain contemporary problems of linguistics and epistemology. Film is an *artificial* language; it is free, as Lawrence Alloway has recently pointed out, of literary and linguistic conventions of iconography and compelled, as Alloway in *Violent America* and Peter Wollen in *Signs and Meaning in the Cinema* have further indicated, to reinvent those conventions through the exigencies of its own drive for meaning.

In the last decade, transformational grammarians like Noam Chomsky and semanticists like Yehoshua Bar-Hillel have revived speculation about the possibility of a mechanical model for human speech, a machine capable of generating, as well as interpreting, meaningful codes in their virtual infinity of variation. It is an important question, perhaps the most important in modern linguistics with its roots, as Chomsky has said, in the origins of Cartesian dualism itself. For at its heart lies another question which we increasingly recognize to be the embattled foundation of romantic humanism— the question to what degree we may believe in the autonomy of human will, upon which our refusal of despair is, if anywhere, based.

But film, of course, *is* such a language—or, at least, as much one as we are likely to witness for some time. It is, formally, a dynamic hybrid between art and technology, the photographic image being, as Walter Benjamin long ago suggested, a development of painting which is also the end of painting. More than a balance, however, film is a continually surprising compromise between creativity and chance, "innocence" and "luck," as Maritain observed of that earlier incarnation of popular mythology, the Dante of the *Commedia*.

In this connection, critics like Pauline Kael in *Going Steady* and Raymond Durgnat in *Films and Feelings* have argued against the over-aestheticized auteur approach to film developed by Bazin and the *Cahiers* theorists. "Whatever the original intention of the writers and director," writes Pauline Kael, "it is usually supplanted, as the production gets under way, by the intention to make money—and the industry judges the film by how well it fulfills that intention."

Ms. Kael is, of course, primarily concerned with debunking the excessive reverence of many contemporary critics (Andrew Sarris is perhaps their chief) toward the poetic vision of directors who, far from being auteurs or even *metteurs-en-scène*, are more properly thought of as mechanical engineers or, in an older parlance, hacks. But her argument carries even deeper implications about the nature of film. Not only is the box office a strong rein upon the chances of a movie's becoming art; so is the very nature of movie-making. The auteur, the presumably omnipotent director who imposes his vision upon the film, is in fact a collaborator with his actors, with his scriptwriter, and with his camera crew; and what he can accomplish is conditioned by their talents and inspirations—or lack thereof. The *Cahiers* critics, of course, made this consideration the chief point of their theory: for a director to succeed *in spite* of such inevitable impingements in making a film "his" should be, they argued, sure proof of an indomitable artistic vision.

What is wrong with this argument is that it gets things backwards. For if we are to take the auteur approach to film seriously, then we must, obviously, assume that film can become art only by betraying or overcoming the contingencies of production that make possible its existence in the first place. Embedded in the theory, in other words, is a deep-rooted contempt for the origins of the form, which is all the more subtle in that it claims to find merit in even the trashiest or most inept works of an established auteur. Bazin's ill-founded enthusiasm for William Wyler's *Best Years of Our Lives* is by now an overused way of embarrassing auteur critics. But we might also cite the lengths to which some recent critics have gone to explicate such bagatelles as John Ford's Civil War segment of *How the West was Won*, or such dreadful inanities as Sam Peckinpah's *Straw Dogs*—a film at once more fascistic than any Leni Riefenstahl ever conceived of and more ostentatiously amateurish than the worst recent production of a college filmmaking course. Or, on the other side of the coin, we might note the contempt in which many critics hold a film like Welles' *Touch of Evil* or *The Stranger* in comparison with his earlier *Kane* or *Ambersons*. Here, so runs a common argument, the auteur has been forced to sell out his genius to the concerns of cheap studio thrillers, manifesting his distinctive *brio* only in virtuoso camera angles or in a few lines of black humor dialogue—when, in fact, *Touch of Evil* and *The Stranger* are among the very best

American films of the postwar period precisely because we have in them a real collaboration between a director of undoubtable genius and a grossly popular form. The collaboration creatively disciplines the genius and inestimably ennobles the form.

Ms. Kael, in the article "Trash, Art, and the Movies" from which I have already quoted, suggests that film is best taken as something midway between art and kitsch, as garbage become self-conscious and serving both as popular therapy and, perhaps, as propaedeutic to higher aesthetic experiences. But we need not be this apologetic in jettisoning the mandarin excesses of auteur criticism. Rather than succeeding as art in spite of its very conditions of existence, cannot film become art exactly because of the impingements, the fundamental political difficulties of making a movie? I have been writing at some length of film as a technological metaphor for precisely those problems of language and reality which possess and disturb the metaphysicians and poets of our century. What I now wish to suggest is that film, through its own internal, ontological dynamics, gives us possible solutions to those problems, solutions which anticipate and frequently surpass the solutions offered by our most valuable writers. Film, in other words, has grown to be a kind of quintessential *writing*, possessed of all the velleities and difficulties we have come to associate with that seemingly innocent word. We have already discussed film as the writing of Cartesian space. It remains to examine how film may also become the writing of that other space, the space of the primal cave, the home, out of which and in contrast to which our idea of the great, difficult world is formed.

During the late forties there was an Italian joke about the remarkable sameness of the working-class, neo-realistic films of De Sica, Visconti, et al.: *Facciamo un film: un uomo cerca lavoro.* The joke catches very nicely the idea, inevitably sociological, of filmmaking: it is a collaboration (*facciamo*), and a collaboration whose ostensive subject (the cliché of "a man seeking work") is, finally, only a pretense for the real subject, which is the technological dream of art, imagination, and heavy machinery all interfering with each other, somehow, to *create*—while what is created, perhaps, makes less difference than we have heretofore been willing to admit.

We are reminded of Flaubert, who articulated the fullest expanse of the romantic dream of imagination when he desired to write *un livre sur rien;* of Henry James and Gertrude Stein, whose writing pushed further and further toward the invisible boundary separating the absolutely (since minimally) significant and the absolutely (since totally) chaotic; or of Robbe-Grillet, the real point of whose fictions is not the meaning concealed beneath their apparent emptiness, but rather the meaning with which their achieved emptiness forces us to fill them. These are not protofilms, but alternative versions of the very imaginative phenomenon which is film itself: art produced by no one or by a cosmos, technology become involuted and self-aware, meaning caught at the moment of emergence from its own originating void. They are a prophetic image of society—not leaving but carrying within itself on its voyage of conquest the primal cave.

These exalted analogues are meant to apply, not to the self-consciously avant-garde tradition of filmmaking celebrated by Amos Vogel, Manny Farber, and Parker Tyler, but to what one has to call the real film: the product of the big studios, whether Hollywood or international. For the studios, through motives more venal than theoretical, have nevertheless remained closest to the true political possibilities of the film—not as propaganda, but as achieved fact. The film *is* a political art, an incarnation of unalienated labor, to the degree that the fluffiest Mervyn LeRoy comedy presents us with an image of industrial and postindustrial mythologies of personality far beyond the possibilities of the most resolutely propagandistic novel. A film by the very fact of its being made presents us with the evidence of the collective personality, technological and artistic, which has produced it; it becomes the real presence of a profoundly political idea of art whose closest analogues are the festival theatre of the Middle Ages or the collaborative tradition of oral poetry that produced both the *Iliad* and *Beowulf.*

We are sustained in this point, of course, by Pudovkin and especially by Eisenstein, for whom the activity itself of filmmaking came to seem more and more a visionary metaphor for the revolutionary society his films were to help bring about. Eisenstein's plans for a film of Marx's *Capital* were, unhappily, never fully crystallized. But his project for an "intellectual cinema," first articulated in his essay "Perspectives" in 1929 (when the *Capital* project was still quite alive), gives us a fair idea of what aura he imagined for his *chef-d'oeuvre:*

> The duality in the spheres of "feeling" and "reasoning" must have new limits by the new art:
> To restore sensuality to science.
> To restore to the intellectual process its fire and passion.
> To plunge the abstract reflective process into the fervour of practical action.
> To give back to emasculated theoretical *formulas* the rich exuberance of life-felt *forms.*
> To give to formal *arbitrariness* the clarity of ideological *formulation.*

It is not really surprising that this should sound so remarkably similar to the programs for aesthetics of Flaubert and Gertrude Stein; for, to Eisenstein, ideology and "pure form" were never really in conflict, the purity of form being itself a version of dialectics and dialectics, in all its tension and self-contradiction, being at the heart of his visionary Marxism. What is surprising, though, is that we should have forgotten so soon the deep wisdom of all this. Eisenstein's enthusiasm for early Walt Disney (particularly *Silly Symphony*) was thus, along his own theoretical lines, a seriously motivated political-aesthetic judgment, not simply an indulgence; just as was his heterodox preference of the bourgeois, melodramatic Balzac to the more "scientific," objective Zola. For Eisenstein, the facts were very simple and very revolutionary (more so, finally, than his own paymasters could bear). Film, a historical and history-making form, became most truly political in becoming most truly itself, in becoming most acutely self-conscious of its own medium, most integrated with the ontological bases of its style.

Indeed, we may chart the history of Eisenstein's own films, from *Potemkin* to *Ivan the Terrible*, both as a growing politicization of the art of the film and as a progressive discovery of the ontological basis of the medium itself. *Battleship Potemkin*, for all its importance in the history of the art, is a relatively crude attempt to imagine on film the "mass man" discovered and analyzed in *Capital*. Eisenstein's reconstruction of the Potemkin mutiny does, indeed, make the point that the revolutionary class exists as a collectivity or not at all: except for the martyred sailor Vakulinchuk, there are in fact no featured actors in the film at all, only the surging masses of the ship's crew, the even larger surging masses of the prerevolutionary city of Odessa, and the continually intercut images of the ship's pistons, its "selfless" machinery grinding inexorably toward the triumph of the rebelling battleship. But if we may assume that Eisenstein's intention, even at the making of *Potemkin*, was to "restore sensuality to science," we must conclude (as he himself seems to have concluded) that the "science" in this early film, the economic and sociological theory of man-in-mass, too far preponderated over any "sensuality"—that is, any *sense* of the individual passions and obsessions out of which a mass movement might effectively be created. It is not entirely frivolous to say that it took the Nazi invasion of Russia to awaken Eisenstein to the full possibilities of revolutionary filmmaking as at once a vision of a unified society and of a more intensely felt private personality. *Alexander Nevsky* is, of course, a propaganda film of the most blatant sort: "operatic" is one of the words most frequently applied to it.

CAVE AND CITY

And yet the vision the film gives us of the stateliness and of the monolithic heroism of Nevsky is a great deal more subtly human than most of *Nevsky's* commentators have indicated. For Nevsky is a public hero brought out of retirement by his long-suffering country and even in his moments of maximum stateliness and authority, is always recognizably a private person. In fact, the film's operatic qualities and Cherkassov's haughtily noble charade of Nevsky underscore the privacy of the hero's personality at the same time that they dramatize the momentousness of the historical events—such as the Battle on the Ice—that Nevsky precipitates. Paul Rotha, in *The Film Till Now*, dismissed *Nevsky* (in favor of the more experimental *Potemkin*) by saying that the director "seemed absorbed in recreating the face of the legendary past at the expense of any but the most elementary political theme." But this most elementary political theme may also—in terms of the drama of film and even, perhaps, in terms of the theory of social revolution—be the most important and perennial political theme of which art can make us aware. Visually and symbolically, Nevsky is posed between two contradictory alternatives: the soulless, totalitarian iron-helmeted Teutonic Knights (the principle of absolute publicity) whom he drives out of Russia; and the good-natured, brawling, flirtatious peasant warriors (a lyrical but innately powerless privacy), whose love affairs provide the curious subplot of the film. By returning, after *Potemkin*, to a more traditionally melodramatic film narrative, Eisenstein—and this surely is a mark of his genius—managed to produce an even more movingly political, humanizing film than was his first success.

This process reaches a kind of apotheosis in *Ivan*, Parts One and Two. Stalin may or may not have been correct to see in the character of Czar Ivan a bitter parody of his own terrorist methods. But we are surely justified in seeing *Ivan the Terrible* as marking one limit of the possibilities of film as a political art. It succeeds, finally, in transmuting melodrama into tragedy. Ivan's terrible loneliness, his imprisonment within the exigencies of state and—literally—within the stiff postures and shadows of absolute power are given profound depth, not in spite of, but because of the high artifice and high sentimentality of Eisenstein's chiaroscuro direction. From Ivan's first defiant speech to the grasping, capitalistic Boyars about the unity of Russia and the sacredness of the soil, there is no doubt that this sixteenth-century czar is actually a twentieth-century nationalist revolutionary. But by surrounding and almost overwhelming his contemporary hero with the ritual, trappings, and icons of medieval Slavic superstition, Eisenstein achieves startling effects of irony and analysis. Early in Part Two, after he has decided upon his campaign of summary executions against the noble Boyars, Ivan ascends to his bedroom and, eyes cast upward, soliloquizes: "If it is possible, let this cup pass from me." It is an outrageous parallel, but one that works in the context of the film and, moreover, works as a brilliant revelation of the suffering, self-conscious humanity seething beneath the hierarchical, iconic, public figure of the Czar. Cherkassov, so runs the legend, was in physical agony throughout much of the filming of *Ivan* because of the exaggerated, hawk- and vulture-like postures Eisenstein forced him to take for long, almost motionless scenes. And we may remember, in this connection, that the intellectual Russian school of filmmaking tended to regard actors more or less as props to be moved and managed in the construction (*montage*) of a dialectical cinema. But, after all, *Ivan* was made after Eisenstein's visit to—and enthusiastic discovery of—Hollywood, the most popular (as opposed to populist) and melodramatic school of filmmaking the world cinema has produced. And perhaps we can see in the iconic poses of Eisenstein and Cherkassov's Ivan not only an extension of the Marxist cinema born in *Potemkin* and articulated in the director's project for an "intellectual cinema" but also a wedding of the popular techniques of melodrama (family feuds and dying wives, after all, account for much of the footage of *Ivan*) with the high seriousness of a political, revolutionary purpose. Eisenstein's last and by far greatest film includes, in other words, the impulses of the cave-home and the exigencies of the crowd-city, the double tendency of film narrative toward unabashed sentimentalizing and clinical analysis; and by including both so explicitly, it becomes perhaps the most definitive political—and, in a deep sense, popular—film we have so far witnessed.

We need not belabor the literary and dramatic analogues to this creative vision—the slang lyricism of Apollinaire, the epic theatre of Brecht and Weill, the *Welthistorische* ragtime of T. S. Eliot and, even more abrasively, Hart Crane. But what bears examination is the sense this aesthetic makes of even minor, unredeemedly popular manifestations of art. Let us compare, for instance, the Mervyn Le-Roy-Busby Berkeley *Gold Diggers of 1933* and John Steinbeck's *In Dubious Battle* (1936). Both have the same theme, the economic crisis of America in the thirties.

In Steinbeck's novel the hero, Jim Nolan, begins by quitting his job and joining the Party. The early scenes of the book all underscore Jim's rootlessness, his anxious willingness to be reborn as the "group-man" of Party orthodoxy. As Jim pursues his initiation into the Party by organizing a strike among itinerant workers in California, he approximates closer and closer the depersonalized, selfless ideal of group-man; and he finally sacrifices his life and his face in a martyrdom which will unite the proletarians of the strike. In a revision of the Platonic myth, Jim finds his home precisely in the homelessness of Marxist revolutionism, in the oddly Christlike role of being a "man for others."

In Dubious Battle is a propagandistic novel in the best sense of the word. Moving, and gracefully structured, it is one of the finest and most mature political novels written in America. Its deep intelligence is manifest, more than anywhere else, in Steinbeck's careful and continual counterpoint between Jim Nolan's psychic development (his growth toward the incarnation of group-identity) and Jim's fictive development (his growth away from the narrative possibilities of the novel as a form). Steinbeck realizes, and makes the point again and again, that the Marxist vision of revolutionary mass man is formally and psychically inimical to the individualistic, radically bourgeois presumptions of the traditional novel; and his book's subtlety is to pose what Eisenstein called the claims of "formal arbitrariness" (the novel) and "ideological formulation" (the revolution) in a complex tension which is "dubious," finally, of everything except the narrator's own anarchic humanism. It is one of the most perspicuous uses of a traditional literary form for antitraditional motives in American writing. Even the prose describing the formation of the striker's camp is a *tour de force* of political style:

> The new tents went up along the streets. Dr. Burton superintended the cooking arrangements. Trucks went out to the city dump and brought back three rusty, discarded stoves. Pieces of tin covered the gaping tops. Cooks were assigned, washtubs filled with water, the cow cut up and potatoes and onions set to cooking in tremendous stews. Buckets of beans were boiled. In the dusk, when the picking was over, the men came in and found tubs of stew waiting for them.

If the strike is for Steinbeck a parturition of mass man from a scattering of oppressed workers, this paragraph catches perfectly that birth. Except for Dr. Burton, a fellow traveler who is basically unsympathetic to the selflessness of mass identity, there are no "novelistic" human beings in this passage. The men appear only as a plural noun, and their collective activity is all but unrecognizable as human action; things get done, but no *one* is there to do them. The prose here is bound to remind us of such profoundly Marxist crowd scenes as the revolt of the sailors in *Potemkin* or the digging of the irrigation canal in King Vidor's *Our Daily Bread*. The difference—and it is an important one—is that in film such scenes can be articulated through rather than in spite of the semiological conventions of the form. Dr. Kracauer is correct at least in this in his pontifical *Theory of Film,* when he argues that the crowd is not only an attractive but somehow an integral subject for cinema.

Thus, *Gold Diggers of 1933*. Tawdry where Steinbeck is noble, inane where he is acute, it is nevertheless a political artwork to be taken with equal seriousness, *as* a work of art, with *In Dubious Battle.* The central dichotomy of the film is the disparity between the banal Mervyn LeRoy-directed love plot (Dick Powell and Ruby Keeler proving again that love can survive Broadway and even a big bank account) and the Busby Berkeley musical numbers (ranging in this case from the dadaist "We're in the Money" through the Wagnerian "Pettin' in the Park" to the astounding finale, "The Forgotten Man," which might have come, not from Brecht, but from one of the wiser inhabitants of a Brechtian nightmare). But this dichotomy is also, of course, the dichotomy between two stages of human history—or, at least, of self-consciousness. As in most of the Berkeley musicals, the "plot" is concerned with love backstage, with the difficulties of mounting a Broadway show, and with the problems of unemployed Depression era chorines. And the moments toward which these clichés tend, the Big Numbers, are at once the justification and the annihilation of the plot. The jobless dancers and starcrossed lovers, that is, find their release and fulfillment in massive productions whose totally *filmic* absurdity cancels out the individualistic, "dramatic" world from which its participants come.

This is as simple as saying that none of the famous Berkeley numbers could ever have been done on the musical stages where they pretend to occur. The technique has become standard in show-business and musical films, reaching perhaps its terminal gigantism in the CinemaScope *No Business Like Show Business.* But in the Berkeley originals there is a strong and subtle epistemological point. The solution of the human problems of the characters is not so much in a plot leading them to success and marriage, as in the moments of transcendence and assimilation into staggering group-art reached in the production numbers. (We might notice an anticipation of this kind of tension and transcendence in the much-underrated *Jazz Singer* of 1928: values of tradition and religion are contained within the silent film, values of jazz and radical anomaly in the sound film

—until the sentimental climax, when we hear the jazz singer intoning the Kol Nidre.) In fact, the relative proportions of music and life set up for the musical film by Berkeley remained largely unchallenged until very recently. *Cabaret* has been celebrated by most of its admirers as part of the "renaissance" of the Hollywood musical of the late sixties and early seventies. But it is also a profoundly atypical musical, not only in its storyline—the end of the Weimar Republic and the rise of Nazism—but in its treatment of the metaphor of the stage. The cabaret is, indeed, the only locale of the musical segments of *Cabaret:* none of the musical numbers take place anywhere but on the stage of the Kit Kat Klub, and, perhaps more significantly, none of them are presented in ways that would not be equally possible on a live stage. Stylish reminiscences of Dietrich and *The Blue Angel* aside, the central metaphor of *Cabaret* is that in a society where decadence has reached the level that identifies personality with performance, both privacy and publicity become equally factitious responses, equally vulnerable to the violence of fascist superstition and nostalgia for a more "authentic" past. *Cabaret* is a brilliant film; and a large part of its brilliance depends precisely upon its negations, its refusal to employ many of the conventional film techniques established in musicals like *Gold Diggers of 1933.*

I am not saying, of course, that *Gold Diggers* is a great movie or as great a work as *In Dubious Battle.* Such value judgments, in themselves, are a far greater disservice to criticism and to art than are the arguments that call them into question. We can always deal with the film in other ways: we may see it as a fondly remembered technical milestone (as might Andrew Sarris), as a projection of the national subconscious (as might Parker Tyler), or as old-fashioned, plain fun (as might Pauline Kael). But none of these versions of *Gold Diggers* controverts or, to my mind, diminishes the interesting cultural and political structure of the film—a structure, let me repeat, due not to the efforts of directors, writers, or actors, but to the nature of the art itself, in reaction to a certain historical context.

Do we assume, then, that film is always innately and subtly political, but always unconsciously, deterministically so? That, of course, would be an absurdity, although perhaps a useful corrective to much contemporary writing about film. Too many critics and filmmakers, anxious to assert the artistic independence of film from literature and literary criteria of judgment, have in fact invented a mythology of film creation that is simply a reprise of unfruitful and now outdated ideas of literary genius. The auteurized mind bears an uncomfortable resemblance to the sort of mentality that produces an anthology called "Great Books of the Western World" or a *Golden Treasury.*

Maurice Merleau-Ponty, in his essay "Cinema and the New Psychology" (1945), writes of film and art, technological epistemology and phenomenological humanism in terms that seem much more efficient. "We recognize," he writes, "a certain structure common to the voice, physiognomy, gestures, and aura of every individual—each individual being, for us, nothing other than this structure, this way of being in the world." With an individual, an individual work of art, or an art itself, we need posit neither design nor inadvertence in the manifestation of this identifying structure: we need, rather, to observe it and to recognize its distinctive modes of restructuring our own fluid transactions with reality.

In the case of film, this means that we need to develop a vocabulary that will allow us to "read" a film as at once writing and anti-writing: as, at each moment of its development, raising and transfiguring our expectations about the nature of narrative, story, and history. The reverse exigency, of course, holds for responsible perception of writing in the age of film: we need to reread this ancient and most problematical of structures as itself called into question and reorganized by the competitive presence of film. Such a vocabulary must be an empirical one, based not upon the vested interests of film or literary theorists, but upon a serious and unprejudiced rereading of all our literature and cinema, and upon a rereading, furthermore, which is *present* within the films and books themselves. Such a re-reading is that of the allegory of the cave I cited at the beginning of this chapter, in which Bertolucci and his crew manage not only to redefine their film through Plato but, in addition, Plato through the medium of *The Conformist.* (We are reminded of Lévi-Strauss's argument that all versions of a myth, including its explications and interpretations, are its isotopes: Sophocles and Freud are equally used *by* the primal structure of the Oedipus tale.) And one possible political characteristic of this vocabulary is the distinction I have suggested between Steinbeck and Berkeley: the form of the novel tends to center upon the conflicts of the individual with the mass and to manifest the mass, the group-man, only allusively or self-parodistically, while the form of much film approaches a social totality from the opposite set of coordinates.

Whatever shape such a critique might ultimately take, it cannot exceed the richness and creativity of films and books as they now exist. This is as it should be; and along this line it is appropriate to conclude with the image of a film whose structure seems consciously to call into play many of the elements we have been discussing. Bergman's *The Passion of Anna* (the Swedish title is simply *A Passion*) is only allusively "about" politics—for example, Max von Sydow and Liv Ullman interrupt their chess game to watch the televised self-immolation of a Vietnamese Buddhist monk. But as Bergman unfolds his *pas de trois* of sexual possessiveness, self-deception, and deceit, we realize that this is indeed a profoundly political film in the only sense in which that word can be important to us: it is a film about our chances to live together and not lie. And in a technical feat that surely owes something to Godard's recent practice, Bergman intercuts the story of the passion with the reactions of his principal actors to the characters they play. Each actor, in other words, presents his or her linear, analytic, "literary" response to the cinematic event which is unfolding and of which the actor is a part. The isolation and mutual incomprehension of their analyses, more dramatically even than the sexual paralyses they act out in the film, create the subtle and oppressive complexity of this great work. Bergman's psychic wasteland describes and takes place within the mutual revelations of cinematic and literary form, dignifying both through a tragic despair whose arena is the mind of the artist faced with his work. Like the best of Bertolucci, Welles, Griffith, and any number of lesser men who have created only one masterwork of writing or filmmaking, Bergman's *Passion* is the work, not of an auteur, but of a sensitive man making the best of his time and his craft, being thought through by the forces that inhabit the forms. And that is what film and writing, as well as politics, can finally promise us of most value.

But if the politics of film, and of postromantic art generally, may be taken in this way, we must also ask the more complicated and technical question, What is the relationship between the conventions of the poet's (filmmaker's) craft and the presumably larger, more specifically moral concern of the individual artist? What, that is, can we say about the interplay of genre and creativity in the art of the film? Given that film and writing are complementary in their relative treatments of the mass as opposed to the individual, it should be possible to discuss the conventions of film and literary narrative in terms of their specific historical relevance, their various ways of manifesting a time sense, a politics, that both transcends and motivates the individual creation of the director, screenwriter, star, and so on.

Another way of putting this problem is to say that any artwork, any narrative, attempts at the same time to indicate the reality of the cave in which human perceptions are bound, and to liberate those perceptions from the cinematic bondage of their particular cave. The further question, then, is what sort of cave, what sort of narrative assumption about the conditions and limits of human fate and effort, the filmmaker (or novelist or poet) chooses to liberate us from. The history of a culture, it seems, may be efficiently written in terms of the inherited artistic forms whose assumptions that culture seeks most deliberately to revise. Literary and filmic genres are important to us, not so much in their primitive, unquestioned "pure" forms, as in their declensions from that purity, their manifestations which, attempting to reformulate the generic norms, indicate to us how far the genres have failed to sustain a vision of human, social reality—and how far they have continued, though partially, to succeed in that vision.

The concept of genre, in other words, captures the ideas of reality versus fantasy, language versus silence, and mass versus individual which have thus far formed the basis of our discussion of the art of film; and yet it transforms those concepts into the matter of a fully historical, political discussion of the film as not only the manifestation of an abstract, theoretical aesthetic, but also as the agency of imaginative politics itself, the continual self-definition and redefinition of a society in terms of its dreams of identity. Indeed, film may, like the romantic ideal of poetry, be the process through which the social, collective Adam awakes to find his dream true. But before we can completely understand that metaphor, it is first essential to ask what, precisely, Adam *does* dream at given moments of time, at given junctures of history, and therefore, what kind of truth he finds, upon awaking, to satisfy the expectations of his dream.

Long before the invention of film, William Wordsworth, in "Tintern Abbey," articulated the problems of romantic politics and artistic convention in a manner highly suggestive for our discussion. "Tintern Abbey" is Wordsworth's attempt to locate, in the interplay of imagination with reality, of the world inside with the world outside the head, some principle of unity or continuity that will allow him to believe in the fundamental benevolence of fate, the rationality of human existence and human society. The occasion of this magnificent quest is the deliberately undramatic one of Wordsworth's revisiting the banks of the River Wye, after a five years' absence, and seeing again the landscape that had provided the setting and impulse of his youthful life. In the first stanza of the poem, before he begins his attempt at reconciling "what we half create / and what perceive" in the universe of our experience, he simply looks at the scene before him; but Wordsworth, in what was to be his most lasting gift to English and American poetry, looks at things from a vantage point so

CAVE AND CITY

purified and devoid of rationalistic, humanizing prejudice as to be radically innovative in the history of writing. His vision of the banks of the Wye, and of the farmers' cottages located along those banks, has been justly celebrated as one of the strangest and most disturbing passages in poetry. For it is the world seen cinematically, the world seen without a self and without the sense that any other selves may, through their organizing efforts, have transformed the mute, alien landscape into a semblance of human reason.

> Once again
> Do I behold these steep and lofty cliffs,
> That on a wild secluded scene impress
> Thoughts of more deep seclusion; and connect
> The landscape with the quiet of the sky.
> The day is come when I again repose
> Here, under this dark sycamore, and view
> These plots of cottage-ground, these orchard-tufts,
> Which at this season, with their unripe fruits,
> Are clad in one green hue, and lose themselves
> 'Mid groves and copses. Once again I see
> These hedge-rows, hardly hedge-rows, little lines
> Of sportive wood run wild: these pastoral farms,
> Green to the very door; and wreaths of smoke
> Sent up, in silence, from among the trees!
> With some uncertain notice, as might seem
> Of vagrant dwellers in the houseless woods,
> Or of some Hermit's cave, where by his fire
> The Hermit sits alone.

The farms "green to the very door" and the orchards that "lose themselves" amid the untended fruitfulness of nature are far from being the pleasant, idyllic version of rural landscape that generations of incautious readers have seen in "Tintern Abbey." Instead, they represent the return of domesticated nature to the inchoate state of nature as *other*, a self-conscious primitivization of the world which is all the more striking because it takes place, not amid volcanoes or cataclysms, but in the quiet afternoon of a poet in the English countryside. So complete is the primitivization that, by the end of the passage, Wordsworth even refuses to allow himself the natural (i.e., conventionally realistic) explanation for the wreaths of smoke he sees. The smoke, obviously from the domestic hearths of the local farmers, becomes for him the prime datum of a reverie about originating consciousness in its natural isolation in space. The Hermit is the only other human being besides Wordsworth to appear in the first half of the poem; and the Hermit (as we have frequently observed of the wraiths of the film experience) is not really there. The cave in which the Hermit sits alone may not be a direct descendant of the Platonic cave, but it is at the very least a cousin germane. For the function of the Hermit—the thought of a "more deep seclusion" even than the poet's own isolation with his thoughts—is to give rise to a series of reflections about the interrelationship of mind and cosmos which are, ultimately, political and social in their lyric implications. For—as all readers of the poem have surely been surprised to find—Wordsworth's final answer to the question, How do we make sense of our lives as a succession of mental experiences within an unthinking universe? will be in terms of human society. I am referring, of course, to the great moment when he turns to his previously unnamed companion (the "dear, dear Friend," who is his sister Dorothy) and discovers that the mind's isolation within itself is resolved by the presence of *other people,* by the possibility of loving and imaginative discourse with our companions in the uniqueness of the human experiment. It is a moment which releases the tensions of isolation implied by the fantasy figure of the lonely Hermit, and a moment in which the originating isolation of the cave becomes the communion of what we may call the minimal city —the coexistence of two human beings in mutual charity on the verge of the primal landscape.

"Tintern Abbey" has rightly been thought of as the premiere poem of English romanticism and very possibly the greatest, most inexhaustible poem of the nineteenth century. The point I wish to make, though, is that its visionary politics, its resolution of the problem of mind and mind's uneasy peace with matter, is engineered not only in terms we can properly call prefilmic, but in terms of well-established genre conventions which Wordsworth systematically inverts. It is not necessary here to reexamine the long tradition of eighteenth-century nature poetry upon which he was building when he wrote "Tintern Abbey." It is sufficient simply to observe that the poem, as a "Lyrical Ballad," depends both upon our understanding the private conventions of the lyric form and the public, sociological conventions of the ballad—and upon our seeing that both conventions are being radically manipulated, interpenetrated, in order to locate a new idea of personality and the individual voice within their generic implications.

Film, for all the reasons we have already stated, is on the surface an even less individualistic mode than poetry, although the uniqueness of poetic creation as well as the mass-produced nature of filmmaking have probably been overemphasized. Nevertheless, the idea of genre undeniably plays a more noticeable role in the history of the narrative film than it does in the history of romantic and postromantic poetry and fiction. Precisely because of this greater reliance upon the conventions of genre, however, the film can often give us parables of visionary politics that are superior to many of their more official literary cousins—at least in their ability to transform a given moment of history or of social relationships into the stuff of myth. For film the genre is history and politics incarnate: that is, there is a *presence* of history within the most technical details of the work of art unrivaled in any other form of storytelling.

As a proleptic image of the concerns of the next chapter, we may conclude with a film which embodies many of the points we have so far discussed, and which, through its technical perfection, links those concerns to the problem of artistic convention and inherited modes or genres of narrative. Claude Chabrol's *The Butcher* is at once a fable of French provincial life, a thriller (Chabrol, alone among the "New Wave" filmmakers, has remained true to his Hitchcockian heritage), and a film about the birth of and chances for civilization. The story is relatively simple: in a provincial town of France, the citizens are terrorized by a series of brutal sex murders. From the beginning of the film (by the very title of the film, in fact), suspicion is thrown upon the town's butcher, a former soldier given to expansive descriptions of the carnage he witnessed while serving with the French Army, although there always remains, in the minds of the viewers and of the investigators, some doubt about his guilt. The local schoolteacher, a tense intellectual who has had a disastrous love affair, befriends the butcher and rapidly finds herself convinced not only that he is the murderer, but also that she cannot betray him to the authorities. In a harrowing scene reminiscent of *Psycho* the butcher enters her house one night and, holding a knife on her, confesses his pathetic obsession with blood and his guilt in the sex crimes—only to stab, not the schoolteacher, but himself. The teacher rushes him to the hospital, where he dies; she returns to her home and, in our last sight in the film, blankly watches the lights blink off and on across the river from her house.

It is a sad tale—or would be so, were it not for Chabrol's treatment of it. The film begins with a shot of a cave, decorated with what seem to be Cro-Magnon drawings of bison, deer, hunters, and so forth. Before we see any human beings in the film, we hear a voice, which we later learn to be that of the schoolteacher, discoursing (to children on a field trip? to the film audience viewing *The Butcher?*)

about the art of primitive man. "And what do we call an appetite when it becomes civilized? A passion," the teacher tells her audience. The observation and the image of the primitive cave are keys to the profound humanity of the film. Chabrol's treatment of the tawdry and disgusting story of the butcher is, finally, an assertion that the civilizing impulse may coexist, paradoxically and scandalously, even with the psychotic urgings to murder and rape. The butcher is a human being, capable not only of brutality but also of love and idealized passion: at the end of the film we shall see him kill himself for shame, having exposed his criminality to the woman he loves. He is, that is to say, no more nor less civilized than the caveman who scrawled the records of his killings on the walls of his home and created out of those scrawls the first and perhaps still the greatest manifestations of the human impulse to art. In his previous film, *This Man Must Die,* Chabrol presented the story of a man driven to avenge the murder of his son and finally unable to bear the moral responsibility of having achieved his vengeance. *The Butcher* carries Chabrol's moral obsession to a level that we can only call metaphysical. For the implication is strong in the film that the butcher, the sex-killer, is somehow guiltless in his carnage, or at least absolved of the guilt of his carnage, because with the frigid schoolteacher he has found the ability to love—even to love an unattainable object. A lust, grown civilized, is to be called a passion.

Throughout the film, there are frequent references to and quotations of the thriller films of Alfred Hitchcock; and *The Butcher* as a whole may be viewed simply as a thriller film. But to do so, I think, is like reading such a novel as Graham Greene's *Brighton Rock* as "simply" a murder mystery. Hitchcock's grim parables of guilt and innocence may concentrate on the insight that all men are ultimately reprehensible before an inscrutable destiny. But Chabrol at his best, and certainly in *The Butcher,* inverts the Hitchcockian lesson to assert that all men, though guilty, are ultimately pardonable before the jury of a truly humane civilization. His is a cinema of forgiveness, even of charity in the oldest and most political sense of that very political word. The humanism of his film, however, does not totally depend upon his use of the detective genre as established in the films of Hitchcock. In one of the most moving scenes of *The Butcher,* the title character, in a pathetic attempt at love-offering, brings a fresh leg of lamb to the school, in which the teacher is just concluding a lesson on French literature. The children, giggling, file out of the classroom; and killer and intellectual, body and spirit of civilization, victim of instinct and priestess of reason are left to face each other, in a delicately unstated dialogue of mutual affection, before a black-board on which is written the single word "BALZAC." It is perhaps one of the most highly "literary" moments of self-revelation in the history of filmmaking; but more importantly, with its multiple reference both to the "Human Comedy" of Balzac's novels and to the whole tradi-tion of narrative—filmic and novelistic—which informs the ironies and ambiguities of *The Butcher*, it is a warning to film theoreticians that the problems of film genre are more deeply ingrained with mat-ters of history, politics, and the individual talent than most of our theories have been able to comprehend. It is to those problems that we now turn.

5

LEOPARDS AND HISTORY: THE PROBLEM OF FILM GENRE

Who is the creator of a film? The question, on the face of it, sounds academic, quite unrelated to any enjoyment, instruction, or edification we might actually get from a film or a series of films. But at a rather more serious level, it is indeed a crucial question. Films are a particularly fascinating mode of art because they call so many of our ordinary assumptions about art into question: neither realistic nor fantastic, they draw us into a new imaginative world which is at the same time a real one and a fantasy; neither language nor silence, they compel us to reinvent a relationship between the word and the space surrounding the word; neither private creations nor public acts, they raise again the problem of the political valence of art. Thus, if we ask, Who is the creator of a film? we are in fact asking, not for a single answer, but for a set of answers, for an attitude, that will allow us to take into account the double existence of any given film as artwork and public dream, as made object and communal expression of the anxieties and hopes of the culture which welcomes and patronizes it.

The image from Claude Chabrol's *The Butcher* with which we concluded the last chapter is a premonitory parable of this question and of the related problem of genre in film. In a thriller set in provincial France, two people—one a frigid intellectual and one an elemental sex-killer—face each other across a blackboard on which the name "BALZAC" is written. In order for us actually to *see* the film, that is, Chabrol expects us to understand that it arises from the intricate interplay of the thriller genre (with particular relevance to Hitchcock) with the conventions of the French provincial *conte,* and of course also with the personal obsessions and idiosyncratic vision of Claude Chabrol. So that to ask, Whose film is it? is not really to seek a definite answer, but rather to engage ourselves with the forces—personal, historic, and generic—out of which the individual film arises.

Kafka's short parable of the leopards also has a bearing on the concerns of this chapter because it suggests the deep relevance of the question of film genre to the parallel and, in our century, equally complex question of literary genre, the relationships between what T. S. Eliot christened "tradition and the individual talent." Kafka's statement of the problem is this: "Leopards break into the temple and drink to the dregs what is in the sacrificial pitchers; this is repeated over and over again; finally it can be calculated in advance, and it becomes a part of the ceremony." The interruption of ritual, the explosive revision of historically established expectation, is of course what constitutes the prophetic moment of art. But as Kafka suggests, that explosion itself continually tends to become assimilated *into* the ritual, necessitating new modes of interruption, new varieties of creative outrage. History and individuality, Kafka tells us, create art through their eternal struggle against each other; and in an art as highly collective, as undeniably historical, and as potentially disruptive as film, we may expect the paradox of the leopards to operate with special appropriateness.

Recently, two colleagues and I had a conversation which, through its mutual incomprehension, raised some of these points in an unusually practical way. One of my friends was a teacher of English who has also taught and written widely—and influentially—about film. The other is a specialist in medieval English and Latin literature and goes to very few films at all. Friend One was remarking that all the most interesting young directors in America were self-conscious genre directors (i.e., Bogdanovich, Coppola, Altman, Lucas). Friend Two then asked, disingenuously, what we meant by "genre director": weren't *all* films, in one way or another, "generic" works, just as all coherent works of literature establish their coherence through the reestablishment and revision of genre norms? Friend One and I proceeded to mumble things like "Western . . . thriller . . . *film noir* . . . audience expectation," all the while watching the bemused (or amused?) smile on the medievalist's face grow more so.

I am sure we failed to convince the medievalist that the concept of genre in film criticism has attained anything like the sophistication with which medieval scholars imbue it. And we failed, I think, not because of his obstinacy or miscomprehension, but because of ours. After our conversation, I began to realize how very uncertain the idea of genre is, in both filmic and literary exegesis, and therefore with how great a degree of subtlety and perspicuity we need to approach it—whether we are dealing with *Piers Plowman* or *Pickup on South Street*.

It took, I think, a medievalist to remind me of the real difficulties of talking about genre. For medievalists deal with a literature and an idea of literature that is largely innocent of the prejudices about individuality and history which have so profoundly affected later literary criticism and almost all film criticism. What is especially surprising, though, is the way in which film, the premiere postromantic art form, tends to return, in its actual manifestation of individual and collective vantage points upon reality, to the assumptions of the medieval, rather than of the romantic, poets. This is not to say, of course, that film is simply a new popular art like the popular entertainments of the medieval period. But it is to insist that in our approach to film as an heir of the last two centuries of art and poetry, we must imagine it also as a reconstitution of poetic and generic ideas far predating those centuries—ideas which return us to the primal Western concerns of the individual work and its relation to history, of which the individual work is at once the constituent and the betrayal.

The idea of genre, as commonly used by film and literary critics, is of course an inheritance from the Renaissance, from the rediscovery of the logic of categories during the Enlightenment, and (perhaps preeminently) from the wedding, during the romantic era, of that logic with the myth of the poet as prophet, of art as individual negotiation between mind and universe, what Wordsworth calls

> all this mighty world
> Of eye and ear, both what we half create
> And what perceive.

It is, in other words, a notion involving a kind of adversary relationship between the creator and the genre in which he creates. A genre, or type, of writing, of storytelling, of presentation, is assumed to preexist the individual work in some sort of Platonic limbo of possibilities; and what we look for, in judging the particular work of art, is the way in which individual talent wrestles with tradition, the way the artist *uses*—i.e., rearranges and decomposes—the "rules" of the form he has selected. This is a distinctively romantic attitude toward genre; we know that the great romantic poets and novelists, from Blake to Flaubert and Joyce, never used a form which they did not also parody and invert. But it also pushes our idea of romanticism much farther back in time than conventional histories of literature suggest. When John Dryden faulted Shakespeare's *Antony and Cleopatra* for not observing the rules of tragic unity laid down by Aristotle, he was judging like a good neoclassical critic. Yet his judgment was romantic or modern to the extent that it, too, assumed that using a genre was a kind of test: can the poet or can he not fit his genius into the abstract, generic norms governing the work?

While Dryden and his age thought that this fitting was by and large a good thing, and while Shelley or Gide regarded it as, at best, a dubious achievement, nevertheless all are in fundamental agreement that the relationship between artist and form is one of contrariety, and that the artist's individuality (a prime value for Dryden no less than for Shelley) manifests itself only *in tension with* the genre within which he works. And this sense of genre and talent informs what is still the dominant and most productive form of film criticism, the auteur theory. To say that film represents the imposition of individual imagination—that of the director-auteur—upon the hackneyed and unpromising matter of his conventional subject is not only the extreme romanticism of film theory, but is also a kind of terminal, absolutist romanticism of literary aesthetics in general. But there are qualifications, if not refutations.

First, we might note the Promethean overtones in the word *auteur* itself. As recently (in the long view) as the early seventeenth century, Ben Jonson was ridiculed for publishing his collected poems under the title *Opera*—for claiming, that is, the status of a classical auteur. But romanticism, if nothing else, is the visionary lyricism of chutzpah. And film, a child of the romantic quest for a perfectly representational language, has spawned a theory of interpretation that exalts the individual personality of the creator beyond any comparable literary theory precisely because the individual touch, the signature of a sole creator, is so much less immediately apparent in film than in the novel or the lyric. In his important essay "La Politique des Auteurs," André Bazin put it this way: "The evolution of Western art towards greater personalisation should definitely be considered as a step forward, as a refinement of culture, but only as long as this individualisation remains only a final perfection and does not claim to *define* culture. At this point, we should remember that irrefutable commonplace we learnt at school: the individual transcends society, but society is also and above all *within* him." Bazin, the founder of the auteurist school, could be less disingenuous than his followers about his final beliefs. And in this crucial passage we see the profoundly nineteenth-century roots of the school: we might almost be reading this as the conclusion to an essay on Byron or Flaubert. The "personalisation" of the artwork has become, not only the point, but the genesis of the impulse to create. Bazin gives society, history, and genre their due, but only as settings for the consciousness of the auteur, to be subsumed and transcended in his performance.

Of course, the celebration of individual genius does not necessarily imply contempt for the idea of genre conventions. But there is a tendency—even in studies directly concerned with film genres— to regard them more or less as backdrops for the flaring-forth of individual creative genius. And though this treatment may be an inevitable feature of postromantic art criticism, it raises problems. These problems have also been raised, more seriously and with more deleterious effect, in the parallel development of literary criticism. Every year, thousands of fledgling Ph.D.'s in English are bullied into reading reams of minor Elizabethan tragedies or Victorian novels, precisely so that they can recognize the true glory of a Shakespeare or a Dickens who rose above and transformed the popular generic matter. I have always found this process confusing, and a little distasteful—not because those minor plays and novels are dull (they are not, really), but just because of the implicit assumption of the method and of its key word, "minor." The assumption is that they are and ought to be dull.

We might say that this sort of criticism of either literature or film is unable to *see* a genre except out of the corner of its eye, for the genre disappears or fades out in the neighborhood of the single artist's corrosive brilliance. Film critics, of course, have a harder time preserving this myopia than do their literary colleagues, since the art of the film—particularly the magnificent, scandalous art of the American film—is so drenched in the operation of generic, nonindividualistic norms of presentation. But when the auteur critic comes to the examination of a director who obeys rather than upsets the laws of his chosen genres, he usually runs for the semantic shelter of that most romantic of concepts, the "primitive." Whether we read Chateaubriand on the American Indian or Andrew Sarris on Samuel

Fuller or Sam Peckinpah, the use of the term "primitive" remains essentially the same: a way of saluting the individual genius of the creator at the expense of the conventions governing his art, even when those conventions and that genius are inseparable.

"Primitive" means "prehistoric." And there is a crucial relationship between the ideas of genius we have been discussing and theories of history—not simply those of the history of art, but those of the history of civilization itself. If, as Bazin, Sarris, and most departments of English believe, the history of an art is the history of its great figures in a spiral of ever-growing "personalisation," then the role of genre in art is like the role of society, tradition, or conservative economics in the established liberal view of cultural change: a shady, primarily negative background for the bloodlessly revolutionary acts of the enlightened. Bazin's colleagues at *Cahiers du Cinéma* probably did not recognize how acute they were in inventing the phrase "*politique des auteurs.*" As the later careers of *Cahiers* critics Godard, Chabrol, and even Truffaut were to make clear, the theory of the journal represented a particularly traditional (we might almost say a classically French, Voltairean) transformation of politics and history into style.

Surely, we can argue that Godard was never more political or more liberally and satirically profound than in his first film, *Breathless*, in which the depersonalizing conventions of the gangster film (Belmondo's famous, heartfelt "Bogey!") are systematically corroded and rearranged by the director's anarchic focus on the stereotypical nature of those conventions. Godard himself plays the anonymous bystander who tips off the police to fugitive Belmondo's whereabouts, bringing to birth the film's absurd and predestined catastrophe—a sure sign of *this* auteur's adversary relationship with the primitiveness of his genre. *Breathless* gives us, with remarkable purity, the myth of creative genius divorced from and in conflict with history, with genre. Belmondo's first words to the audience, after stealing a car, are *J'aime la France:* his immersion in the American thriller has turned him into a tourist in his own country, the first of those alienated *hommes revoltés* who will become Godard's most important contribution to the narrative traditions of the film.

But—"the narrative *traditions* of the film"! Is this not a refutation of the myth which generates *Breathless*, the myth of an unstructured, free art, utilizing established conventions only self-consciously and parodistically? I return to my medievalist friend's ironic smile. Most films are not *Breathless:* indeed, it is only because they are not that we can recognize a *Breathless* for what it is. The myth of genius in conflict with genre thus becomes a self-fulfilling prophecy. But there is another way we can imagine the relationship between the specific creation and the historic conditions of that creation. Who is the author of *The Canterbury Tales*? Chaucer or the age? Jacques Maritain, in his famous essay "Dante's Innocence and Luck," argues that the *Commedia* is the product not so much of its creator's genius as of the sublime *receptivity* of that genius to the total influence of an era. And, of course, we know a great deal more about Dante and Chaucer than we do about the authors of most of the great works of the Middle Ages. In the cases of *Piers Plowman*, the *Njalsaga*, or *Sir Gawain and the Green Knight* we not only know nothing about the personality of the creator, but more essentially, we cannot tell to what degree the excellence of the work is due to a putative individual creator, or to the accretion of influence, convention, and digressions from the hands of any number of anonymous contributors, redactors, and scribes. The analogy between such cumulative production and the art of medieval architecture is by now hackneyed beyond redemption, though not, I think, beyond repetition, especially if we can see the further analogy to the contemporary film studio.

Comparisons such as this have been drawn before. One of the best early essays on film aesthetics is "Style and Medium in the Motion Pictures," by the master scholar of medieval and Renaissance iconography, Erwin Panofsky. And writers like Parker Tyler, Dwight MacDonald, and Leslie Fiedler consistently (and perversely, in the view of many film theoreticians) "read" film as the unconscious projection of archetypes of the public mind. But this sort of psychic exegesis can scarcely be called a genre approach to film. The pursuit of hidden archetypes, however valuable, tends to reduce even the most formalized characteristics of an artistic convention to a dead level of Freudian or Jungian sameness. The same problem results from archetypal approaches in literary or dramatic criticism. Once you have identified the monomyth at the center of all human imagination, it becomes ridiculously difficult to discriminate between any two versions of it, even if the versions are as dissimilar as *As You Like It* and *Sergeant Pepper's Lonely Hearts Club Band*, or *The Trial* and *Straw Dogs*.

A more fruitful approach may be the recently popular "structuralist" analysis of film and literature. Indeed, if there is a point in considering film from a preromantic, medievalist sense of its conventions, structuralism is an attractive candidate for the methodology of that consideration. Itself a product of romantic ideas of language and consciousness, it has evolved into what amounts to a new scholasticism of the imagination. The structuralist attitude is nowhere better epitomized than by Claude Lévi-Strauss, in the "overture" to his study *The Raw and the Cooked:* "Mythological analysis has not, and cannot have, as its aim to show how men think. . . . I therefore claim to show, not how men think in myths, but how myths operate in men's minds without their being aware of the fact." If we substitute "genre" for "myth" in this passage, we get a fair idea of where the structuralist critique of literature and film tends. Just as language, the great human structure of structures, not only has a history but is its own history, so the forms of narrative art may be viewed as creating their own masterpieces—operating in men's minds—with a kind of trans- or super-personal determinism which exceeds factors like individual genius or creativity.

Undoubtedly, the structuralist approach I have outlined leads, in its extreme versions, to an obliteration of the idea of the individual work itself, which is just as wrongheaded as the overly romantic auteurism we are trying to escape. But as a corrective to previous trends and as a rich mine of new insights into the operation of myths, it is invaluable. Just as romanticism itself is best comprehended, not simply as the revolutionary myth of personality, but as a tension and contrast with older myths of depersonalization, against which it achieved its moments of maximum power; so our approach to film— particularly to the problem of genre in film—can be illuminated by a set of theoretical considerations whose very contradictoriness ensures that we will not be trapped, in our reading of a specific film, in a single dogmatic and distorting aesthetics.

In his history *Aesthetics and Art Theory*, Harold Osborne offers interesting, nonstructuralist corroboration for the idea of film creation we are trying to describe. Osborne remarks that the technologization of art, particularly architecture, in the last two centuries has produced a new kind of artist, for whom traditional aesthetics gives us no very good name: he is the designer, or planner, whose conception of the work is at once realized, transformed, and re-created by the technologists who bring it into being. Osborne's description of the artist as planner applies equally well to film. One remembers the clever review of Visconti's *Ludwig* by Pauline Kael, with its insight that filmmakers are the archetypal mad kings, manic Master Builders of our era. Insofar as he is planner or Master Builder, the filmmaker deals, for his raw materials, not so much in plot, character, or visual effects—the shibboleths of conventional criticism—as in the sheer possibilities that generic norms bestow upon art. He deals, that is, in many-times-told tales which are a result of the collaboration among the planner's own imagination, the expectations and imaginations of his audience, and the "thinking which takes place in man" represented by the generic structures themselves. Nowhere, perhaps, is this complex and difficult relationship between producer and audience, artist and mass subconscious better caught than in F. Scott Fitzgerald's unfinished novel, *The Last Tycoon*. There, the narrator muses about the career of the book's hero, Stahr, a driven and tragic filmmaker: "This [Hollywood] was where Stahr had come to earth after that extraordinary illuminating flight where he saw which way we were going, and how we looked doing it, and how much of it mattered. You could say that this was where an accidental wind blew him, but I don't think so. I would rather think that in a 'long shot' he saw a new way of measuring our jerky hopes and graceful rogueries and awkward sorrows, and that he came here from choice to be with us to the end." To see "which way we were going, and how we looked doing it, and how much of it mattered": if the interplay of convention and originality, cliché and archetype that is the narrative film can successfully do that, then it has achieved no more nor less political and artistic sophistication than the nineteenth-century French novel, or the eighteenth-century English satire.

The remainder of this chapter is an exercise in what used to be called "practical criticism," as a way of developing some of the arguments I have already advanced and of indicating how these arguments can facilitate our understanding of a given film. I shall deal with three films, each one representative of one of the most perennial and productive narrative genres: detective thriller, horror film, and Western. None of the films is by a director who can really be called great, although all three directors—Samuel Fuller, Jack Arnold, and Edward Dmytryk—have produced a large number of exceptionally fine films. And, perhaps most importantly, the three films—*Pickup on South Street, The Creature from the Black Lagoon*, and *Warlock*—date from that most inwardly turbulent and perhaps manic period of American political life, the Eisenhower-McCarthy fifties.

There is good reason for considering the decade of the fifties a most interesting one for American genre film. Hollywood began that decade under the double trauma of the Red Scare, which drove so many talented film artists out of the business for more than ten years, and television, whose growing grip on the nation's leisure time spelled the death of the successful B-movie—previously the richest and most problematically creative area of American filmmaking. The American film industry reeled under this one-two punch for most of the decade and also struggled with the disturbing presentiment that the great achievements of the thriller, the horror film, and the Western—such as *The Maltese Falcon, The Bride of Frankenstein* or *The Wolfman,* and *Stagecoach* or *Red River*—were irrecoverably in the past. It was not a sanguine time for filmmakers. But precisely because of this complex of internal and external obstacles, the film studios of the fifties managed to create films in the classic popular narrative genres that shed new light (perhaps the light of a dawning and reductive self-consciousness) on the psychological and political underpinnings of their basic myths. I am interested in examining how these films, each one a firmly established genre film, incorporate and comment upon, *through the conventions of the genre itself,* the psychic life of their times—"where we were going and how we looked going there."

Pickup on South Street and the Thriller

Nicholas Garnham's *Samuel Fuller* is a valuable and complete survey of Fuller's productions. But it is Andrew Sarris, in his indispensable and infuriating compendium *The American Cinema,* who articulates the dominant attitude toward the director. "Fuller," Sarris writes, "is an authentic American primitive whose works have to be seen to be understood. . . . It is time the cinema followed the other arts in honoring its primitives. Fuller belongs to the cinema, and not to literature and sociology."

Most of what is wrong with the auteur theory, and much of what is wrong with the growing Fuller cult, is embedded in Sarris's remarks. Taken one by one, in fact, they almost amount to a bad parody of the worst of academic literary criticism. Fuller's works have to be seen to be understood, we are told; and behind this statement we hear the echo of all those critics from Sarris to Gene Young-blood who piously insist upon the "autonomy" of the film experience as if it were somehow different from and more austere than the autonomy of any other artistic experience. What artistic creation, from that of Homer to Shelley's to Don Siegel's, does *not* need to be seen to be understood? But the semantic well poisoning becomes more serious. Fuller as an "American primitive" is at once easier to take and harder to take seriously than Fuller as the maker of a few brilliant movies and a few more awful ones. And Fuller as belonging to "the cinema, and not to literature and sociology" may be forgiven such absurdities as *The Naked Kiss* (1965) since he is, after all, "cinematic" and not "literary"—but is by the same token denied full credit for the complexity and subtlety of a masterpiece like *Pickup on South Street* (1953) since he is, after all, "cinematic" and not "literary."

What I wish to suggest is that Fuller is important, not as a cinematic Grant Wood or a kind of holy barbarian, but as the maker of two or three exceptionally fine and exceptionally rich films. And, further, I wish to suggest that Fuller's true value for film history is in itself an unanswerable refutation of the worst excesses of contemporary film aesthetics. For not only is he an uneven director, capable of major achievements and major disasters, but he is also a director whose productions, far from being the work of a single-minded, creatively obsessed primitive, are, at their best, the products not only of his own direction but also of the traditions and the world in which he finds himself enmeshed. If we can honestly say that Fuller belongs to cinema and not to literature or sociology, then we are working either with a terribly simple-minded concept of literary and sociological meaning, or with a terribly impoverished concept of the range of true cinema. "Trust the tale, not the teller," D. H. Lawrence said some years ago. Fuller, in his occasional genius, helps us look past the romantic fascism of "autonomous art" film theory to the perilous, and perilously maintained, truth of his tales.

Pickup on South Street may be Fuller's best film, not only for what it does, but for what it means in the history of the American thriller and, more largely, in the history of American popular mythology and political aesthetics. Made in the still-warm afterglow of Senator Joseph McCarthy's heyday, it incorporates on its surface all of Fuller's primitive, he-mannishly American fixations. Skip McCoy (Richard Widmark), a pickpocket just released from prison, robs a girl named Candy (Jean Peters) of her purse on the New York subway. Although Skip does not know it, Candy is carrying some microfilm vital to U.S. defense, which she is about to deliver to the head of a Communist spy ring. Candy herself does not know what she is carrying, but believes that she is simply engaged in industrial espionage for her boyfriend Joey (Richard Kiley)—unbeknownst to her, a Red agent. FBI agent MacGregor (Willis Bouchey), who has been trailing Candy, sees Skip make his pickup but cannot stop him before he leaves the subway. After this exposition—roughly the first five minutes of the film—the rest of the plot is almost preordained. The FBI, aided by police captain Dan Tiger (Murvyn Vye), tracks Skip down, tries to get him to give up the film, fails, and enlists Candy to help them. Candy, at first repulsed by Skip (he has a habit of hitting women he dislikes), gradually falls in love with him, acts as a double agent for the FBI to save Skip from himself—who is rather like a lovesick Herbert Philbrick—and is found out by Joey and shot. Skip, realizing that Candy really loves him, determines to work for her cause and the cause of America, tracks down Joey, beats him to a pulp in the subway, and helps the authorities clear up the spy ring. The movie ends with Candy and Skip leaving the police station together, about to start a new life, and Candy promising Captain Tiger that her man will never again stray from the narrow paths of honesty and good citizenship.

A crude parable at best: all the values simple, all the shots uncluttered, all the problems soluble in the simplest human terms. Except that *Pickup* is not just a fine Fuller film, but a fine film—and fine precisely because of the vast set of literary, sociological, and filmic traditions upon which it builds. Paradoxically, it is a film that could not have been made in any era less repressed or paranoid than the McCarthy years ("Are you now, or *have you ever been . . .*"), and yet a film that, like all major art, transcends and even negates the premises of its origin.

It is a thriller; more than that, it is a spy thriller, pitting the American underworld against the greater, more sinister underworld of old Europe, of Russia, of the intellectual invaders from Over There. And here we are forced to note what few historians have remarked: the supreme good fortune, for the preservation of our national xenophobia, that our first enemies in the Cold War were the Russians. Eastern Europeans are close enough to us to be truly hateful aliens, whereas true Orientals like the Chinese could never have generated such a full but intimately familiar panic. Dr. Mabuse is a necessary predecessor of Fu Manchu in our nightmares.

The grounds of Fuller's thriller, furthermore, are well established from propaganda films of the Second World War, the era which gave birth to the full-fledged thriller and the film noir. After Czechoslovakia and Pearl Harbor, the assumption was very early adopted and fostered that the comparatively innocent, openhearted vice of the capitalist crook would always win out over the more satanic criminality of the foreign invader. One remembers a movie like *All Through the Night* (1942), where Bogart as a middle-aged Bowery Boy defeats the German Fifth Column; a scene like the one in *Sherlock Holmes and the Voice of Terror* (1942) where Rathbone enlists the entire Soho underworld in support of King and Country against the Hun;

or, perhaps definitively, a line like the one in *Casablanca* (1942) where Bogart tells Conrad Veidt (Major Strasse) that there are certain sections of New York where even the Wehrmacht would be ill-advised to go.

It is all rather lighthearted, and a permanent resource of America's mythic foreign policy, as if the siege of Leningrad were to be endured by a nation of Huckleberry Finns. And Fuller, with a sure eye to the traditions of his art, adopts its assumption. But between the golden age of movie propaganda, 1942, and *Pickup on South Street* lies that other great product of wartime and postwar American filmmaking, the film noir. The two traditions, thriller and film noir, have been discussed enough by now that their differences need little elaboration here (if, in fact, the differences have not been in many ways overelaborated and exaggerated). Fuller's brilliant achievement in *Pickup* is to superimpose these two genres upon each other, thereby redefining the moral and filmic assumptions of each and transcending them to form a new genre, a new way of seeing the world, that has become more and more the most important political vision of American films in the sixties.

Structurally, the difference between the spy thriller circa 1942 and the film noir is a difference in modes of tribalization, ways of dividing the world. In the spy thriller, the opposition is between the world of the just and its assailers, the City of God and that of Mammon. It is a division that cuts across such boundaries as legal-illegal and heroic-cowardly (Holmes *and* the Soho thieves resist the Hun; Rick *and* Renault conspire in killing Major Strasse). Its vocabulary is primarily political and economic (nationalism and capitalism against fascism), and only secondarily, if at all, psychological or sexual. In the film noir, on the other hand, sexual and psychological concerns govern the playing-out of the action—to the degree, finally, that politics either becomes irrelevant or takes on oddly mutated dimensions. The central assumption of the film noir—that any man, no matter how honest, may become a criminal—in fact tribalizes the world in terms of innocence and experience, the unconsciously normal and the wisely but more sadly monstrous. The first scene of Lang's *Woman in the Window* (1945) epitomizes the ambiguities of the film noir. Professor Wanley (Edward G. Robinson) is lecturing to his psychology class with the name "Sigmund Freud" written on the blackboard behind him. Wanley's lecture is about the impingements of Freudian psychology on the ancient sanction of the Decalogue: he blithely explains that there are certain circumstances in which, psychologically speaking, the inhibition "Thou Shalt Not Kill" may be put in abeyance. And the story of *Woman in the Window*, of course, is to play out the manner in which the warfare of those two dispensations is to destroy Wanley. (Even the controversial dream-ending of the film bears out our point, for it makes little difference whether Wanley is shattered in the "real" world or only in the world of his unconscious; the shattering, the revelation of the inescapable beast under the skin, are equally complete in either case.)

In *Pickup*, as I have said, these two traditions of filmmaking cohabit and interfere with each other. Politics and sexuality, psychology and economics are jumbled together in a pattern of shifting allegiances that broadens the timbre of American films. First, the tradition of the film noir is inverted by the competitive pressure of the spy thriller. Instead of a parable of an honest man grown suddenly and inexplicably corrupt, we are confronted with the spectacle of a corrupt, petty criminal grown heroic—but heroic without sacrificing the basic instincts and behavior patterns of his criminality. Widmark's beautiful performance as Skip McCoy echoes and builds upon the psychotic iconography he had established in *Kiss of Death* (1947): as opposed to the benevolent gangsters of early spy thrillers, he is *really* a criminal, *really* a man on the razor-edge of civilization, living in an abandoned lean-to at the verge of the ocean. He slugs Jean Peters when he returns to his hut and finds her searching there. But he is also, if not entirely moral, generous and ethical. For much of the film we watch him investigating, à la Bogart's Philip Marlowe or Lloyd Nolan's Michael Kane, independently of and yet supportive of the police, the source and nature of the microfilm he has acquired. The identification of the criminal with the private investigator seems inevitable to us now, after such revelations as Welles's Hank Quinlan in *Touch of Evil* (1957) or Lee Marvin's Charlie in Don Siegel's *The Killers* (1964). But so far as I know, the explicit identification of the two roles had to wait for Fuller's film, the closest approximation being perhaps the symbiosis of Edmund O'Brien and James Cagney in *White Heat* (1949).

Indeed, the figure of Skip McCoy cuts across two well-established axes of character, that of capitalist-enemy and that of normal-corrupt. Skip lives and moves in both worlds at once—fortunately for America, since the whole mythology of the Red Menace in the McCarthy years was that the Communists also were not only the enemy Over There but also the Enemy Within, indistinguishable from the most pacific and ordinary of your neighbors. Skip is an entrepreneur, and his criminal business is, to him, no more nor less than a job, a job involving a high degree of initiative and private enterprise, in fact. And this characteristic of the underworld is also important for *Pickup on South Street*. Skip is first identified for the police by the old woman Mo (Thelma Ritter), herself a hustler, who sells Skip out for money to buy herself a burial plot. Mo is all but a mother to Skip in the film, and her betrayal of him is motivated only by the dispassionate requirements of business. "Skip's gotta eat, too," she remarks on discovering that he has returned to pickpocketing so soon after his release from prison. This remark, catching so well the resonance of life in a cash-and-carry culture, is brilliantly echoed by Skip when he learns from Candy that Mo has been his betrayer: "Oh well, Mo's gotta make a living, too."

This sort of easy cynicism might be identified with the acid vision of a self-sufficient underworld in Lang's *M* (1932) or with some of the musical dramas of Brecht and Weill. But Fuller's vision is less concentrated and more suggestive than the comic despair of Weimar Germany. If Skip is at once investigator, crook, hero, and businessman, the same confusion of roles obtains in the world he inhabits. One of the crucial discoveries of McCarthy-era paranoia was that capitalism and Communism were not only antagonistic but competitive systems. The threat of a worldwide Red plot that the senator announced to the nation was doubly frightening because it was so like the monolithic, incomprehensible image that large-scale industrial capitalism had become by the late forties. The era of terror at the beehive Red menace is also the era of those complementary myths of escape from and defeat by the American corporate machine, *The Wild One* and *The Man in the Grey Flannel Suit*. Our fear of the alien political machine, in other words, was in many ways a psychological projection of postwar fears of the economic machine, the Detroit which had beat the Germans but could provide only Levittowns for the families of the victors. Film noir and international thriller, in other words, were integrated not only in Fuller's vision, but also in the psychic life of the country itself.

Thus, in *Pickup* there is the curious detail about Candy's involvement in the original espionage. In terms of the surface-level, romantic plot, she is "innocent"—the hooker with a heart of gold who saves Widmark from himself. But her innocence consists in her believing that she is engaged in "mere" industrial spying for her boyfriend. Explaining the importance of the lost film, Joey tells Candy, "This is big business"; and he is both lying and telling the absolute truth. The worlds of the film mirror each other uncomfortably and even, from the vantage-point of HUAC as it was then constituted, subversively. The masters of the spy ring themselves, when Candy finally is ushered into their presence, sit around a plush hotel suite, their faces caught in oppressive but heraldically impressive closeup. They are not just spies, but a cartel, a board of directors, a corporate entity. (How appropriate for Fuller that "commune" and "corporation" can be regarded as having almost the same root meaning, the collapse of the many into the one, the triumph of Leviathan.) FBI agent MacGregor is a double for these impersonal, almost Olympian manipulators, especially since he is played by Willis Bouchey, whose uncanny resemblance to Eisenhower guaranteed him a series of important character roles all through the fifties.

In the midst of these impersonal and depersonalizing powers Skip McCoy is caught. And in his entrapment, we begin to recognize the distinctive genius of *Pickup*. McCoy's disease at the beginning of the movie is an isolation from personality itself. His final decision to help the FBI is not so much a conversion to patriotism as his private discovery of identity in a world that, capitalist *and* Communist, legal *and* criminal, has begun to militate all but overwhelmingly against such privacy. For the first twenty minutes or so of the film Widmark has no dialogue; we see him only as a silent, anonymous pickpocket in a subway crowd or as a mug shot, that photographic archetype of modern anonymity, identified by Mo in the police station. Fuller carefully establishes that, to the police, the FBI, and the Reds, McCoy is an object; and McCoy's cockiness with brutal Captain Tiger in their first interview is the cunning of a man used to being treated as a thing by the machine of the modern city. "Go on, hit me," he taunts Tiger after insulting him, using his own vulnerability as his only defense. In two important scenes—his first interview with Tiger and a later confrontation with Candy, both of them occurring at Skip's waterfront lean-to—Fuller places Widmark prone in the foreground with his interviewer towering over him. This visual suggestion of passivity is central to the film: Skip must be made to stand up, not for America, but for the preservation of his own selfhood.

Such self-preservation, in fact, is the real America which unmistakably emerges from the film. And far from being the conservatism of a film primitive, it is as subtle as the structure of Jeffersonian democracy or as adventurous as the revolutionism of Herbert Marcuse. For it is a fragmentation of the monolithic one *back* into the many, the reformation of society on a principle of pleasure rather than profit, sexual generosity rather than sexual repression. And at this point we come to the center of irony in *Pickup on South Street*, the implications of the title itself. The "pickup" is, of course, Skip's theft of Candy's purse. But the much stronger connotation of "pickup," i.e., casual sexual liaison, is underscored again and again. The theft scene itself is simply astonishing. As Skip stands before Candy on the subway, rifling her purse, she is staring up (looking at him? thinking of Joey?) with an unmistakable expression of sexual excitement on her face, her lips half-parted, her eyes half-closed. There is a classic association in Freudian dream-analysis between woman's purse and woman's vagina, of course; but this is exactly the association which Fuller does *not* wish to invoke. Rather, his film is a careful and subtle plot to convert the one meaning of "pickup" (economic) into the other (sexual) and then to fix the sexuality of the second meaning as a real salvation for both Skip and Candy. In the same terms we might apply to a brilliant novel or lyric poem, we may say that the movie is a process to make the prophecy of the first scene come true. After their first clinch, Candy leers at Skip and says, "When you drill for oil, sometimes you hit a gusher"—an extremely crude image of sex as economics, of intercourse as mechanism (almost literally as "screwing") that their developing attachment and love will not cancel but, rather, purge of its economic, acquisitive overtones, just as the title, "Pickup," will be purged.

Almost every major detail of the film contributes to this motif of sexual awakening. Midway through the film, Mo is killed by the spies after revealing Skip's whereabouts to Candy; the aging and death-oriented mother cedes to the young and life-bringing lover. In the same fashion, Candy remarks to Skip in their first serious clinch, "You've got your hand where it's not supposed to be"—an obvious and splendid inversion of Skip's purse-rifling in the first scene. But the point is sufficiently clear: whereas the film noir of the forties (especially *Double Indemnity, Woman in the Window,* and *Laura*) assumed that sexuality is the unacknowledged, repressed energy that can turn a law-abiding citizen into a criminal (a simplistic interpretation of the libido, if ever there was one), Fuller's film establishes the cinematic myth of liberating sexuality we have since come to associate with the films of Don Siegel and Sam Peckinpah. And while the spy-thriller of the pre-Yalta age conceived of criminality as a harmless bagatelle capable of being converted into patriotic energy, *Pickup on South Street* gives us an underworld way of life which is in fact the best preparation for and a mirror-image of the *Surrealpolitik* of clashing superpowers.

Jim Morrison, leader-singer of the rock group The Doors, raised eyebrows when in the late sixties he described himself as an "erotic politician." Actually, Morrison was describing himself in terms of a set of attitudes that had been long established by such thinkers as

Marx, Norman O. Brown, and Herbert Marcuse, and by such film-makers as Siegel, Luchino Visconti, Jean-Luc Godard—and, perhaps preeminently, Samuel Fuller. *Pickup on South Street* is the earliest and best example of erotic radicalism in the American cinema, a transformation of earlier modes of the thriller into an art that is the obvious progenitor of *Invasion of the Body Snatchers*, *Kiss Me, Deadly*, and even *Touch of Evil*—to say nothing of Siegel's 1964 *The Killers* or John Boorman's 1967 *Point Blank*.

The genius of *Pickup* is not the genius of an auteur shaping the world to the exigencies of his imagination. Rather, it is the genius of a brilliant director and cast whose historical circumstances provided them with a perfect situation against which to play out their various artistic strategies. In making a conventional anti-Communist thriller in the midst of the McCarthy era, Fuller was lucky and brilliant enough to forge a parable about liberation and love that abrogates the twin economics of Communism and capitalism both. The final politics of Fuller's film is the politics of the brain-cage, of the individual trapped and all but lost in an inhospitable system. And in the struggles of Fuller against his medium, and of Widmark against the plot in which he finds himself, we read the hieroglyphic of our own films and our own difficulties, the thriller whose central crime and central solution is not in the world at all, but in the scandalous and irrefutably political ground of human consciousness.

The Creature from the Black Lagoon and the Horror Film

As the popular film and popular culture generally become more and more a subject of serious academic interest, we are likely to be treated to more and more thoughtful excurses upon those works which many of us enjoyed years ago in the cool unthinking darkness of Saturday afternoon. Not that this multilevel coming to light is a bad thing: on the contrary, it is one of the best signs of the continuing health of our culture. And reading the criticism of a Leslie Fiedler or a Parker Tyler, or the "pop" fictions of a Thomas Pynchon (*The Crying of Lot 49*) or a Brock Brower (*The Late Great Creature*), is, for a generation trained to be abashed about enjoying films later than *Potemkin*, itself a kind of liberation. But there is a danger in the meeting of academicism and pop culture, one implicit in the term "pop" itself. The danger is simply that critics—and their readers and students—might too easily forget that pop culture is, after all, *culture*: that, on its own terms, it is no less serious, and potentially no less moving, than the culture which produced an Ovid or a George Herbert. Those Saturday afternoons—how could we deny it?—were wonderful. But we cannot and should not go back there; and a criticism which tries to, which turns a serious appreciation of these films into an excuse for returning there, is actually ducking the duties of the more complex and dangerous fun of which, at their best, they were a prophecy.

The film I wish to discuss is, in its way, a parable of this problem, a fable for pop critics. In histories of the horror film, Jack Arnold's 1954 *Creature from the Black Lagoon* is most often regarded as a late and degenerate variant of the Frankenstein motif, a fast-buck piece of sensationalism, a B-picture even by the standards of a B-picture genre. There is, certainly, something ludicrously adventitious about the existence of the "gill-man." He is not a monstrous threat to society nor to the world at large: the scientists have to *go* to the Lagoon to be terrorized by him, and unlike his oriental cousins Godzilla and Reptilicus, he is vulnerable to bullets and spear guns. The charge of silliness, moreover, may well apply to Arnold's sequels to the first film (*Revenge of the Creature*, 1955; *The Creature Walks among Us*, 1957), although those productions, too, are not without their delights for the horror afficionado.

The original *Creature*, though, is a far better and far more important film than has yet been recognized. Much more than such relatively celebrated efforts as Don Siegel's 1956 *Invasion of the Body Snatchers* or Howard Hawks and Christian Nyby's 1951 *The Thing*, it is definitively a film of the fifties. In terms of his popular success—an index of quality frowned upon, sometimes with good reason, by serious film critics—the Creature has established himself along with Dracula, Frankenstein's monster, and the Wolfman as one of the staples of the national crop of fear. I refer, of course, to the series of monster models produced in the mid-sixties, with great success, by Aurora Plastics, Inc. And I also invoke the fact that almost any moviegoer between twenty-five and thirty-five, while he may not recognize the provenance of the Man from Planet X, the Thing, or the phrase "seed-pod," will unquestionably know upon sight from what movie comes a photo of the gill-man. The Creature, against all odds of believability, official recognition, and even artistic quality, has *made* it. It behooves us to ask why.

The tradition of horror, as we are coming to realize, is one of the oldest and most continuous of cinematic genres. That this is so should not surprise anyone who has even a minimal acquaintance with the imaginative life of the West, since terrifying tales are among the most ancient and most persistent stories in our inheritance, perhaps, indeed, in the inheritance of the human subconscious. A psychic history of culture, in fact, could be written very efficiently from the morphology of its monsters, the history of those personifications of the void which successive generations have selected as their central nightmares. Roy Huss and T. J. Ross' anthology *Focus on the Horror Film* classifies varieties of horror into gothic (or supernatural), "monster horror" (mechnical men, zombies, etc.), and "psychological horror" (the terrors of dementia). It is a convincing catalogue for the history of film and, indeed, for the history of literature since the romantic era, developing from the satanic villains of the gothic tale, through the demonic puppets of Mary Shelley and Dickens, into the frozen mental landscapes of Kafka and Beckett. But these phases of horror are not stages in an evolutionary sense. According to the particular needs for fear of a given age, any one of the "later" phases of the monster may revert or collapse into a more primal incarnation of the unspeakable, though perhaps overlaid with the trappings of contemporary, "scientific" verisimilitude. Each era chooses the monster it deserves and projects; and all of them are, in their terribleness, blood brothers.

The Creature from the Black Lagoon is a significant case of this interpenetration of levels of horror. During the fifties, the most dominant form of the monster was the alien invader—the hyperrational saucerman, or the subrational insect mutant—whose threat was not so much personal violence as an insidious, fiendishly cold undermining of the normally (i.e., bourgeois American) human. I have already mentioned *Invasion of the Body Snatchers* and *The Thing*, both of which exploit the undermining of civilization by vegetable life. There are also such classics of apocalypticism as *The Day the Earth Stood Still* (1951) and *The Man from Planet X* (1951), in both of which the alien is originally well intentioned but stung to malevolence by human mistrust; *Them!* (1954), *Tarantula* (1956), and *The Beast from 20,000 Fathoms* (1953), in which the alien is a fearful result of nuclear alchemy; and *This Island Earth* (1955), *Earth Versus the Flying Saucers* (1956), and *Not of This Earth* (1957), true types of the evil-bug-eyed-invader movie.

For a long time now, sociologists and psychoanalysts of the film have been making clear the political paranoia underlying these movies —their deep connection with the McCarthyist fear of the subtle Red Menace, with the threat of a massive and nefarious Fifth Column infesting the entire fabric of American society, and, in the case of the gigantic reptilian or insect mutations, with the fear of the Bomb.

Raymond Durgnat's splendid essay on *This Island Earth* in *Films and Feelings* may conveniently stand as example and consummation of such readings.

But valuable as these interpretations are, they do not explain the peculiar power of the Creature; and their failure to do so makes one suspect that the Creature himself might lead us to a better insight into the life of the decade. He is, as I have said, neither alien invader nor atomic mutant: he is, as one of the scientists in the film observes, "an evolutionary dead end," a man-fish who has, simply and absurdly, survived the eons since his race was spawned. He survives, furthermore, because he is the Creature from the Black Lagoon—an out-of-the-way South American inlet where time has stood still. His very existence, in other words, is the reason for his peculiar horror. Unlike any other monster one can think of, he is the result of no cause, neither accident nor devilish science nor the supernatural: he simply *is*, primal and eldest, and the outrage he generates is the curse only of those unlucky enough to discover his existence. The story begins with the discovery, by an archaeologist, of a claw fossil belonging to one of the Creature's ancient race. The action of the film is the story of what happens to those who seek out and seek to capture the primal secrets which have been there all along in the innocence and blandness of their unharassed privacy.

In what, then, does the terror of the Creature's being there (almost exactly in the sense of Heideggerian *Dasein*) consist? To answer this is to analyze the tightly conceived plot of the film and to realize, first of all, that the Creature is almost as adventitious within the plot itself as he is in the larger tradition of horror monsters. For while most films in the genre involve some (usually sketchy) love interest between the young scientist—evil or benign— and the horror's intended female victim, in *The Creature from the Black Lagoon*, unusually and brilliantly, the love story all but displaces the horror element of the plot. This is for the very good reason, I shall suggest, that the love story is another version of the horror plot.

After the discovery of the initial fossil, a team of scientists take a small boat to the remote Black Lagoon, hoping to locate more fossils and establish a definite date for their find. The team, besides the mandatory old sage and a pipe-smoking, middle-aged establishment figure, consists of Mark (Richard Denning), David (Richard Carlson), and Kay (Julie Adams). Mark is a brilliant and ambitious young archaeologist with a string of important discoveries already behind him and anxious to consolidate his fame; David, his assistant, is a more reflective, sensitive and as yet unproved man; and Kay, Mark's colleague and girlfriend from childhood, is beginning to fall in love with David, much to Mark's chagrin. It is in terms of this triangle— Kay's instincts, Mark's possessive jealousy, and David's uncertainty and self-doubt—that the action will develop. And as the Creature gradually emerges into the center of that action, we see him—perhaps subconsciously, but inevitably and crucially—as a strange symbol and projection of the murderous sexual tension. For *The Creature from the Black Lagoon* is a demonic pastoral, and its titular monster is, if anything, an almost allegorical vision of sexual terror.

I do not mean to identify the Creature as that shibboleth of critical oversimplification, a "phallic symbol." He is much more than a sublimation: he is a realization of the psychic violence of the phallus itself. He is a *gill-man*, a man-fish, a dweller in the aboriginal bath of the world's youth, a rigid swimmer in the generative fluid. I have mentioned that he is one of the most recognizable and memorable of monsters. And surely part of the reason for this is that his makeup is exactly in tune with his deep-structure function in the plot: to put it simply, his now famous head looks like a penis. And his behavior in the film, an ambiguous meld of canniness and sheerly instinctual reaction, is not a symbol as much as it is a hieroglyph, an icon for the infinitely variable but single-minded urging of the libido.

As is usual for pastoral, the Creature's identifying locale is central to his meaning. The Black Lagoon, physically at least, is hardly black at all. Only a few of the film's scenes take place at night, and as both Kay and David note, the lagoon itself is lovely, with deceptively deep, still waters. The lagoon's blackness is not a matter of its depth, on the naturalistic level of the plot—but of the preconsciously "black," on the symbolic level of the film. For the *Black* Lagoon, in this sense, invokes inevitable associations of the cloacal, which, as we now know, has strong implications—particularly in the maturely infantile world of the pastoral—with the genital. The very word "lagoon," in the popular mythology of American art, has an inevitable tinge of the exotic and erotic about it via innumerable love songs and Dorothy Lamour: imagine the tonal difference in a Creature from the Black Lake, or the Black Estuary.

Two years after *The Creature*, Fred Wilcox's *Forbidden Planet* was to earn a justifiable but overblown reputation for its evocation, within a science-fiction context, of Shakespearian pastoral and "the monster from the Id," projected and finally abhorred by its physicist-Prospero. The great advantage of *The Creature* both as art and as sociopolitical history is that it represents a confrontation, not with a futuristic monster from the Id, but, in a timescape contemporary to the decade which spawned it, with the Id itself. If *Forbidden Planet* is, as many have insisted, Hollywood's *Tempest*, then *The Creature from the Black Lagoon* is its *As You Like It:* less perfect, even less profound, in a sense—but ultimately richer, truer to generic form, and more humanly inclusive.

To go to the Black Lagoon, then, is to return to the primal sink, the nursery site and origin of the species' sexual jealousy. The lagoon is a place, like all true pastoral places (Arcadia, Arden, Shangri-la), of clarification and terror. And in this respect, the casting of *The Creature* is a marvel of subtlety and wit. For throughout the first part of the film, we simply do not know with whom our sympathies are to lie. Granted that the Creature himself is phallus fascination and phallus fear, *whose* fascination and fear is he? Richard Denning and Richard Carlson, Mark and David, are two of the most perennial starring leads of all fifties B-movies and thus present the viewer with a serious uncertainty of identification. If Mark is sometimes overbearing, David is sometimes too feckless; they even look alike, a fact which complicates their sexual contest with overtones of sibling rivalry, older against younger brother. And Julie Adams, as Kay, may also—though less predictably—emerge as the dominant member of the trio. Ms. Adams was, simply, one of the sexiest leading ladies that Hollywood managed to produce in the fifties, a tantalizing combination of chippie and girl-next-door (the raped schoolteacher in *Blackboard Jungle*, the standoffish school nurse in *The Private War of Major Benson*), at once statuesque and approachable. As sexual motivation for both horror and psychodrama in *The Creature*, she is usually photographed—with great good sense—from below and in a one-piece bathing suit.

David (Carlson) emerges at the end of the film as our agent of identification but not without a good deal of vacillation in the story line. Even before that, though, the film establishes itself as what we might today call a "sexist" tale, that is, a tale about the warfare *for* Kay which never takes into account Kay's own emotions in the matter. Bound to Mark by nostalgia and loyalty, she is bound to David by the stronger tie of love. And, in fact, once she admits this tie, the central action of the film can begin. Her function is simply to love, and the problem of Mark and David is how to come to terms with the promise and threat to their masculinity caused by her decision.

After the characters enter the lagoon, their rivalry and mutual tension becomes increasingly explicit; that, after all, is what pastoral landscapes are there for. The culmination of the first (nonmonstrous) part of the film is surely the scene—almost absurdly obvious for a generation of Freudian cineastes—where David and Kay, pledging their love on the deck of the ship, are interrupted by Mark, who is preparing to dive for gill-man fossils armed with flippers, oxygen mask, and spear-gun. Mark makes a pointed demonstration of the spear-gun's power by firing it into the ship's mast and then gruffly commands David to prepare for their dive. He has become, visually and psychologically, a mirror-image of the archaic monster who will destroy him.

This scene is terribly important, since it establishes for us the nature of the sexual warfare between David and Mark. Possession of Kay is, in reality, only a strategic objective in that war, since the real issue is the nature of manhood itself. Who shall have, finally, the courage to appropriate to himself the energies and violences of the libido, to be, in other words, a *man* for the decade? Both David and Mark—siblings, twins, coscientists—are good, job-oriented, middle-class rationalists exploring the cloacal-genetic lagoon; and their contest is a *Kulturkampf*, a definition of what sort of manhood their culture will tolerate or sanction. Mark, as owner of the murderous, phallic spear-gun, as "older brother," begins with the upper hand; but this itself is a tip-off, since, at least in fiction, upper hands are always dealt to be called. So the tale of the monster will, among other things, chasten Mark's individualism and ambition, leading us to recognize in gentle, self-effacing David the awaited dragonmaster of the Eisenhower decade.

Immediately after the spear-gun scene comes the central and most famous passage in the movie, Kay's swimming excursion in the lagoon. As Kay swims at the surface of the water, the Creature, making his first extended appearance, swims only a few feet below her, his body exactly synchronized with hers, looking up at her. It is a wonderfully balletic sequence and one of the most striking allegories of sexual desire in the history of the art. For the Creature certainly *does* desire Kay, and all the more intensely since he is himself a highly abstract, nearly "disembodied" projection of that desire in David and Mark. He is, to repeat, that force which men face only in the simplified world of the lagoon, which civilization, indeed, refuses to let them face.

The great horror-film analogue for this situation, of course, is King Kong's lust for Fay Wray. But *King Kong* (1933) is a far more conventional, perhaps simpler exploitation of erotic panic. The giant gorilla, after all, is not a projection of the psyches of the film's two male leads, the slick showman-entrepreneur and the rough-edged but human sea captain. He is, as innumerable commentators have pointed out, a pathetic, all-but-human victim of that rage for beauty which is man's cross and crown in this tradition of mythology. *Kong,* then, is one of the uncounted retellings of the Beauty and the Beast story, which in film run from James Whale and Cocteau to Chabrol's brilliant *The Butcher. The Creature,* however, belongs to the older, sterner archetype of the dragon and the dragon-slayer. In that archaic contest we recognize the ultimate stakes to be the re-creation of the world through control of the antihuman, instinctual chaos which the dragon incarnates and which the hero must slay in himself before meeting his apocalyptic adversary.

As the film develops, the Creature manages to kill three of the crew and, escaping from momentary capture, to maim another. Mark, the assertive sexual and intellectual bully, insists on staying to capture or kill the monster—insists, in other words, upon being the simple hero which the archetype demands, on *mastering* the penis-fear of the Creature and thus establishing his right to Kay. David, however, is kinder. He realizes that the Creature is himself an innocent monster, provoked only by human intrusion, as he also realizes that his older-brother adversary, Mark, is the prey of emotions over which he has no control. After the last attack, supported by the remaining crew, David insists that the ship leave the lagoon for the safety of all. Nor can it be accidental that the last attack is the maiming of the middle-aged, establishment figure of the team (Whit Bissel), whose judicious yet still-productive place in the microcosmic society of the science ship needs now to be filled.

It is the first time in the film that David has usurped Mark's authority and is a decisive, though not a final, moment in his struggle for manhood. For psychosexually, *The Creature* is a much subtler movie than many recent "serious" films in the same area (to take one among many, Schlesinger's *Sunday, Bloody Sunday*). David's public assertion of control must be supported by a more difficult, privately won self-assurance. And the film, without ever suggesting the least dramatic agony in the character of David and with a tact almost like that of medieval allegory, brilliantly projects that struggle in its final movement.

A psychoanalyst might conjecture that the young David's early, forced assertion of dominance might well lead to a kind of sexual paralysis, an uneasy standoff between the adult and the adolescent within him. In terms of the movie itself—and in terms of a long tradition of Western allegory—it is not enough to escape from the phallic Creature and all he represents: he must be faced, and faced maturely. How appropriate, then, that as the ship, under David's command, begins to sail out of the lagoon, the crew finds that the exit channel has been blocked by the Creature. Exit and entrance channel, one should say, since it is an exit from the clarified world of erotic drives in the lagoon and an entrance to the real world of grownup life: a real *limen*, a threshhold, with all the associations Freud, Jung, and Jack Arnold are capable of giving that word.

Crossing the threshhold is the traditional duty of initiates and, in our culture, of bridegrooms about to take on the full rights of manhood. No less so for David. To cross this threshhold is at once to overcome the final terror of the Creature, to establish his professional and societal usurpation of Mark, and to win his intended bride, Kay. If the film as a whole has been, on one level, a parable of occlusions to sexual maturity, this last movement is its beautiful (both in physical and filmic terms) culmination and resolution.

In order to remove the blockade the Creature has placed across the channel, Mark and David once again go under water, but now with David directing operations. Once they are below, the Creature, predictably enough, attacks, grabbing Mark. And now David takes the spear-gun, already established as the emblem of Mark's self-confidence, to save his partner. The transfer of power made socially on the deck of the ship is now being ratified in the lagoon-world. And it is important to note that David seizes the spear-gun, as he had seized power, out of a kind of higher selflessness, a primarily corporate sexuality and psychic maturity.

But this, too, is not enough. There has to follow the climactic test upon David, his confrontation with the Creature himself. In the well-known sequence that follows, the wounded Creature summons the strength to take Kay from the ship through his secret underground passage into his own subterranean lair. David, of course, follows; and by now, in this film, we are not surprised to see the reemergence of such an archetypal motif as the night-journey through the labyrinth (cf. Theseus searching for the Minotaur, Aeneas in the Underworld, Leopold Bloom in Nighttown). To meet the Creature face-to-face is to meet, in a preternaturally violent atmosphere, the *full* terror of maturity; and it is thus a brilliant touch that the Creature wrests away from David his spear-gun, robbing him of any of the mechanical attributes of manhood in a terminal—sexually, an apocalyptic—crisis. But David is a corporate hero to the end. As he has sacrificed his own *rite de passage* to the good of society, so society intervenes to complete that rite for him. He stands his ground, facing the unspeakable gill-man. And in an ending that can only be called *civitas ex machina*, we find that the other crew members have followed him through the labyrinth, and shoot—though they do not kill—the Creature, driving him back to the lagoon so that they, David, and Kay may rejoin the daylight world to which all pastorals ultimately lead back.

A strange film, a strange blend of insight and inadvertence, of the archaic and the postindustrial. And, I suggest, a film which, like all major works of art, makes sense only by making sense of its age. *The Creature from the Black Lagoon* confronts, as frankly as fifties' reticence will allow and more subtly, perhaps, than the frankness of the sixties and seventies can manage, the tangled skein of sexual, social, and violent impulses out of which politics is made. It is a horror story whose true theme is the refusal of heroism, a story of battle against the monstrous almost without battle. And as such, it makes deeper sense of those other monster movies of the 1950s that I have mentioned. Far beyond the political, anti-Communist implications of the seed-pods in *Invasion of the Body Snatchers* or the withered, dessicated saucer-men of *Earth Versus the Flying Saucers*, we glimpse in *The Creature* the central evasion of energy, the central fear of the life-force itself which underlay the witch-hunts and HUAC purges. In his celebrated attack on Joseph McCarthy in *Generation of Vipers*, Philip Wylie identified the real power of the charismatic senator as an extension of the timidity and protracted adolescence of "Momism." *The Creature* helps to see beautifully, in every sense of the word, how right Wylie was.

In a film produced the year before *The Creature*—Samuel Fuller's 1953 *Pickup on South Street*—one can see the traditions of the thriller and the film noir undergoing a metamorphosis into the political shadings of the decade: the enemy has become The Enemy, the mysterious and incredibly resourceful Fifth Column, and the hero's battle against the crooks has become Richard Widmark's quest for the ability to love Jean Peters. Arnold's film gives us the same transformation, but from the other side of the spectrum. If the thriller was turning into sexually timid romance, the sexually timid romance of the horror film was turning into political thriller, in a more subtle way. David's wetsuit in *The Creature*, at least symbolically, is made of gray flannel. Like Hugh Marlowe in *Earth Versus the Flying Saucers*, Rex Reason in *This Island Earth*, James Whitmore in *Them!*, and John Foster Dulles in the Suez crisis or Eisenhower in Vietnam, David fights only when provoked by the eruptive terror of the insidious, the anarchic, the asocial. And his fight, although it may seem an entry into maturity, is in reality a struggle to *maintain* the innocence, the happy consciousness of a man who knows his place in the system and comfortably functions therein. The threshhold becomes a circle: the labyrinth, the maze of a standardized IQ test.

This is what I mean by insisting that the Creature, unlike other and earlier versions of horror, is almost not there. He is what threatens: but it is an abyss glimpsed only in three-quarter profile. It is not surprising that the horror film, after its late heyday in the mid-fifties should diverge along two lines of development quite different from anything that had gone before. The Roger Corman Poe-cycle, featuring Vincent Price, is almost a nonhorror genre; Price is usually cast, not in the role of villain, but of perturbed and deranged *victim* of forces too awful and too complex to be even visualized (*House of Usher*, 1960; *The Haunted Palace*, 1963). It is as if he were at once David and the fearsome Creature. The nostalgic revivals of Dracula and Frankenstein produced by Hammer films, on the other hand, represent a kind of vision of America from abroad that insists—like British rock of the sixties (the Beatles, the Who, the Rolling Stones)—upon rediscovering, in a continental context, the true roots of the American vision of the abyss. Their great popularity in the States, like the successes of the rock groups, are in fact a testimony to the persistence of those dangerous visions, even throughout the relative doldrums of the Eisenhower and Kennedy years.

Even later horror films, like *Rosemary's Baby* and *The Exorcist*, may be seen in a kind of paradigmatic relationship to the discoveries and ironies of *The Creature from the Black Lagoon*. For the sexual-mythic point of *The Creature* is that to possess Kay is also, necessarily, to face and overcome the demonic threat of the Monster. But in both *Rosemary's Baby* and *The Exorcist* (which I am tempted to call horror films of the Watergate era) the point of the horror is that the monster has already *achieved* sexual possession of the maiden whose winning is the quest of the film. It is as if both these later films bring that subtle water ballet between the Creature and Ms. Adams to its crude, predestined consummation. In the latter film, especially, a large part of the very real horror of the story is that the worst has already happened: the copulation of demon and innocent young girl is the unspeakable situation which the film exists to find a cure for. It is, in fact, a compilation of the most time-worn situations and shots of classic horror films from *The Mummy* on. But in *The Exorcist* each one of those shots retains its power because now we know—are *meant* to know—that the worst has already happened, that the maiden has been possessed, that the devil is in the driver's seat of this world and needs to be purged. How many other horror films, indeed, are named, not for their destructive monster, but for their distinctive monster slayer?

The Creature from the Black Lagoon, then, brilliant in its truth to its own form and era, is also a landmark in the psychic history of the horror film. Song of innocence it may well be, but in its final (unintentional?) implications it is not only an exploration but also a criticism of those monsters our younger selves found fit to tremble at. And in the sad, abandoned figure of the Creature himself we may read an equally powerful, maybe even more compelling version of that insight into the tragedy of the human denial contained in Robert Lowell's 1956 song of experience, "Skunk Hour":

> I stand on top
> of our back steps and breathe the rich air—
> a mother skunk with her column of kittens swills the
> garbage pail.
> She jabs her wedge-head in a cup
> of sour cream, drops her ostrich tail,
> and will not scare.

It is what Saturday afternoon was really *about*, and its darkness is central to whatever of light we may since have achieved.

Warlock and the Western

In its 25 May 1959 issue, *Time* carried the following review:

Warlock (20th Century-Fox) is a two-hour $2,000,000 western with three major stars (Richard Widmark, Henry Fonda, Anthony Quinn), two main villains, three main plots, five subplots, eight cooling corpses, and nine major outbreaks of violence. Hero No. 1 (Fonda), a sort of Good Bad Guy, is a notorious gunman who wears gold-handled Colts. The townspeople of Warlock ask him to protect them from Villain No. 1 (Tom Drake), a Bad Bad Guy with a slow sneer, a fast draw, and plenty of sneaking dry-gulchers on his payroll. Unfortunately, Hero No. 1 refuses to take the job without his sidekick, Villain No. 2 (Quinn), a G.B.G. who turns out to be a B.B.G.—the sort of lowdown skunk that makes his girlfriend keep him. So the scriptwriter rings in Hero No. 2 (Widmark), a G.B.G. who develops into a G.G.G. and goes after the bad guys like a blackbird picking ticks off a cow. In the end, with the villains all gone, the heroes have nothing left to do but answer the all-important questions: 1) Who is faster on the draw? 2) Who is slower on the drawl?

Newsweek (20 April 1959) had given the film an even briefer review, but one which ended on the capsule comment, more intelligent than anything in *Time*, "The Jamesian West—Henry, not Jesse."

In Jack Nachbar's "Seventy Years on the Trail: A Selected Chronology of the Western Movie," an exhaustive catalogue prepared for *The Journal of Popular Film*, the year 1959 is one of the briefest entries, tagged only as the year of Howard Hawks's *Rio Bravo*. Edward Dmytryk directed *Warlock*: also, among other films, *Murder, My Sweet* (1944), *The Caine Mutiny* (1954), *The Left Hand of God* (1955), *Raintree County* (1957), and *The Young Lions* (1958). There is, however, no mention of Dmytryk in Andrew Sarris's survey, *The American Cinema: Directors and Directions, 1929–1968*—a volume which *does* include filmographies and analytic paragraphs on such luminaries as Jack Smight, Paul Fejos, and Theodore J. Flicker.

I do not wish to belabor the point. But apparently, *Warlock* enjoys something less than a position of celebrity among Westerns, and its director, whatever triumphs he may have scored, has not risen to the critically acclaimed rank of auteur. It is not, of course, my concern here to discuss or attempt to resurrect the critical reputation of Edward Dmytryk, although, for reasons which I shall indicate, the reputation of the director exerts a curious influence on our viewing of *Warlock*. I am concerned, though, with examining the film itself; and that means, at least in part, examining the reasons why this remarkably subtle, powerful Western should have been relegated to a double anonymity, both among the mass audience which follows the tastes of *Time* and *Newsweek*, and among the cinematic-literary intellectuals who enjoy talking about the "vision" of *Red River* or *Rio Bravo* and make up critical histories of the Western movie.

Part of the problem, surely, is the sheer immensity of the genre, the Western movie. Of all the genres of the narrative film, none has been a more perennial staple of the Hollywood and international studios, and none has generated a more widely inclusive, more infinitely variable, or more rigorously established set of plot conventions. Since *The Great Train Robbery* (1903) established, at the same time, the potentialities of the narrative film and the basic situation of the Western romance in film, the Western has developed into the most complete mythology, the most totally self-contained and self-explanatory structure, that film has yet evolved. And in the spate of cowboy films released every year, year after year, it is perhaps not too surprising that even a film as good as *Warlock* should have been lost temporarily in the crowd.

THE PROBLEM OF FILM GENRE   147

On a more complicated level, too, the overwhelming conventionality of the Westerns might militate against adequate recognition of a particular film. The *Time* review is especially interesting in this respect. Aside from its flip vulgarity and—as we shall see—serious miscomprehension of the basic plot of *Warlock*, the review manages to pan the film by the clever techniques of assimilating it to the very conventions (or clichés) of which any Western film, insofar as it *is* a Western film, is made up. "Good good guys, bad bad guys," and the phoney sagebrushisms of "sneaking dry-gulchers" or "a blackbird picking ticks off a cow" (Do blackbirds pick ticks off cows? Would a *Time* reviewer know such things?)—the phrases themselves are an interesting, if unfair, critique of the film. For, they imply, this two-hour, expensive fiasco, for all the complexity of its plot, is "just another Western." It is revealing, I think, that such a semantic trick could not be played in a popular review of any sort of film besides a Western. As familiar as we have become with the assumptions and preordained climaxes of the love story, the detective thriller, the war epic, and the horror film, only the Western has entered deeply and blatantly enough into our common lexicon to establish its own, instantly recognizable shorthand.

Indeed, critics and theoreticians of the film have found the Western a rich field for the discovery of "genius"—precisely *because* of the assumed blandness of the generic background. Here again is the highly romantic assumption at the heart of the auteur theory that the creative genius of the filmmaker manifests itself at its strongest and most triumphant *against* the grain of the artwork, in contravention of the established rules of the genre, with a kind of Shelleyan rage and contempt for the limitations of the chosen form. Thus, directors like John Ford, Budd Boetticher, and Anthony Mann are celebrated Western auteurs (justly, of course), not so much for the great Westerns they make, but for what they do to (or with or about) the inherited certainties of the Western plot. Their innovations are Kafkaesque leopards breaking into the ritual and thus becoming the cynosure of the ritual.

But what of the genre itself? John Cawelti's fine book *The Six Gun Mystique* is one of the few studies to analyze seriously and perceptively the assumptions of the Western for their own sake, viewing them as an important and perhaps determinative contemporary mythology. And even Cawelti's book leaves certain basic questions unanswered. How could an auteurist critic, with his deeply embedded assumptions about the relative importance of genius and convention, deal with a Western film whose brilliance was exactly its manifestation of the conventional forms, its penetration to and restatement of the originating myth? I do not think he could. I think he would simply pass such a film by. As evidence, I submit the banishment of *Warlock* to the sad immortality of scattered groups of silent admirers and infrequent resurrections on late-night, local TV.

Warlock, that is, is a film whose power consists, paradoxically, in its unoriginality, in its quiet and flawless working-out of its own deepest archetypes. That such unoriginality ultimately becomes another, higher kind of originality is, of course, implicit in such a reading of the film. John Crowe Ransom, in an essay on Milton's great pastoral "Lycidas," explained the genius of Milton's poem, its astoundingly creative resuscitation of the moribund pastoral genre, by calling it "a poem almost anonymous." It is a useful phrase and a useful attitude to bear in mind when approaching a film like *Warlock*.

The plot, though complex, is not nearly so muddled or stupid as *Time* would have it. Warlock is a frontier town with a drunken, ineffectual sheriff; it is being terrorized by the rancher-gangster Abe McQuown (Tom Drake). McQuown's gang includes the Gannon brothers: Billy (Frank Gorshin), a hotheaded young gunman, and Johnny (Richard Widmark), a feckless hanger-on who is simply tolerated for Billy's sake. After McQuown's gang publicly humiliates and banishes the sheriff, the townspeople decide to hire a "town marshal" (that is, an unofficial, popularly appointed lawman) to save them from chaos. There is strong resistance to this by the one official left in Warlock, Judge Holloway (Wallace Ford), a bitter, cynical old cripple. But the businessmen, concerned for the safety of their property, hire Clay Blaisdell (Henry Fonda), a legendary fast gun. Blaisdell arrives in town accompanied by his longtime friend and fellow gunfighter Tom Morgan (Anthony Quinn). Morgan, who is a fanatic admirer of Blaisdell and of his reputation as a gunfighter, purchases a saloon and sets up a profitable business while he and Blaisdell clean up Warlock.

Meanwhile, Johnny Gannon has become progressively disenchanted with the McQuown gang and finally disassociates himself from them, although the citizens of Warlock only barely tolerate him in town. Lily Dollar (Dorothy Malone), a lady of notoriously loose virtue, former mistress of both Blaisdell and Morgan, has arrived in town—much to Morgan's displeasure—and Johnny becomes interested in her. Morgan, it grows more and more obvious, has a homosexual fixation upon Blaisdell: Morgan is lame and ugly, a barroom brawler whose subtlest technique is to get the drop on his adversary with a sawed-off shotgun, while Blaisdell, resplendent in his black suit and gold pistols, is a living symbol not only of our own most cherished myth of the gunfighter but of the beauty Morgan does not possess. Blaisdell, unaware of or unwilling to admit the nature of Morgan's friendship, is tired of the town-to-town, evanescent life of a six-gun shaman; he contemplates throwing it all over and marrying a local "nice girl," Jessie Marlowe (Dolores Michaels). Morgan, of course, is outraged both at the involvement of his friend with normal, stable heterosexuality, and at his possible descent from a heroic to a quotidian lifestyle.

As my synopsis indicates, the gunfighting elements of *Warlock* are transformed, about midway in the film, into a very different, much more psychological kind of battle: *Newsweek*'s squib about the "Jamesian West" is, in fact, altogether appropriate. But this is not to say that *Warlock* is an "anti-Western," a "novelistic Western," or that long and justifiably dead oxymoron of post-*High Noon* press-agentry, an "adult Western." For the crippling mental problems of the characters—Gannon's disgust with the outlaw life, Blaisdell's ennui with the role of peacemaker, Morgan's pathetic confusion about his own sexual identity and his attitude toward the West—arise out of the basic matter of the Western movie plot; they are, as I have already suggested, particularly intelligent and faithful penetrations to the visionary conflicts implicit in the Western situation. The power of *Warlock*, to reiterate, is its innocence; but that innocence is carefully and cannily *constructed*, and consists, at least on this level, in projecting onto the characters in the Western movie the dubieties and ambiguities of identification which are normally implicit in the movie audience.

If it is out of the typical action plot that such ambiguities are evolved, it is back to such an action plot that *Warlock* returns for its resolution. Blaisdell and Morgan—as Blaisdell has already wearily predicted—become almost as much an annoyance to the good citizens of Warlock as had been the now-chastened McQuown gang. The citizens, led by Judge Holloway, ask for someone to volunteer to be sworn in as sheriff. Johnny Gannon volunteers and, amid laughter and derision, is sworn in. He then visits the remaining members of the McQuown gang to try and talk them out of their proposed warfare on the town and is terribly beaten by them and stabbed in his gun hand. Returning bloodied and humiliated to town, he prepares for what promises to be a suicidal confrontation with the gang on the morrow. But the next day, miraculously, with bandaged hand and no help from the citizens of Warlock, he defeats the McQuown gang and establishes himself as the law.

Morgan, meanwhile, has been driven mad by Blaisdell's uncon-
cern over the decline of his (Blaisdell's) image and by Blaisdell's
benevolence toward the usurper Gannon. Morgan gets drunk that
night and, in tearful recriminations and taunting, forces Blaisdell to
draw on him and kill him. And while the simple-minded may view
this part of the action as a cliché about the sadomasochistic character
of all homosexual love, it is nevertheless a compelling scene: Morgan's
lover and hero has "died" into normalcy and history, and Morgan has
nothing left to do but sacrifice himself at the pyre of his lost image
of glory. The pyre, in fact, becomes literally realized: Blaisdell,
shocked at having finally learned the truth about Morgan (and about
himself), herds the good citizens of Warlock into Morgan's bar,
humiliates and brutalizes Judge Holloway (who has been voicing
smug satisfaction at the murder), and sets fire to bar, hotel, and
corpse in a primitive funeral service for which the adjective "Homeric" is not inappropriate.

The final crisis of the film has then been established. For Blaisdell, deprived of Morgan and confronted with a legal peacemaker, has
no more function in the world of Warlock. Gannon tells Blaisdell that
he must leave town the next day, and Blaisdell, still hoping to settle
down with Jessie, threatens to kill Gannon. But over a night's reflection, Blaisdell decides that there really is no future for him in this or
any town. Gannon, of course, does not know this and is certain that
Blaisdell will gun him down. In what he presumes to be his last
night, he becomes the lover of the cynical, generous Lily Dollar. The
next day, in a confrontation which is actually the confrontation between two eras of mythic time, Blaisdell meets Gannon, outdraws
him twice, with both gold pistols, but refuses to fire. After giving
his guns a last, flamboyant flourish, he throws them in the dust and
rides out of town, leaving Warlock in the care of its new sheriff and
his new lady, and leaving his own chances for a normal life forever—
and, one must add, tragically—behind him.

The screenplay, by Robert Alan Aurthur, may well be one of the
most literate ever filmed in Hollywood—except that the adjective
"literate" has come to be faint praise indeed among some circles of
cineastes. It is better, and more accurate, to call it one of the most
filmic screenplays of the fifties. For while the Western, as a genre, has
developed so many possible motifs that it would be impossible (or
deliberately ludicrous, as in Cat Ballou or Mel Brooks's Blazing Sad-
dles) to include most of them in a single film, Warlock does manage
to include and raise to a high level of consciousness one of the central
—perhaps the central—mythic possibilities of the form. Warlock is

a town, and *Warlock* is one of the surprisingly few Western movies named for the place in which the action occurs. But the film helps us see that the paradigmatic action—to found a city—is in fact the real concern of many of the most important films in the Western genre, that, indeed, the epic theme and the epic risk are more appropriate to the Western than perhaps to any other narrative film genre.

"Strangers and pilgrims fare we here, declaring we seek a city": the lovely image from the Protestant hymnal would be out of place in a detective thriller or a horror film, but perfectly appropriate as a theme for most of the great Westerns. *The Virginian, The Westerner, Stagecoach, The Ox-Bow Incident, Red River, High Noon,* and many others all involve, at a very deep level, energies which other narrative genres touch only allusively. The thriller, for example, deals primarily in a bifurcation, a tribalization of the urban world (into crooks and detectives, guilty and innocent). Such compartmentalization can reveal the complexities and ambiguities of political identity within the city, but fundamentally has little to say about the originating impulses which make the city. The horror film—always some version or another of that most primal of human myths, the hero and the dragon—is indeed a myth of civilizing origins (the conquest of the dragon is the archetypal creation of human order out of alien chaos). But it is probably too *large* a mythos for the theme of city-founding, just as myth itself has to become diminished, civilized, before it can produce the reduced—and hence more interesting, more complex— matter of epic.

In scene 10 of *The Great Train Robbery*, the railroad clerk who had been bound and gagged by the train robbers bursts into a country square dance, announces the robbery, and helps form a posse to track down the desperadoes. The scene is usually heralded by film historians as the "first use of simultaneous time in narrative film," since the action of scene 10 is parallel to the previous action, the escape of the robbers. But if it is the first suspension of time in film, it is also the first scene in which the Western community, in its peculiarly vulnerable and exemplary relationship to violence, is established. The technical detail of narrative time, in other words, is significant because of the narrative point it makes. The train robbery has literally suspended the normal time of an organized polity—as all violence or crime is antihistorical, a violation of the ordered ritual of civilized time—and therefore must be cured by the posse (from *posse comitatus,* "the body of men that a peace officer or a county is empowered to call to assist him in preserving the peace," i.e., in restoring history to its normal course).

That most of the major (and all of the minor) Westerns are about establishing or reestablishing a polity, a group of civilized individuals living on the edge of the nonhuman Other, is one way of saying that the Western may well be the most naturally filmic of genres. In the previous chapter we observed that one formal distinction between filmic and novelistic narrative may be that while the novel has a strong tendency to realize individualities, and only secondarily imply the mass out of which individuals arise, film seems to have the opposite and complementary tendency. This tendency is most congenial to the hidden theme of the Western—the description of the origin of the city, of a civilized mass of human beings, with individualities defined only in a secondary relationship to that fundamental idea of the human crowd. And indeed, the Western hero, whether marshal, cowboy, or good-bad outlaw, has always had this curious kind of identity in film: he is a mythic personage, terribly distinct from others in his world, both through his behavior and through the wonderfully elaborate paraphernalia of hats, outfits, sixguns, and spurs which attach to him. But he is distinct as a player of roles rather than as a real, private self; he is distinct, in other words, only in the way in which primitive shaman or priest are distinct from the community—*distinguished* for the very service they perform.

This, indeed, is probably the main reason for a very curious fact: that, of all the popular genres film and literary of narrative, the Western has risen to true greatness only in film. There is no Dashiell Hammett, Raymond Chandler, Robert Heinlein, or Arthur C. Clarke of the Western novel (even the legendary Max Brand is an unredeemed hack writer with scattered poetic yearnings); and there could not be, because film, the direct incarnation of romantic aesthetics, is so much more attuned, technologically and phenomenologically, to the central myth of the Western tale. To find a great Western novelist, in fact, we must go back *to* the romantic era, to perhaps the only true romantic novelist America has produced. I am referring, of course, to James Fenimore Cooper and his creation Natty Bumppo, the first American cowboy (there were European versions in the eighteenth century).

Cooper, of course, thought he was creating a national American epic theme—and he was right. Cooper was an ardent aristocrat (enemy of the radical Articles of Confederation and friend to the conservative, bourgeois Constitution which replaced them); and his Leatherstocking Tales, particularly *The Prairie*, use the rugged individualistic figure of Natty Bumppo as a patriarch whose proper and melancholy role is to protect the innocent and the young exiled into the forest, precisely so that those innocent and young may establish an organized decent society which, in turn, holds no place for Natty. It is no accident that, as he dies at the end of *The Prairie*, Natty's last words to the rising sun are "Here I am!"—the *Hineni* with which Abraham, another wandering patriarch and father of lawgivers, responds to God's summons in Genesis.

Much nonsense has been written and taught about rugged individualism as the burden of Western allegories and as the distinguishing characteristic of the Western hero. But the individualism is there only as a means to the much more important end of established collectivity, of the construction of a city in the wilderness which can at once deal efficiently with the wilderness (both without and within the human personality) and yet function as the beachhead of civilization, preserving intact the values that have sustained us from cave to city. Michael Marsden, in an interesting article entitled "Savior in the Saddle: The Sagebrush Testament" (*Illinois Quarterly*, December 1973), suggests that the cowboy hero, isolated and yet serving through his isolation the good of the community, is the most legitimate American type of Christ: "The Western Savior needs the confrontation with civilization (formal religion) to tame him, but he can easily arrive at heroic stature because of his essential goodness." While the association with Christ is overstated, it helps substantiate the association I wish to insist on, that of pontifex, mediator for civilization against the universe.

But as anthropology and Western films have been telling us for almost a century now, there are two kinds of pontifices, two varieties of mediators, involved in the origin of civilization; and the transition from one to the other is perhaps one of the crucial events in the history of civilized man. Shaman and priest are their most useful names and, as described in Joseph Campbell's *The Masks of God* or in the epochal works of Mircea Eliade, their most suggestive differentiation for our purposes.

Scenario: if we wish to imagine the primal horde gathered at the verge of their assembly into a structured unit, a civilization, then the first person to organize them into a religious and law-abiding group will have been the mysterious figure of the shaman. The shaman (witch doctor, medicine man, crazed prophet or old man of the mountain) is the mediator, the voice of the divine, for the seminomadic society of man as hunter. Radically individualistic, erratic, even (as Géza Róheim suggests in *The Origin and Function of Culture*) schizophrenic, he represents the religious impulse, the impulse to law and social morality, in its most problematic state. For he has no church, no doctrine, no codified set of precepts: his messages from the divine are delivered through his own ecstatic voice, and are as ad hoc, as wandering as the life of the hunter group to whom he ministers.

With the organization of hunter groups into stable agrarian societies, however, and with the consequent formation of settled towns rather than portable, nonce villages, the shaman is displaced by his less dramatic, less energetic, but more predictable cousin, the priest. The priest—true pontifex, builder but not crosser of bridges to the Moral Imperative—is no longer the erratic voice of a divine order assumed to lie beyond human attempts at understanding or codification. Rather, he is the representative of an established, divinely revealed form of worship and uprightness—the Law as constitution of society rather than the law as initial, socializing impulse. Unlike the Prophets, he is not gifted with and cursed by a special predisposition to violent possessions, but instead, is the herald of the people, calling them to a recognition of their already-ordained duties and responsibilities: he is, in other words, *one of them* singled out for service. If the shaman's peculiar talent is for possession, magic, and ecstasy, the priest's is for self-possession, social cohesiveness, and the rectitude of liturgy (*leitourgia*, "public service, public duty, the commonweal").

The distinction between shamanic and priestly functions is a richly suggestive one and one which retains a perennial tension in the history of culture: Moses and Aaron, Peter and Paul, or (more to the point of *Warlock*) McCarthy and Eisenhower. It is also a tension which has produced the two basic and most permanently interesting varieties of "mediatorship" in the Western film, what we may loosely call the *Stagecoach* and *Westerner* varieties, after the two films of 1939 and 1940 which establish their norms with such authority.

The society in *Stagecoach* is the explicitly nomadic one of the travelers in the coach to Lordsburg. These travelers are a microcosm of interpersonal tensions (the "normal" family, the bad woman, the drunken doctor, the suave crook, the hearty sidekick) threatened both by the invading savagery of the Indians and by the brooding, magnificently alien landscape of Monument Valley. The Ringo Kid (John Wayne) saves the group and holds it together against danger from within and without because, like a good shaman, he is a kind of holy outlaw, erratic and a law unto himself.

In *The Westerner*, on the other hand, the nomadic tribe has already settled into a town, the town of Langtry, under the ambiguous dispensation of Judge Roy Bean (Walter Brennan), a kind of primitive shaman gone to seed. The hero of the film, Cole Hardin (Gary Cooper), drifts into Langtry and ultimately civilizes it, turns it into a true city by establishing a code of normal rationality and justice against the erratic lynch-rule of Bean. Unlike the "magically" named Ringo Kid, Cole Hardin is an emissary of normalcy, a priest of the everyday whose very calmness and reluctance to "draw" are his most salient characteristics. (This was, in fact, to be Cooper's permanent contribution to the Western, as against Wayne's shamanism.)

Both kinds of plots have had a long and rich life, extending even to relatively recent films. As examples of the shaman plot, we have exploration of the West films like *Northwest Passage*, most cattle-drive films (particularly, of course, *Red River*, with Wayne now the jealous old shaman protecting his regime against his "son" and rival, Montgomery Clift), Anthony Mann's *The Naked Spur*, and John Sturges's vastly underrated *The Law and Jake Wade*. In all of these, the basic situation is the pilgrimage of a minisociety through hostile territory, under the tutelage of an ambivalent (buckskin-Byronic?) hero-villain. (We might include, as a mythic spinoff from this Western plot, all the films depicting disaster in planes, ships, buses, trains, or other enclosed, moving spaces, the prime example being *The High and the Mighty*, starring—inevitably—John Wayne as the airline pilot.) The priestly, town-centered film is perhaps an even richer tradition: these include *The Ox-Bow Incident*, *Destry Rides Again* (Jimmy Stewart being an even more successful incarnation of the normal than Cooper), *My Darling Clementine*, *Gunfight at the O.K. Corral*, and of course *High Noon*.

But in *Warlock*, if not for the first time, at least more explicitly and in more complicated fashion than ever before, these two traditions are deliberately intertwined; and that, if nothing else, should establish the great importance of the film for all that has happened since 1959 in the so-called contemporary Western film. The name "Warlock" itself is of course not simply the name of the town, but an ancient name for a sorcerer; and Robert Alan Aurthur surely means us to form vague magical and mythical associations about the film from the opening titles. Warlock is a town that has slipped back from civilization into the primal anarchy. The sheriff, representative of civic religion, is humiliated in the first sequence and driven out; and all that remains are the outlaws, incarnations of chaos, and the bitter old judge, the lame, ruined deity whose dispensation is past. The town, then, must re-evolve up the scale of political mythography. And it begins that process, naturally, with the shamanic Blaisdell. His name, too, is significant: "Clay Blaisdell" is the only predictable, stereotyped cowboy name in a film otherwise populated by McQuowns, Gannons, Marlowes, and Holloways. Clay Blaisdell is a legend, in other words; and his special uniform (reminiscent of Fonda's Wyatt Earp role in *Clementine*) and fetishistic, totemic golden pistols reinforce that legendary role.

But from the vantage point of civilization, the shaman's order is not enough, or too much: it is disruptive, murderously indiscriminate. Blaisdell's double in *Warlock* is the lame, brutal, repressed homosexual Morgan. But if Morgan is, in one sense, the dark side of Blaisdell's own personality, he is also, in a more important sense, the living *effect* of Blaisdell's dispensation upon the lesser normal members of society. Morgan, after all, is Blaisdell's biggest fan (and the associations of that word with movie-oriented daydreaming are deliberate); his lameness reminds us of Judge Holloway's lameness, for both men are ordinary citizens whose psychic health has been shattered by the eruption either of chaos (in the case of Holloway) or of an intolerably unapproachable, vatic energy (in the case of Morgan).

It is a subtle and accurate insight of the screenplay that Blaisdell's own primal civilizing action—his reconversion of Warlock back from a violent mob into an organized community—is also the very act that necessitates his exile and replacement by the new priest-sheriff. Johnny Gannon has previously been a member of the outlaw gang, and acquires his new vocation as agent of normal law and normal order only after his almost ritual wounding in the hand on his nighttime visit to McQuown's headquarters. And here, too, the casting of the film is brilliant. For if Fonda, in his sheer presence, conjures up images of the gunfighter from the classic Westerns of the forties, Widmark's John Gannon is a perfect and beautiful extension of his previous roles as primarily urban, nervous, flawed good-bad men (as in *Pickup on South Street*). His delineation is not neurotic, but just tense enough to indicate to us that in moving from the reign of Blaisdell to that of Sheriff Gannon, we are moving from the world of legend to that of our own time, to our own quotidian history.

If *Warlock* works as such a profound revision and restatement of the fundamental myths of the Western film, though, it also works subtly as the cancellation, or at least the transcendence, of those myths. For it is a peculiarly modern discovery that once you understand a myth, it has ceased to be—at least for you—a myth at all. *Warlock* transforms the energies that had been mostly latent in earlier Westerns into the very structure of its tale; and in doing so, the film actually initiates the tradition of the contemporary, or abstract, Western, which has given us films like Sergio Leone's *Once upon a Time in the West*, Brando's *One-Eyed Jacks*, Robert Altman's *McCabe and Mrs. Miller*, George Roy Hill's *Butch Cassidy and the*

Sundance Kid, and even Michael Crichton's *Westworld.* What these very disparate films have in common—and what makes them perhaps the most interesting Westerns of the sixties and seventies—is their concentration, in one way or another, upon the Western film as mythology, as a rich vision of the sources of the contemporary psyche, and their various attempts to articulate and influence the health of that psyche by manipulating the mythic vision of the Western. It may or may not be a matter of specific, perceived influence; as I have said, Warlock has enjoyed a strange anonymity since its initial release. But whether we concern ourselves with the operatic, baroque textures and rhythms of Leone, the semiparodic obsession with social evolution and urban cosmogony of Altman, or Brando's fascination with the West as a schematic model of power politics, we are confronting films that are distinct heirs and extensions of *Warlock.*

It is interesting to speculate what should have brought about a film such as *Warlock.* In part, of course, artistic forms evolve under their own impetus, and it was inevitable that sooner or later the Western film should have achieved the self-consciousness explicit in Aurthur's script. But another circumstance—the troubled political life of America in the fifties—seems to have exerted a peculiar pressure on the film, as, indeed, it has continued to exert a peculiar pressure on our own social consciousness, whether in or out of films. In my discussion of the film, I have concentrated on the brilliance of the screenplay and of the acting, rather than upon the direction. Even *Warlock's* most ardent admirers would admit, I think, that the direction is, at most, adequate. Edward Dmytryk's career as a director has been largely characterized by a workmanlike, sometimes plodding efficiency which, at its best, can allow fine screenplays and fine performances to pass uninhibited by directorial interference onto the screen. This is not to dispraise Dmytryk: if one way of thinking about the director of a film is as auteur, by analogy with the creator of a literary work, Dmytryk reminds us that another, equally valid and important analogy is to think of the director as publisher, that is, as a craftsman of taste rather than of creativity, whose crucial talent is to recognize and package attractively original works of value.

But the gift of taste can itself be creative, in particularly subtle ways. And Dmytryk's selection of and obvious recognition of the structure of *Warlock* resonates interestingly with his own career, with the history of Westerns in the fifties, and with the political neuroses of America in that decade. I have already identified John Wayne as the archetypal individualistic and potentially murderous shaman of the Western mythology; and of course, to American conservatives, Wayne has for some time now represented the incarnation of those good, old frontier values which, it is felt, radicals and the welfare state are in process of subverting. Here is Wayne speaking to *Playboy* (May 1971) about Hollywood in the early forties, the years which would eventuate in the salad days of HUAC and Senator Joseph Mc-Carthy:

> The State Department . . . sent the poor bastard [an Army Colonel, a loyal American] out to be the technical director on my picture *Back to Bataan*, which was being made by Eddie Dmytryk. I knew that he and a whole group of actors in the picture were pro-Reds, and when I wasn't there, these pro-Reds went to work on the colonel. He was a Catholic, so they kidded him about his religion: they even sang the *Internationale* at lunchtime. . . . So I went to Dmytryk and said, "Hey, are you a Commie?" He said, "No, I'm not a Commie. My father was a Russian. I was born in Canada. But if the masses of the American people want communism, I think it'd be good for our country." When he used the word "masses," he exposed himself. That word is not a part of Western terminology. So I knew he was a Commie. Well, it later came out.

What "later came out," of course, was Dmytryk's harassment by the House Un-American Activities Committee and the near-wreckage of his career in the same era which actually did destroy so many promising filmmakers and performers. And Wayne's recounting of the incident is a nearly perfect example of the kind of institutionalized paranoia (if not something worse) that gripped much of the country in those terrible days: a man's use of the word "masses" was grounds for character assassination of the most nearly literal sort. Dmytryk did survive (though not without some damage to his self-respect), and his film of 1954, *The Caine Mutiny*, is a fascinating if bitter parable about the ambiguities of vested power and the dubious limits of obedience to insane authority (Was it wrong to have relieved the madman Queeg? Would it have been right to face up to the madman McCarthy?). The fact that Dmytryk, after his initial investigation by HUAC, later recanted and became the only friendly witness to the committee from the celebrated Hollywood Ten adds a poignant if somewhat tarnished allure to his political allegories like *The Caine Mutiny* and *Warlock*. For if such films, among all the films of the decade, seem in retrospect to be the most replete with the real ambiguities of political life, the real terrors and self-betrayals attendant upon being a truly political man, we may say that Dmytryk, more fully and more agonizingly than any other filmmaker of his generation, had explored the lower as well as the higher reaches of such terror and such betrayal.

But the same era which nearly shipwrecked Dmytryk's career and which gave us our present-day images of John Wayne and Ronald Reagan also brought about a change in the mythography of the Western, which, more blatantly than in any other film genre, reflects the contemporary crisis. In the paragraph immediately following the one I have quoted from the *Playboy* interview, Wayne goes on to lambast some "other fellas who really did things that were detrimental to our way of life." One of them is Carl Foreman, the screenwriter for Fred Zinneman's 1952 *High Noon*, the Western that first concentrated upon the possibility that the *town itself* to which the priest-sheriff ministers may be corrupt, and corrupt at the heart, unable to muster courage to help him outface the invading hordes who are minions of chaos. (This myth of the corruption of the normal was, of course, anticipated during the forties by such non-Western films as Frank Capra's *It's a Wonderful Life* and by nearly all the abrasive comedies of Preston Sturges.) *High Noon*, from its first showing, was understood to be a grim parable of Hollywood's lack of courage under fire from manic Washington. But it has not, perhaps, been clearly enough understood that this brilliant film could have chosen no better allegorical scene for its despair than that of the classic Western—a mode and a genre which its own bitterness permanently altered. The one just man, Sheriff Will Kane, is inevitably played by Gary Cooper, for this film is in many ways a cancellation of the optimistic town-myth of *The Westerner*. And if *High Noon* is a filmic revision of one of the primary Western plots we have been tracing, George Stevens's *Shane* (1953) seems to be a revision of the other, shamanic plot. Alan Ladd's gunfighter-savior, Shane, is a reluctant dragon-slayer at best: only in the climactic scene does he draw his guns, to kill Jack Palance. But his reluctance, as the film makes clear, is not the slow, deadly self-restraint of gunmen in the William S. Hart tradition; rather, it is a kind of existential ennui with the role itself, a disgust with the necessity of being a private bearer of justice. *Shane* has not retained the high regard in which it was held upon original release, but it remains one of the most singularly weary Westerns of all time: perhaps even more tellingly than *High Noon*, it reflects the shattering pressure of politics upon the most political of American popular daydreams.

Warlock was made in 1958–59, of course; the nightmare years of the early fifties were long past, and the Eisenhower regime itself was fast drawing to a conclusion. And the film has none of the implicit edge, the implicit bitterness, of *High Noon* or *Shane*, or even of John Sturges's 1955 film *Bad Day at Black Rock*. In fact, it is a crucially transitional film made in a highly transitional year, the last year of one of the most distinctive decades in American history. But the fable of Warlock looks back upon the transformation of the Western myth in the fifties, no less than it prophesies future transformations for the following decades. In the figure of Clay Blaisdell, Shane (and the Ringo Kid and all their cousins-german) once again finds a purpose in his shamanic role of man on the razor's edge, political prophet of the primal tribe; but it is a purpose tinged with self-distrust and cynicism at the very society which requires such prophets. And in Johnny Gannon, Will Kane seems to pick up again the badge he dropped in the dust at the end of *High Noon*; but if this is a priest-sheriff *redivivus*, it is a priest-sheriff who knows more painfully than most of his predecessors the terrible risk of being herald of the people, and the terrible losses and failures, diminishings of energy and of trust, involved in again moving up the scale of civilized existence. The final, mock gun battle between Gannon and Blaisdell is a defeat for both of them, for the stronger man has renounced his strength and banished himself to eternal wandering on the edge of nature and civilization, while the weaker one has achieved his vocation at the expense of learning his weakness—and at the deeper expense of losing a friend.

Perhaps the most striking filmic inheritance from the ambience (if not specifically the film) of *Warlock* is a scene from that strange Eastern-Western *Midnight Cowboy*—a vision of the West by a European, and hence (as with Leone's films), a particularly abstract vision. Joe Buck (Jon Voight) has come to New York from the Southwest to make a living as a male prostitute for wealthy women (rather an ithyphallic Blaisdell wandering into a town, not uncivilized, but rottenly overcivilized). He wears absurdly emblematic, fringed and stitched cowboy clothes, and can find no success and no friend but the consumptive thief Ratso Rizzo (Dustin Hoffman). And in one wonderfully brutal scene in their shared hovel in an abandoned tenement, Ratso tells Joe that he has to get a new suit of clothes if he wants to score with the "rich broads"; "That shit you're wearing is just fag stuff," he says. Joe whirls around to face Ratso, outraged and shaken to the core. "Fag stuff!" he sputters; and reaching for the most indisputably masculine image he knows, shouts: "J—J—John Wayne! You think *John Wayne's* a faggot?"

In this transformation of an archetype into a cliché perhaps Dmytryk, Aurthur, Foreman, and all the professional casualties of the fifties have their revenge. At any rate, the point of Joe's explosive question—addressed to us as well as to Ratso—is to remind us how complex and dangerous has become our sense of our own most definitive self-image, and to indicate how much all of us in this age are desperately perturbed citizens of the state of Warlock.

THE PROBLEM OF FILM GENRE   161

6

ADAM AWAKING:
PERSONALITY,
PERSONA, AND
PERSON IN FILM

With a film like *Warlock*, part of our understanding of the revision and redefinition of Western archetypes taking place is a function of the personalities who take part in the action. Henry Fonda as the all but ritualistic gunfighter Clay Blaisdell is not just a performer, but also a creator of the film, since in his weary, cynical performance we see (or, at least, are surely meant to see) an ironic commentary on his previous performances as Wyatt Earp in *My Darling Clementine* or as the "one just man" in *The Ox-Bow Incident*. Nor would Richard Widmark be as convincing as he is in the role of the self-mistrustful sheriff Johnny Gannon if we did not know that before *Warlock* Widmark's roles were confined primarily to contemporary, big-city gangster films; for, as I have already observed, the transition from Blaisdell as town marshal to Gannon as sheriff is in fact a transition from mythical, "Western movie" time to our time—the time of everyday political history, partial victories, difficult decisions, and situational ethics.

This use of an actor's established screen personality is, of course, one of the oldest and most continually effective ways in which film comments on its own meaning. To take a very recent example: Michael Crichton's 1973 *Westworld* is a fantasy about an amusement park of the near future, a kind of existential Disneyland, where one can live out one's dreams of being a cowboy hero, killing robot gunfighters (programmed to be slower on the draw than their human adversaries) and copulating with robot dance hall girls (programmed to respond to every partner as if he were a paragon of virility). The automation, predictably, goes awry; and the human, overcivilized hero (Richard Benjamin) finds himself pursued by a deadly robot gunfighter who now not only fires real bullets, but aims to kill. The parable itself is an interesting counter-myth of filmic and social assumptions: we are to learn, presumably, how much we *actually* pay for the dreams which nourish us, and how deeply those heroic dreams are rooted in bloodshed and bestiality. But the film, dully directed and slowly paced, acquires its undeniably rich effect primarily from the casting of the berserk robot, who is played by Yul Brynner dressed exactly as he was and behaving exactly as he did in that most successful and most unabashedly heroic of Westerns, John Sturges's *Magnificent Seven*. It is a cruel and precise self-parody and one which makes Crichton's point about the artificiality of the Western *macho* myth more tellingly than perhaps even Crichton's own plodding screenplay.

Examples of this self-referential use of the star proliferate, ranging from the simply and pleasantly witty to the complex. In an oddly ignored yet splendid political satire, *The Senator Was Indiscreet* (1948), William Powell plays an aging, wonderfully corrupt, deadhead senator who almost grafts his way into the White House and who continually makes phone calls back to "Momma," his ambitious wife, promising her great things to come. In the end, when the senator has been defeated and exiled to a South Seas island (where he becomes, predictably, the blustering headman of a native tribe), we see him apologizing to the white-haired, faceless Momma for not having made President. Momma assures him that it is all right, turns to face him and us—and we see, framed by phony white hair, the smiling face of Myrna Loy. The moment has nothing whatsoever to do with the literate, elegant plot of the film, but no one who has seen and remembered the *Thin Man* films can fail to appreciate the humor and the pathos of this completely unmotivated reunion of two beautiful performers now past their youthful sleekness—especially if we remember that when they played Nick and Nora Charles, Powell's favorite pet name for Myrna Loy was "Mommy."

In a very different (though superficially similar) fashion, Buster

Keaton acknowledges his own screen identity in *Steamboat Bill, Jr.* Bill, Jr., has returned to the waterfront town where his father is a crusty old steamboat captain. Disgusted with his son's foppish manners and dress, Bill, Sr., takes Keaton to a general store to buy him a suit of clothes fit for a real man. And in one rather long scene, Keaton tries on a succession of hats, each one of which looks more ridiculous than the last, each one of which Keaton admires, and each one of which his father throws angrily aside. But midway through the series, as the father's back is turned, Keaton reaches for the characteristic black, wide-brimmed boater which was his signature in his early comic triumphs. He looks at himself for the briefest of moments—during which we see *our* Buster Keaton, *the* Buster Keaton—and then, grimacing in disgust, throws the hat aside. It is the most elegant of ironic comments by Keaton on the audience's expectations about his behavior. But more than that, it is one of the hidden thematic statements in this most understated and richest of Keaton's films. For Steamboat Bill, Jr., will have proved by the end of the film that he is, and has been all along, the "real man" his father desires—in spite of his foppishness and in spite of the slapstick situations in which he continually finds himself. During the climactic hurricane sequence, Keaton as Bill, Jr., will prove himself that graceful master of threatening space which I called him in a previous chapter, handling his boat, saving his father, his girl, his girl's father, etc., etc., with a deadpan assurance for which "beautiful" is too impoverished a word. And his brief rejection of the "Keaton" hat, his instantaneous departure from his previously established (or, at least, previously assumed) role is an important, inimitable prophecy of the major theme of *Steamboat Bill, Jr.*

I adduce these examples of the actor's creative function in the inmost meaning of a film because it is the least understood, least discussed, and, presently, most deliberately ignored of all the component functions of the film art. The much-touted decline of the Hollywood star system during the sixties and into the seventies is partially a matter of economics, contract law, trade unionism, and (among both stars and producers) cussedness. But it is also a phenomenon of great significance for the nature of film and one which film theory, not unexpectedly, has been quick to justify and institutionalize rather than examine. The disappearance of glamor as a marketable commodity, and the rise of the so-called ugly–i.e., normal-looking–star (Dustin Hoffman, Sandy Dennis, Gene Hackman, Al Pacino, Barbra Streisand) is one relatively simple aspect of what seems to be a movement, on the part of many filmmakers, away from earlier ideas of film acting toward a more theoretical, anonymous idea of the filmed work. At a more serious level, we may observe that such major, affecting films as George Romero's *Night of the Living Dead*, Peter Fonda and Dennis Hopper's *Easy Rider*, and George Lucas's *American Graffiti* not only do not feature recognizable, established actors in the major roles (Romero's film, indeed, used only one professional actor), but depend for much of their extraordinary energy on the non-star, almost nondramatic quality of the performances. An important early influence on this trend was probably John Cassavetes's 1961 *Shadows*, where the actors managed to deliver their written lines in such a way as to make them seem improvised. We have now reached a stage where films of high seriousness can be made in deliberate contravention of the idea of performance. Robert Altman's 1973 *The Long Goodbye*, for example, is a rather childish satire on the Hollywood thriller, the detective film in general, and the Raymond Chandler mystique in particular. Whatever satiric edge the film delivers is achieved by the ostentatiously perverse cross-casting of the major roles: Elliott Gould is Philip Marlowe (a friend of mine was prompted to ask, "What next—Woody Allen as Sam Spade?" anticipating the news that *The Maltese Falcon* is being remade with George Segal as Spade), and Nina Van Palandt and Jim Bouton, two enthusiastic non-actors, play the other major roles.

Perhaps the most important film in the recent history of film acting is Fred Zinneman's 1973 *The Day of the Jackal*. Neither perversely counter-cast nor making showy use of non-performers or unrecognizable performers, *The Day of the Jackal* makes important points about the political and technical reasons for the demise of stardom. The film narrates a fictitious attempt on Charles DeGaulle's life by a professional assassin known only as "the Jackal" (icily played by Edward Fox). But, of course, as a film made in post-Kennedy America, it is only superficially about DeGaulle's potential assassination: the audience knows and the filmmakers surely knew that *The Day of the Jackal* is about assassination as an idea—and an idea with particular poignance for anyone who lived through 22 November 1963. As we follow the Jackal's intricate, cruel maneuvers to get his one clear shot at DeGaulle, we become more and more aware that, though we participate in the Jackal's point of view—and even, in a strange way, are concerned for his success—the real star of the film is not Edward Fox, but the man we see only in long shots, in the midst of crowds and guards, the man who plays "Charles De-Gaulle," and who bears such an uncanny resemblance to the real Charles DeGaulle. The "star" of the film, in other words, is public history, or our idea of public history, the emblematic and untouchable great whose shocking vulnerability and terrifying ability to bleed like the rest of us only becomes real through the demonic mediatorship of the Jackal (or, in the real world, of Oswald, of Sirhan, of Ray). Zinneman reinforces this sense of conflicting public and private realities, that of DeGaulle versus that of the Jackal and our own, in a series of quite subtle technical devices. At one point, for example, a motorcycle policeman is delivering a letter to DeGaulle's office in the Invalides. As he drives to the Invalides, we follow him in a conventional, extremely smooth and filmic tracking shot. But when the officer dismounts and enters the president's outer office—that is, when he and we approach the scene of actual, official history—Zinneman shifts to a track from a hand-held camera and to a much grainier texture of film. The jumpy, poor, documentary quality of the shot creates a convincing illusion of DeGaulle's presence. And it also, I think, reminds us of the most effective horror film in the history of the art: Abraham Zapruder's home movie of the presidential cavalcade, which did more than we could have suspected at the time to revise our ideas of fantasy and reality in film and in history.

Whatever the reasons for the current underemphasis on stardom in the narrative film, however, I wish in this chapter to take a rather old-fashioned view of its importance, to insist that it remains, even if in a different modality, one of the crucial aspects of film; and I want to suggest that we take those self-conscious, self-effacing quotation marks off the word "star." If criticism is mainly an attempt to understand and consolidate our immediate experience of an art—to possess it as only remembered experience can be possessed—then the serious study of film should have a great deal to say about actors, particularly those actors who have achieved the indelible and—so runs the cliché—indefinable quality of stardom. After all, even the most passionately intellectual theoretician still probably goes to as many films because of their leading actors as he does because of their directors or cameramen. And unless we want to take an impossibly puritan stance about what makes art Art, it has to be admitted that a film can—and usually does—become good or, sometimes, great precisely because of its stars, and even in spite of inept direction or absurd plot.

But what I have just said "has to be admitted" is heresy to many students of film. Indeed, when theorists of any stripe come to examine the role of the actor's personality in shaping the complete film, they usually descend to one or another well-worn truism about film acting: its essential difference from stage performance; its ten-

ADAM AWAKING

dency to escape from, rather than become absorbed in, a particular role; its deep connection with audience expectation and daydreaming; etc. While there is no denying the validity of these stances, what interests me is their comparative scarcity—and, beyond that, the great scarcity of serious discussions of the movie star in supposedly complete discussions of film aesthetics. One of the few relevant surveys of the question, indeed, has been produced by probably the most perceptive film critic now functioning. In *Play It Again, Sam*, Woody Allen—as an impotent, neurotic film reviewer—finds himself revitalized and saved, not by "film as film," but by the sheer, fictive but nonetheless humanizing force of Bogart's persona. In contradiction to the vision of Zinneman's film, *Play it Again, Sam* works as a kind of triumphant, cannily innocent "Day of the Schlimihl." But not many critics have achieved Allen's insight.

To take a specific instance: I think that Stanley Kramer's 1967 *Guess Who's Coming to Dinner?* is a major film and needs to be included in any full canon of Hollywood art. And yet its plot (as usual for Kramer) is a ridiculously simple-minded exercise in California liberalism, and its direction (as equally usual) is uninteresting and glossy. What makes it important for me and, I want to insist, for the history of film is Spencer Tracy. It is his last performance (he died less than two weeks after production ended), and he is visibly aged and tired on the screen. But the energy with which he carries his role—that of a liberal newspaperman whose daughter wants to marry Sidney Poitier—and particularly his long concluding speech about acceptance, charity, and so on, raise the film, and even the candy-cane sentimentality of that last speech, to a very high level of genius. It sounds more than a little ghoulish to say that the film moves me so deeply because I know Tracy was dying when he made it. But, I think, it only sounds that way because we have not yet invented an honest vocabulary for the art that will allow us to discuss such things. For if *Guess Who's Coming to Dinner?* is the record of the last, tragically difficult role of a great actor, it is not simply the sad memento of his decline, an expensive urn for his ashes. Tracy acts with dignity and tremendous, suicidal energy. And his performance is ultimately a statement of life and persistence whose existential profundity goes far beyond the simple morality which the film intends to convey.

But these considerations are not very widely discussed ones. I would, I am sure, feel embarrassed arguing my affection for *Guess Who's Coming to Dinner?* (or for James Cagney's *Love Me or Leave Me* or Rosalind Russell's *Majority of One*) in conversation with most of my cinema-theorist colleagues. And this seems a great pity. It is another indication that, in film as in literary criticism, we often allow a specious sense of "respectability" to betray us into reducing the full impact, the full and dangerous complexity of the very experience we are trying to preserve. A key word for this problem may be the word "record," which I used in referring to Tracy's presence in Kramer's film; and as I write the word, I am reminded again of the grim knowledge incarnated in the Zapruder film. Whatever else it may be, film is a record of life. (Bazin once argued the evolution of film from the primitive art of mummification.) Though no one is really there on the screen, people are also more really *there* than most of us ever manage to be in our daily lives. This existential paradox of film presence is a continual scandal to formalist theories of art, theories which attempt to discuss the artwork as if it were a proportioned, elegant object with only tangential connections to our own disorderly act of living. It may well be that the failure of film criticism to discuss adequately the role of the actor is a function of its failure ever adequately to come to terms with the truly radical, romantic antiformalism of the medium.

Pauline Kael, to be sure, never fails to take full account of her own response to the stars of the films she reviews, but her healthy honesty in this regard is overbalanced by her resolute refusal to be speculative about any of her responses. And although Raymond Durgnat, one of our most sensitive film critics, attempts in *Films and Feelings* to discuss the importance of star actors, it is without his usual self-assurance and range of speculation (a kind of shyness carried through in his recent discussion, in *Film Comment* for March 1974, of the Marilyn Monroe mystique). But the majority of critics shy away from examining the importance of the star *in* the film, the actor as a functioning part of the total aesthetics of the work, for a reason, I think, implicit in the word "star" itself.

Samuel Goldwyn, who knew as much about it as anyone did, once defined "star quality" as follows: when an actor like Walter Pidgeon walks on screen, you know he's got balls; but when Gable walks on, you can hear them clacking together. Goldwyn did not go on—or has not been reported—to give a corresponding definition of female stardom. But his observation is, in many ways, unimpeachable. Whatever we mean by the word "star," it inevitably conjures up all we feel to be most vulgar, antiartistic, and "popular" in the worst sense about the movie industry. In our associative lexicon, "star" always implies and is completed by "fan." And between them, those two words invoke the whole aura of filmland magazines, personality cults, the cynical marketing of a performer's private life, and the thinly disguised sexual hysteria of premiere-night mobs: in short, the passion of the lonely crowd to hear those balls clacking. It is not surprising, then, that as film becomes more respectable as a serious art and a serious academic study, the aspect of it most difficult to assimilate into critical discourse should be the aspect most intimately connected with its scruffy box-office origins. Not surprising, but not rational, for in slighting the reality, both aesthetic and commercial, of the star as central to the art of the film, critics and filmmakers also slight the reality of the art itself.

I have been arguing all along that film and literary narrative are more intimate sister arts than we have really understood. But as anyone who has had siblings knows, that relationship is sometimes as revealing for its bitterness as for its harmony. In the present context, it is interesting that the most vituperative—and most brilliant—anti-Hollywood novels concentrate upon the star system not simply as an economic, but also as the imaginative perversion at the center of their satiric target. From Nathanael West's *The Day of the Locust* to Muriel Spark's *The Public Image* even to Norman Mailer's nonnovel *Marilyn*, the most violent attacks of literary artists upon film art have been in terms of its tendency to elevate certain personalities, certain collections of face, body, gesture, and voice, to a quasi-divine status of permanence and glory. It is a tawdry eminence, compounded of the impotent dreams of the masses and their sacrificial reflection in the hollow, depersonalized life of the star. It is a reduction of screen performance, in other words, to the shallowness of the wafer-thin celluloid image, a metaphorical insistence that, since nobody is there as we watch the film, nobody is there in the personalities we see performing in the film. Even Gore Vidal's *Myra Breckinridge*, a novel written with a deliberately camp, childlike enthusiasm for the trappings of Hollywood, incarnates this attitude: Myron-Myra becomes a star only at the expense of his-her sexual and psychic identity. And F. Scott Fitzgerald's *The Last Tycoon*, which may well be the most sensitive and intelligent novel ever written about Hollywood or about the art of the film, elaborates the warfare of film and fiction into a complex set of relationships that are as much a self-critique of the novel itself as they are an attack upon the Hollywood system. If Vidal found it necessary to alter the sex of his star, Fitzgerald performs a far more suggestive sex-change upon his own artistic personality. His first-person narrative is that of a young girl, helplessly in love with the sensitive, virile, and doomed movie producer Monroe Stahr. Just as Fitzgerald himself was both dazzled and appalled by Hollywood—and saw his job as screenwriter both as a creative challenge and as a murderous threat to his ability to write at all—so his female narrator longs for Stahr and yet clinically comprehends his problems. Stahr, as his name indicates, is the *real* star of the movie business, a man whose art is the manipulation, not of an individual role or even an individual film, but of a whole industry, an immense factory of dreams and myths. And in an early, exquisitely ironic scene, he gives brilliant advice on how to write a film and on how a film differs from a novel to a confused British novelist hired by the studio. But Stahr's yearning for the art is deeply flawed by his lack of culture and poise, and as we know from Fitzgerald's notes for the novel, he was finally to have died with his dreams of art and love pathetically un-realized—a larger, in fact, colossal Gatsby. Thus, the novel was to have had, in its own way, its revenge for acknowledging the pro-ducer's genius. And, indeed, in the only scene in the book in which we see an actual star, a Hollywood leading man, that character comes to Monroe Stahr pathetically seeking advice on how to deal with his sexual impotence.

Oddly, whenever Hollywood decides to become "serious" about itself, it too accedes to this well-established myth of the star's psychic and sexual emptiness—a fact which should serve critics and novelists clear notice that the myth contains a fallacy. In all three versions of *A Star Is Born*, the female Star leads a life of frustration and off-screen agony caused by her "discoverer" and lover, the ineffectual, alcoholic male Star. (In the first version, the 1932 *What Price Hollywood?*, this feckless alcoholic was a director; his later transformation into an actor is almost a history of the growing prestige of the auteur theory.) Particularly in the Judy Garland version (1954), the film, in explicit and vampire-like fashion, trades on Judy Garland's well-known personal difficulties, so that it has the unpleasant aura of an *auto-da-fé*—and not a very sincere one. In *The Barefoot Contessa* (1954), a more palatable version of the same myth, Ava Gardner (playing Maria Vargas, the peasant girl "made" by a seedy collection of producers and PR men) achieves stardom and the adulation of her inane fans only at the price of sexual fulfillment: the man she finally falls in love with and marries, an Italian nobleman, turns out to be impotent. *Man of a Thousand Faces* (1957), important for Cagney's stunning performance as Lon Chaney, concentrates upon Chaney's difficulties with his shrewish, unresponsive wife and his estrangement from his son. And although Ruth Etting, Lillian Roth, and Helen Morgan were, at best, adequate cabaret performers and by no means film stars, their respective biographies—which after all *star* film stars

(Doris Day in *Love Me or Leave Me,* Susan Hayward in *I'll Cry Tomorrow,* Ann Blyth in *The Helen Morgan Story*)—take fiendish delight in festooning these show business exempla with all manner of overdone alcoholism and sexual frustration. Apparently the commandment for the star—at least à la Hollywood's own prissier kind of self-consciousness—is, Send not to know for whom the balls clack, 'tis not for *thee.*

Most revealing of all, though, is the recent film *The Way We Were* (1973), with Robert Redford and Barbra Streisand. Here, all the elements we have been discussing come together in a confused mélange: the reality of the star as an element within the film, coupled with the odd embarrassment about that reality when the commercial film grows self-conscious, with the attendant set of "literary," "novelistic" prejudices which subtly support that embarrassment. Except for its stars, *The Way We Were* is an unremarkable film in every way. Redford and Streisand, of course, are as "major," as indisputably estellated, as anyone currently above the horizon: and their being there is what inspirits the film and carries it in two very different directions. Barbra Streisand's talent for mugging, for a kind of kinetic, joyful neurosis—she is the first actress since Marilyn Monroe who can be funny and sensuous at the same time—finds a natural vehicle in her role as Katie Morowski, a New York-Jewish (the hyphen is put there by Streisand's own persona) Communist. And Redford's flawless, wooden handsomeness—his face has the abstract perfection of a comic-book hero, with the same inevitable sense that something has not been drawn in—eminently suits him to play Hubbel Gardner, WASP, decathlon champion, and fledgling writer. But this suitability of actors to roles, like most instances of "perfect casting," finally corrodes the reality of the roles themselves. We know, at every point in the film, that we are not watching, not Morowski and Gardner, but Streisand and Redford; and we also know that that is precisely what we paid to see. *The Way We Were* is that most venerable of box-office conspiracies, the "star vehicle"—a movie that exists primarily, if not solely, for displaying its leading players in as many of their famous postures as possible. It is a conspiracy, moreover, in which the audience is complicit.

But film has grown less innocent since the heyday of the star vehicle. And *The Way We Were* is diffident about, even self-contemptuous of, its own greatest merit, in a way that an existentialist would probably refer to as "bad faith." It becomes, in fact, a film about Hollywood, about film, and about the loss of that innocence now associated with the forties, the clear moral issues of the Second

World War, the way Glenn Miller played, and the American film from *The Grapes of Wrath* to *The Best Years of Our Lives*. An important stage in the love affair of Streisand and Redford, in fact, is marked when they walk beneath a marquee advertising *The Best Years of Our Lives*. Later, when they have moved to Hollywood and Streisand (in one of the many clichés out of which this mosaic of clichés is made) announces her pregnancy to Redford, she coyly describes it as the plot of a movie she is writing—as, indeed, it is the plot of the movie she is in. Film, I have suggested throughout my discussion, is one of the most revealing historical arts available to us, a deep insight into the psyche of its age. But *The Way We Were* tends to reverse, unpleasantly on the whole, the thrust of that assertion. Trapped into being a star's movie in an age which officially and academically demands greater seriousness, it attempts to cannibalize history, to reach *through* its stars to some apprehension of the greater deeds outside mere film. And in the end, it resembles nothing so much as the provincial state of mind of those young cineastes for whom the Second World War can be remembered as the era, not of the London Blitz or of Stalingrad, but of the Andrews Sisters and *Buck Privates*.

The final breakup between the lovers is explicitly paralleled with their contrasting reactions to the HUAC witch hunts of the early fifties, Streisand taking it as a vital civil-rights issue and Redford trying simply to survive and keep his job as a scriptwriter. They both lose. They lose each other, and they are, after all, *stars:* what worse punishment can be inflicted on them than to have to marry bit-players? But in the final scene, when they meet again after years of separation, we ask, What are they being punished *for?* Streisand, of course, for her idealism; Redford for his moral cowardice (he has degenerated, in a self-contemptuous metaphor that would have delighted Fitzgerald, from novelist to screenwriter to television hack).

But I think it is more than that. I think they are being punished —have to be punished, in this curious mixture of ersatz innocence and low seriousness—for being stars. Just as the film self-consciously undervalues its own art vis-à-vis the "serious" craft of the novelist, so its plot has to do penance, in the end, for having been a star vehicle. It is the same bundle of impulses and embarrassments that has manipulated the plots of a number of recent films involving pairings of major actors with major actresses: Glenda Jackson and George Segal in *A Touch of Class*, Ryan O'Neal and Ali McGraw in *Love Story*, Sarah Miles and Richard Chamberlain in *Lady Caroline Lamb*. One claim, of course, is that these are simply "mature" love stories. But is a love affair more mature because it ends unhappily? Rather, these films seem evidence of the industry's sensitivity to its new-found artistic status and its diffidence about presenting Films (the capital is appropriate) which rely for their appeal on anything so crass as stars. We might well call it the it-didn't-happen-one-night syndrome: stars need to be chastened by the art whose purity their distracting presence debases. (We might cite as corroborative evidence one of the few recent films in which two major stars live happily ever after, *What's Up, Doc?*, Peter Bogdanovich's deliberate reminiscence of the Grant-Hepburn, Gable-Colbert days.)

This attitude is reassuring, both to the novelist jealous of film's power and preeminence and to the critic or intellectual who wants to escape the stigma of being simply a "fan" or a "buff." And, of course, for the viewer with a knowledge of film history, it even has official sanction. Lev Kuleshov long ago performed his famous experiment in film acting, the effect of which was to negate the very concept of the need for actors. Kuleshov alternated shots of a man's expressionless face with shots of a bowl of soup, a female corpse, and a child; the effect, presumably, was to register—without any effort at performance on the actor's part—such emotions as hunger, grief, and nostalgia. The "Kuleshov effect" has come to be one of the most celebrated truisms about the construction of a film and of course is ideal justification for the formalist, as opposed to the existentialist, approach to film art. (Not until V. F. Perkins's recent study, *Film as Film*, in fact, has anyone had the great good sense to remark that since no one for fifty years has actually *seen* the Kuleshov film, learned disquisitions on its significance are, at best, dubious.) But Pudovkin and Eisenstein, under the dispensation of Kuleshov, tended to think and write of actors as mannequins, to be manipulated by the omnipotent director and editor. (Does anyone remember the name of a single actor in *Potemkin?* in *Mother?* in *Nevsky* or *Ivan*, except that most elegant of mannequins, Cherkassov?) Hitchcock, too, has frequently referred to actors as "cattle." And the European film industry seems to have generated considerably fewer stars than its American cousin, while at the same time achieving a remarkably high level of perfection—at least in some respects. It is no surprise, therefore, to see Siegfried Kracauer, in his *Theory of Film*, dismiss the function of the actor in film as simply that of a mobile, unusually pliant prop, like the features of landscape or furniture. And it is easy to assume that film becomes a major art not because of but despite its stars; that the director-editor, if anyone, is the creator of the film; and that the star, if he deserves discussion at all, deserves it as a kind of sociopathic phenomenon who may be utilized by a director for a particular, socioanalytic effect (here I am thinking specifically of Andrew Sarris's remarkably imperceptive essay on James Stewart in *The Primal Screen*).

We have seen that, in film, terms like "reality," "fantasy," "tradition," and "genre" have especially far-reaching complexity. With the concept of the actor in film, and with the limiting case of his or her presence as star, we come to what may be the most energetic and potentially the richest contribution of film art to the contemporary imagination.

Conventional formalist film theory, with its idea of directorial authority as the true creative presence in cinema, has been an immensely valuable, creative approach to the viewing of films. But the theory originates in a really quite unoriginal, nineteenth-century concept of artistic creation. The romantic author, a combination of prophet and high priest of art, has been preserved by literary mythology in Flaubert's ideal of the artist as God of his invented universe, in Joyce's utterances on disinterested creation in *A Portrait of the Artist as a Young Man*, and in T. S. Eliot's famous dictum that poetry is, not the expression of, but an escape from, emotion. The romantic myth of art, that is, insists upon the importance of the individual creator, but at the same time insists upon the hierarchical nature of the artistic medium through which that individuality is manifested. It is to be expected that a film criticism deriving from this concept would look for the uniqueness of film as its essential revelation, but would look for that uniqueness in a remote and abstract rather than obvious manifestation. Thus the displacement of the actor by the anonymous, remote, manipulating person of the director, cinematographer, and so on.

On the contrary, however, the structural interplay of creation and repetition, of individual talent and tradition, that is at the heart of film and of all art is most powerfully manifested in a quite different, more obvious area than in the relationship of film and director: that is, in the relationship of film and performance. This is, more generally, the relationship between the technological-aesthetic complex that is the film as medium, and the real presence of human figures and faces who, although they are never really there as we watch the screen, are nevertheless the best and only reason anyone has for looking at the screen at all. If film does tend to concentrate primarily on masses of people and to portray individual personality only by its derivation from the mass, then we may also say that film, in its struggle toward the manifestation of individuality, moves toward the transcendence of its own medium, and consequently toward that moment of self-realization and self-cancellation that is the highest reach of romantic art.

This sense of human personality as simultaneously present and absent in the work of art is, after all, an alternative and historically more accurate version of the romantic idea of the artist-in-the-work. Flaubert, Joyce, and Eliot, with their pronouncements about artistic disinterest, are in reaction against and therefore, ironically, continuators of the distinctively romantic problem of mediating between the artwork as objectivity and the artwork as expression and potential salvation of the private personality. The other side of the myth of the poet as prophet is the myth of poetry as the poet's one chance for prophecy: the sense, terrifying to writers from Keats to Malcolm Lowry, that the personality may be absorbed, fragmented, dissipated in the formal, linguistic structures which are that personality's expressive medium. Film—Adam's dream, which he awoke to find true —carries this conflict to its most extreme pitch, a pitch so extreme, indeed, that the warfare between personality and mechanism is the prime datum of our experience of film narrative. Modern fiction, from *Notes from Underground* to *Gravity's Rainbow,* has been exploring the ways we entrap ourselves within fictions, sacrificing our humanity to an inhuman rigidity of thought. And film, characteristically, incarnates the same crucial problem in an inverted way. It is a technology, a mechanism, which has the peculiar power of manifesting the presence of absence, a "reality" which is not there, a nostalgia for the present. And its drive, therefore, is to elucidate a myth of personality out of the mechanism, to separate out from the preordained nature of its operations the idea of the human.

This view of personality in film, implicit in all I have said about film language, genre, and politics, is brilliantly caught in one of Kafka's strange little parables "Von den Gleichnissen" ("On Parables"):

Concerning this a man once said: Why such reluctance? If you only followed the parables you yourselves would become parables and with that rid of all your daily cares.
Another said: I bet that is also a parable.
The first said: You have won.
The second said: But unfortunately only in parable.
The first said: No, in reality: in parable you have lost.

Parable and reality, those twin, mutually reflective mirrors, catch between them the fate of human life, whether it wins or loses. One is reminded of the narrator of John Barth's "Bellerophoniad" in *Chimera*, a man who sets out to imitate perfectly the archetypal career of the mythic hero and finds that he has become a perfect *imitation* of a mythic hero. And if most contemporary fiction assumes, like Kafka's second speaker, that it is only *in* parable that man may win, if at all, most films, like Kafka's first speaker, assume that it is only in liberation *from* the mirror of parable, liberation from form, that he can succeed. The two assumptions, like the two speakers and the two mirrors, are in fact the complementary halves of a unity, the unity of our quest for a creative *self*-consciousness. Adam's dream becomes problematic and can become Adam's nightmare if Adam fails to distinguish his waking from his dreaming, or thinks he only *dreams* that he awakens. For what is the quest of his dream if not Eve, the necessary other person who is both his completion and his longed-for fall into history?

It is worth noting, in this regard, that of the very few film performers whom theoreticians are willing to elevate to the rank of auteur, by far the largest number are the slapstick comedians. Eisenstein, Bazin, Kracauer, and Sarris are in agreement (if about nothing else) that Chaplin and, to a lesser degree, Keaton, Langdon, and the Marx Brothers belong among the greatest creators of film art. And surely, in this curious and universal lapse of theoretical rigor, we can see an important truth about film. Why is Chaplin, for example, included in the pantheon of auteurs? Not really because he happened to write and direct his most important films; no one, by the same token, could seriously attribute the genius of *Duck Soup* to Leo McCarey. Chaplin's greatness is, simply, to have incorporated within his film personality a crucial, archetypal aspect of all film personality: that struggle of the human to show itself *within* the mechanical, which we have described as film's deepest romanticism. Slapstick is the purest structural version of this struggle, the manifestation of the mechanical opening of *City Lights*—trying to survive among the marmoreal, mythicized versions of the self with which tradition has surrounded and nearly strangled us.

In *Film: The Creative Process*, John Howard Lawson makes the point that Chaplin's acting style probably owes a large debt to the disastrous screen appearance of Sarah Bernhardt in *Queen Elizabeth* (1912): "Her performance before the camera exposed and mocked gestures that were charged with real emotion on the stage. Chaplin's genius discovered that the mockery was a key to the camera's peculiar intimacy; it could show the absurdity of passionate gesture and at the same time register the sincerity and despair of the gesticulating figure, seeking vainly to attain a dignity which the merciless camera denied him." The last phrases of Lawson's observation articulate perfectly that quality of tension, of contrast and contest between medium and personality, that I have been describing as endemic to all film acting, not only slapstick comedy.

Indeed, Lawson's choice of the term "absurdity" to label the quality of stage gestures when transferred to film should remind us not only of Chaplin but also of another great comedian and warrior in the battles of modern consciousness. Albert Camus never established his credentials as a film critic. But in *The Myth of Sisyphus*, as indeed throughout his career, he dealt with exactly those concerns—the humanization of technology, the acquisition of humanity and language in the heart of an alien universe, the Coming of the secular Word—which we have discussed as central to both film and writing in our postromantic era: "Men, too, secrete the inhuman. At certain moments of lucidity, the mechanical aspect of their gesture, their meaningless pantomine makes silly everything that surrounds them. A man is talking on the telephone behind a glass partition; you cannot hear him, but you see his incomprehensible dumb show: you wonder why he is alive. . . . Likewise the stranger who at certain seconds comes to meet us in a mirror, the familiar and yet alarming brother we encounter in our own photographs is also the absurd." The gestures and unheard speech of the man in the phone booth announce the mechanistic, inhuman void which only the human word can fill. And this is, I submit, the best and richest definition we have not only of silent film comedy but also of the art of acting in the film itself.

We shall do better, indeed, to forget the word "acting"—or else to take it at its most basic, untheatrical level of significance. "Acting" as the thespian art does not and cannot exist in the film: this is the reason for Kuleshov, Pudovkin, and Eisenstein's contempt for the idea of dramatic performance. The stage actor's craft, whatever else it may be, is the art of assimilating himself to a predetermined dramatic role—to an abstract, demonic potency of action—and of behaving in such a way that that potency becomes realized in his physical presence on the stage. The film performer, on the other hand, is burdened with the necessity of realizing his role—which is to say, his physical presence—through a medium which resists the full reality of that presence.

A suggestive analogy to the difference is the distinction between our expectations at a performance of classical music and at a jazz performance. Listening to Horowitz or Arrau perform Chopin, we are primarily concerned with the artist's ability to incarnate or articulate a preestablished score. But listening to Thelonious Monk play *I Surrender, Dear,* or listening to Cecil Taylor play one of his own compositions, we are concerned with the struggle of the performer against the predetermined nature of his medium (the theme, the chord structure, etc.). Like jazz performance, film acting is improvisatory, on an almost metaphysical level. In the drama, the aim of performance is to achieve a kind of psychophysical translucence, whereby the potencies imagined by the author of the drama "shine through" the immitigable physicality of presence-on-the-stage. In film, however, the dramatic text is—rightly—only a *pre*-text for its eruption into the moving figures, the absurd images, who are not really there but whom the film, at the height of its artifice, can convince us *do* exist in their own lucid physicality.

Nowhere is this quality of film acting better caught than in Marlene Dietrich's performance in *The Blue Angel.* One of the most sensual performances in the history of film, Dietrich's portrayal of Lola Lola inevitably reminds us of Sam Goldwyn's criteria for stardom— or even of Edy Williams's sense of screen reality, quoted in the second chapter. But, of course, that is precisely the point of *The Blue Angel* as film: that Lola Lola, cabaret singer and seductress, can never be as seductive, as monumentally sexual, as Marlene Dietrich, film singer and impersonator. A great deal of misunderstanding has been generated about this film. It is not simply an undistinguished vehicle which triumphs because of Dietrich's indomitable, animal power (an explanation that assumes film to be a kind of transparent record of stage presence). Nor, to cite a more common explanation, is Dietrich the Trilby of Josef von Sternberg's Svengali-like direction. Von Sternberg was a brilliant director. But *The Blue Angel* transcends, as do all great films, the simplicities of traditional aesthetics. Here is a conventional, formalist critic, Alan Casty, discussing (in his *Development of the Film*) the interplay of director and star in *The Blue Angel:* "Von Sternberg's images of Marlene Dietrich's legs (sexual and suggestive beyond the more explicit display of female flesh in later films) are perfect examples of his intricate and meaningful use of the stimuli of physical surface. On a small, tawdry, cluttered stage . . . Dietrich's legs insist on a physical frankness beyond their decadently artificial surroundings."

Surely we may be excused for finding this explanation of the film's power less than adequate to its subject. And given the choice between Casty's version of Dietrich's legs as "Von Sternberg's . . . intricate and meaningful use of the stimuli of physical surface" and the version Sam Goldwyn might have left us, we may be excused—

on both theoretical and experiential grounds—for preferring the mogul to the formalist. Indeed, the weakness of formalistic criticism is implicit in the contortions of Casty's grammar. "Von Sternberg's *images* of Marlene Dietrich's legs" are, after all, not what we see: we see Marlene Dietrich's legs, and the genius of von Sternberg is to create a film which takes account of, and becomes an existential homage to, that shattering, ghostly reality.

The Blue Angel, then, is a film in which the genius of the director and of the leading actress coincide to produce a profound commentary on the nature of film personality. Casty is right to concentrate upon the stage atmosphere of Dietrich's role. But the use of the stage goes far beyond the simple juxtaposition and contrast he sees. In the very first scene of the film, we see an old woman at sunrise washing shop windows. One of the windows displays a large photograph of "Lola Lola," advertising her act at *Der Blaue Engel*. The old woman splashes a pail of soapy water against the window, and we watch the suds run down the picture of Lola without wetting it: we are surprised to discover that the photo is on the other side of the glass, not pasted on from the outside. It is a rich parable of the nature of film presence: the seductive, startlingly sensual reality of the body separated from our experience by an invisible barrier, made absent and untouchable in its very, riotous there-ness. And, of course, von Sternberg's wisdom in beginning with this scene would be pointless without the overwhelming reality of Dietrich herself, that body and voice which neither the photograph nor the stage vision of Lola can fully realize. If "Lola Lola" lies behind the shield of glass (von Sternberg's metaphor for the film medium itself?), Dietrich lies behind the role of "Lola" even more inaccessibly and tantalizingly. The plot of *The Blue Angel*—the seduction of Professor Rath ("Professor Reason," played by Emil Jannings) and his degradation by Lola—will act out the implications of that first shot, the untouchableness, the impossibility of possessing not Lola but Dietrich. We last see her, as Rath staggers back to his abandoned classroom to die, seated on stage singing the weary song which has remained her signature, "Falling in Love Again." The last words of each stanza of that song, *gar nicht* ("not at all," "in no way"), reaffirm the absence-in-presence, the Camus-like absurd, that is the burden and challenge of this kind of acting.

In terms of the nineteenth- and twentieth-century literary associations we have been tracing throughout this study, film as the product of the star offers especially suggestive analogues. The first romantic "star," in a very real sense, was Lord Byron. And Byron's paradoxical vision of person and persona, character and caricature, can teach us a great deal about the reality of these matters in film. The narrative poems that made him the most famous writer in Europe— *Childe Harold's Pilgrimage, The Giaour, The Corsair*—are all popular entertainments with conventionalized plots in quite the same way as are the great bulk of narrative films, be they Westerns, thrillers, horror, war, or love stories. Byron was well aware of this conventionality, as his letters and conversations show. He even exulted, with his peculiar visionary vulgarity, in achieving fame by mastery of genres largely discredited among more serious writers. We can and should think of him as a kind of entrepreneur, producer, director, and sole actor in a long series of literary thrillers. But there is no doubt where, among these various functions, Byron himself assigned primacy. "Poetry is the lava of the imagination," he observed in a letter to his unhappy wife-to-be, "whose eruption prevents an earthquake." Whichever of his heroes he is describing, we and Byron's original audience and Byron himself know that the real subject is George Gordon, sixth Baron Byron in one guise, one assumed experimental personality, or another. And this egocentrism, condemned by a century of solemn critics as puerile and excessive, we have lately come to realize to be an important, perhaps central, romantic transmutation of the creative self.

The Byronic game, played across a potential infinity of roles, poses, and situations, is in fact the struggle of the poetic intelligence to find a voice, to invent a structure for itself which will make it *present* in the poem. Thus Byron becomes the ancestor of all those hero-clowns of modern writing—Baudelaire, Wilde, Proust, Joyce, Genet, Mailer—who have made their lives a pre-text for their work. In all these writers, we find the impulse to sacrifice concerns of form and decorum and of the traditional values of language to the goal of making the work manifest the personality of the artist, making Adam's dream not only a true dream, but distinctively and inalienably his own dream.

Nor is this simply to resurrect the age-old cliché about art as "self-expression." For central to the Byronic line of romantic writing is the assumption of its own impossibility. Self-expression may be the goal of the art, as of the life; but it is a goal militated against and undercut by the art itself. This warfare of aesthetic form against its own ends has become increasingly the theme of our best fiction and poetry, from Kafka's agonized quarrel with the nature of parable to the latest novels of Thomas Pynchon and John Gardner.

This warfare is also, inevitably, part of our experience of the narrative film, because popular entertainment in the form of the narrative film is the crucial articulation of the myths and difficulties of consciousness in our era. Which is to say, of course, that "pop culture"—at least as spoken of by traditional intellectuals—simply does not exist. There is no such thing as a primitive, inarticulate, trashy nonart which lives on in the taste of the masses in opposition and contrast to a mature, serious, self-conscious art which is the property of the imaginatively elect. What exists, rather, is a spectrum or hierarchy of articulation ranging from the most schematic allegory to the most intricately organized elaboration and extension of that same allegory.

The romantics, particularly Byron, were well aware of this interpenetration of levels of culture. And Byron, my nominee for the first star actor of the precinema, created an art which, like the art of Joyce, Chaplin, Cagney, and Pynchon, details the struggle of the self to assert its own existence within a welter of political, cultural, and historical details whose very richness threatens to deprive that self of its vitality. It is an "interesting" art in the highest sense of the word, for it gives us back the image of our own predicament, made tolerable and even joyful by the mummer's gift of significant mimicry.

Parker Tyler, in *The Hollywood Hallucination*, has suggested that film acting should be described not as acting but as *charade*, meaning by that that no film performance can hope to attain the subtlety or range of emotion of a great drama or a great novel. While I disagree with Tyler's strange animus against the art he understands so well, I think that the term "charade" makes a great deal of sense and not only in reference to film acting. It also makes sense in reference to the much more important quality of film *presence*—how film, like our best contemporary writing, makes real the idea and image of human consciousness in an inhospitable world. After all, the game of charades, which seems to bore half the human race and delight the other half, is a game of turning your body into language, of trying in the most elemental of ways to make the word flesh—or flesh the word. We may, to be sure, locate this human presence anywhere in a given film: in the activity of director, producer, scenarist, cameraman, or even clothing and set designer. But in the majority of cases, the profundity and truth of the film experience is due to the presence of the actors—those strange simulacra of personality caught midway between classic dramaturgy and sheer exhibitionism, whose charades of identity motivate our first and our most serious interest in the narrative film. This is largely the point, indeed, of a vastly underrated study of film and literature, Bruce Kawin's *Telling It Again and Again* (Ithaca, 1972). Kawin argues for the Kierkegaardian principle of repetition—the effort of the soul to realize itself against the interminable recapitulation of its processes—as the generating principle of both film art and modern literature.

Pursuing the analogues I have suggested, we can trace at least two stages of film presence for the actor, or two ways in which his physical reality or unreality on the screen functions. Both parallel certain literary and metaphysical responses to the modern problem of articulating one's personality in an invidious environment; and both help constitute the vision of cinema—which is to say, our vision of our best hope for survival. They are the incarnations of the actor as warrior against his medium and of the actor as type, as survival myth in spite of and therefore somehow outside his medium.

The first mode, that of the actor as warrior, is the most primitive and also the most basic and most inescapable. Much of what we have said about film has had to do with the curious nature of the art itself: a mechanical, artificial means for reproducing human existence which strives, in spite of its artificiality, to return that existence to the status of a natural phenomenon. Structuralist anthropology argues that the distinctive quality of human civilization is its absolute *otherness* from nature, its total isolation from the circumambient universe of nonconscious being. It is a compelling argument, especially in the case of the romantic culture which itself spawned structuralism. For Romanticism and its child, film, represent a rupture of the ancient self-assurance of human intelligence, represent the coming-of-age of that intelligence to a sense of its isolation from the rest of the world and, therefore, to the terrible necessity to return—even if only in dream—to the rhythms of that world.

In this sense, then, any performance by an actor in a film is a warfare between personality and mechanism. It is no accident that the two director-founders of narrative film technique, Eisenstein and Griffith, have both acknowledged their indebtedness to the nineteenth-century English novel, particularly to Dickens. The Victorian novel, direct heir of Byronic narrative, catches in a unique way the struggle of characters against a dehumanizing, historically inevitable environment. Those film historians who attempt to trace Dickens's influence on Griffith or Eisenstein in terms of the authorial editing of the directors do not miss but distort the point. The truest Dickensian influence upon *Birth of a Nation*, *Intolerance*, *Potemkin*, or *Ivan the Terrible* is in the interchange between editorial control and the disruptive presence of the actors.

Let us take a famous instance, the concluding sequence of *Ivan the Terrible, Part One.* There we see Ivan looking down upon a file of Pilgrims come to call him back to the throne of Russia. This sequence has its great power not simply because of the editing or composition of its shots, but precisely because Cherkassov's marvelous, distorted pantomine throughout the whole film has prepared us for it. We have been aware all along that starring as Ivan has involved impossible, painful distortions and exaggerations of the human posture (both literally and, in terms of politics, figuratively): Eisenstein reportedly nearly ruined Cherkassov's health in demanding some of the sustained, grotesque poses which are the beauty of *Ivan.* And the mythic point of the film becomes, in this way, a perfect analogue to the basic, experiential point of *watching* the film. We see a great film actor in tension with the painful and stylized constrictions of posture and shot composition, portraying a great man in tension with the stylized, constricted milieu which threatens to sap his identity.

But when the actor-warrior either succeeds or fails splendidly in his battle against the mechanism which is his medium, he tends to become a *type* of that struggle, a star is the only way that term can make sense to us—i.e., and archetype of the human presence in the machine. There are, of course, any number of examples of this sort of typology: my own enthusiasm for Tracy, even in *Guess Who's Coming to Dinner?*, is founded on a sense of Tracy's screen personality as one of the great comic archetypes of survival. But two of the most important and currently celebrated stars of the Hollywood tradition—Humphrey Bogart and James Cagney—capture, in their contrasting styles of presence, many of the dichotomies of film language we have been tracing throughout this book.

Actors, especially film actors, may be regarded as survival types. Just as Joyce's Leopold Bloom or Fitzgerald's Jay Gatsby represent crucial varieties of struggling and surviving consciousnesses, so certain artificially constructed personalities in the presence and nonpresence of their film existence become charades of intelligence surviving against the machine in which they are trapped. Film language, we have said, alternates between the mythic extremes of Tarzan and Frankenstein: between the myth of language, or human meaning, triumphant against any deprivation or dehumanization, and the counter-myth of language self-defeated and self-destroyed in its attempt to create a mechanical replica of itself. Among the geniuses of the silent film, Keaton and Chaplin can be taken as types, respectively, of intelligence supremely competent to survive the Cartesian nightmare of slapstick-space, and of intelligence eternally bewildered, threatened, and annihilated by that space. (Thus, while Keaton's happy endings always satisfy us, Chaplin's strike us again and again as sentimental—i.e., falsifications of his own best instincts.)

But with the coming of sound, the possibilities of realizing these language myths were immensely enriched—even though it took film-makers a while actually to grasp the possibilities. The film, as talkie, suddenly became much truer to life, much more "naturalistic," than it had been before. And with this increased naturalism came the potential of a new kind of hyper-naturalism, a distinctly cinematic surrealism: that of the speaking voice which moves us, not because of what it says, but because it speaks.

Nowhere did the new naturalism of the sound film establish itself more firmly than in the Hollywood gangster epic. And, correspondingly, nowhere did the chances of the film voice—of the act of speech literally mapped onto the screen's symbolic space—more brilliantly realize themselves than in the personae of Bogart and Cagney.

Both men are masters of film presence. Indeed, so dominating are the personalities of "Bogey" and "Jimmy" that very few of their films are considered on their own merits *as* films. It is especially revealing to consider two of the few films in which they appeared together—*Angels with Dirty Faces* (1938) and *The Roaring Twenties* (1939)—for in these films we witness the meeting of, and one of the purest distinctions between, the counter-myths of film language we have been tracing. Cagney in company with Bogart seems to become even lighter, even more blond, and Bogart grows correspondingly darker and more lethargic. Cagney's villainy in *Angels* and *Twenties* is explained away by the plots as environmental conditioning or disappointed honesty; Bogart's villainy, in both cases, is taken as a given, a problematic absolute.

This is precisely the distinction that was to stay with them throughout their careers. We may remember their first major appearances: Cagney's *The Public Enemy* (1931), in which he first realized his unique style of stationary choreography (the little two-step he does after meeting Jean Harlow is one of the greatest dances on film), and Bogart's *The Petrified Forest* (1936), where his Duke Mantee flails and rants in a hysteria of motion that only underscores his fundamental immobility.

The fact is that Bogart—like Chaplin and Chaplin's great archetype, the Frankenstein monster—is one of our most powerful symbols of the defeat of the mind by space; only in Bogart's case, that defeat becomes all the more humanizing for its gift of speech. It is no accident that his first great role was in a film whose title included the word "petrified," or that our memory of his most brilliant performances—*The Maltese Falcon, Key Largo, The Caine Mutiny*—is preeminently the memory of Bogart seated somewhere, paralyzed by his own intelligence and irony while the world goes to hell around him. Bogart's upper lip was paralyzed (the reason so many of his early roles feature him with a moustache), and that paralysis, amounting to a minor speech defect, accounts also for his signal gift to film language. For his words always seem drawn from him, perhaps with a sneer, perhaps (as in the great last scene of the *Falcon*) with a rising panic at their inadequacy. He speaks, always, with difficulty; and that difficulty implies the depth of incertitude from which his words are drawn, as if each of his characters (Spade, Rick, Charlie Allnut, Queeg) were having continually to decide whether or not to continue playing out the part fate and the film had assigned him. The rediscovery and celebration of Bogart some years ago as the first "existential" hero of the American film was right-minded, if only partially correct. For his presence is, indeed, that of the absurd man; but Bogart's absurd man is man exclusively as *victim* of the world's mechanism, a victim whose sad irony reminds us that even in defeat there remain the possibilities of a self-mistrustful honor and dignity. He is not simply the talking film's Chaplin, in other words: he is, in a real sense, its Dostoevsky.

With Cagney the case is altered. If we remember Bogart stationary, it is almost impossible to remember Cagney not moving—even when he is being perfectly still. As with Keaton and Tarzan, Cagney's genius is his ability to hint a victory over the dead certitudes of the preordained universe. So he always moves—with his voice, his face, his feet, or failing all those, his hands. (In the 1933 *Footlight Parade*, codirector Lloyd Bacon almost outdoes Busby Berkeley's dance spectaculars by concentrating in the nonmusical segments upon Cagney's wonderfully expressive hand gestures.) If Bogart gives us nobility against the certitudes of defeat, Cagney acts out for us again and again the charade of grace and lightness in the absence of any certitude whatsoever. He is a man of surfaces, dipping into the lower resonances of his roles (even in the shattering *White Heat* of 1949) only occasionally, only for a stunning instant before he is off again on his career-long masque of assurance. And his voice—tenor to Bogart's baritone—is an impossibly gentle, lilting parody of solemnity, a New York-inflected, lightning-fast clarity of articulation which mocks the words it pronounces, but mocks them with the irony of laughter, not of underlying tragedy. It is natural that the Cagney festivals and the Cagney renaissance should postdate Bogart's. For Cagney incarnates the second phase of modern consciousness, its newfound ability to survive *within* fiction and its hope of locating joy even in the wasteland.

Cagney, in fact, is probably the only great film actor to successfully portray another great film actor. His performance as Lon Chaney in *Man of a Thousand Faces* (1957) is not only a brilliant re-creation of Chaney's own talent but an eloquent and gay *tour de force* in which Cagney himself acts out the *business* of acting—the manifestation of presence-through-absence which he, as talkie actor, carries to an even more delicate subtlety than the silent-film genius of Chaney could reach.

Bogart and Cagney, of course, are only two among many examples we could choose to illustrate the ways in which film manifests its myth of personality. We could also survey the personae developed by Edward G. Robinson, Carole Lombard, Conrad Veidt, or—more recently—Paul Newman, Jean-Pierre Léaud, or Jane Fonda. But the pair I have chosen exemplify, I believe, the alternate possibilities of screen acting as typology; and in their very exaggeration (for Bogart and Cagney are surely the most easily—and frequently—parodied performers in the history of film) they articulate the distinctness of that myth of personality in the history of art. Through the power of his presence, the star may outstrip even the artwork in and through which he is made manifest: the balls, as Goldwyn would have it, may clack so loudly that we hear nothing else. But that, after all, is exactly the point of having a star—and the point of having film at all. In that ribald, anarchic clacking (as with Byron, as with Mailer) we hear the music which a contemporary aesthetic will allow us to regard as truly significant: the music of the self existing through and surviving in spite of the leaden fables of identity that are the landscape of all our minds. Adam has awakened to find his dream shockingly and seductively true; and film, like the literature that can mean the most for us, that can most humanize and brace us, is a way of learning to live with that truth, that dangerous dream.

**THE JOHNS HOPKINS
UNIVERSITY PRESS**

This book was composed in Palatino text
and display type by the Monotype
Composition Company from a design
by Patrick Turner. It was printed on
55 # Sebago Offset Antique paper
and bound by the Murray Printing
Company.